Certified Tropical Timber
and Consumer Behaviour

Karl Ludwig Brockmann · Jens Hemmelskamp
Olav Hohmeyer

Certified Tropical Timber and Consumer Behaviour

The Impact of a Certification Scheme
for Tropical Timber
from Sustainable Forest Management
on German Demand

With 22 Figures

Physica-Verlag
A Springer-Verlag Company

Research Department
Environmental and
Resource Economics,
Logistics, ZEW

Series Editor

Dr. Olav Hohmeyer

Authors

Dipl.-Vw. Karl Ludwig Brockmann
Dipl.-Vw. Jens Hemmelskamp
Dr. Olav Hohmeyer

Centre for European Economic Research (ZEW)
Kaiserring 14–16
D-68161 Mannheim
Germany

Die Deutsche Bibliothek - CIP-Einheitsaufnahme

Brockmann, Karl Ludwig:
Certified tropical timber and consumer behaviour : the impact
of a certification scheme for tropical timber from sustainable
forest management on German demand / Karl Ludwig
Brockmann ; Jens Hemmelskamp ; Olav Hohmeyer. Research
Department Environmental and Resource Economics,
Logistics, ZEW. - Heidelberg : Physica-Verl., 1996
(Umwelt- und Ressourcenökonomie)

ISBN 3-7908-0955-1
NE: Hemmelskamp, Jens:; Hohmeyer, Olav:

ISBN 3-7908-0955-1 Physica-Verlag Heidelberg

SPIN 10542591   88/2202-5 4 3 2 1 0 – Printed on acid-free paper

Foreword

Trade with and use of tropical timber have repeatedly been criticized because of the continued reduction of tropical forest areas. However, it has now been recognized that boycott actions and restrictions imposed on the use of tropical timber are inappropriate measures for countering the causes of the destruction of tropical forests effectively.

In contrast to boycotts and prohibitions the introduction of a credible certification scheme for timber from sustainable forest management is a constructive strategy. A certification scheme offers economic incentives to promote sustainable forest management in the tropics and international trade in timber from environmentally sound management.

This study carried out by the ZEW shows that increasing demand for timber products from sustainable forest management can be expected.

At the same time the results of this study are a signal for the tropical countries to improve market access for tropical timber products by sustainable management of their forests thereby making an important contribution towards the protection and preservation of these natural resources.

Dr. Günter Rexrodt
Federal Minister of Economics

Acknowledgements

This book is the result of a study commissioned by the German Federal Ministry of Economics. However, while acknowledging this support, we wish to point out that the views are those of the authors alone and do not necessarily reflect the position of the Ministry.

Preparation of this book involved a number of people. There were several experts who provided useful details and background information. Where possible, reference to their contributions is made throughout the book. In particular, we benefited from discussions with Hagen Frost, Dr. Wolfgang Karius and Gerhard Schmok (Federal Ministry of Economics), Prof. Dr. Heiner Ollmann (Federal Research Centre for Forestry and Forest Products) and Stefan Schardt (Initiative Tropenwald).

Last not least, we express our warm gratitude to our colleagues Henrike Koschel and Tobias F.N. Schmidt for helpful discussions as well as Jennifer Kirsch, Thomas Schwörer and David Milleker who assisted us throughout the research and production of this book.

Karl Ludwig Brockmann
Jens Hemmelskamp
Olav Hohmeyer

Contents

List of Tables

List of Figures

List of Abbreviations

ATC	Anti-Tropical timber campaign
CMA	Centrale Marketing-Gesellschaft der Deutschen Agrarwirtschaft mbH (Central Marketing Company of German Agriculture)
CO_2	Carbon dioxide
CS	Certification scheme
CT	Coniferous timber
DMD	Brancheninformationsdienst Detail-Marketing-Dienste Baumarktforschung, Essen (Branch Information Service Detail Marketing Services Building Market Research, Essen)
EC	European Community
EU	European Union
FAO	Food and Agriculture Organization of the United Nations
FPL	Forschungsinstitut für Pigmente und Lacke e.V. (Research Institute for Pigments and Lacquers)
FRG	Federal Republic of Germany
GATT	General Agreement on Tariffs and Trade
IBRD	International Bank for Reconstruction and Development/ The World Bank
ITTO	International Tropical Timber Organization
ITW	Initiative Tropenwald (German Tropical Forest Initiative)
IWP	Increased willingness to pay
nCT	Non-coniferous timber
OECD	Organisation for Economic Co-Operation and Development
SFM	Sustainable forest management
TT	Tropical timber
UBA	Umweltbundesamt (German Federal Environmental Agency)
UN	United Nations
UN/ECE	United Nations/European Commission for Europe
WU	Window units

1 Introduction

The latest data issued by the Food and Agriculture Organization (FAO) show that destruction of tropical forests is proceeding at unabated pace (see Table 1). At the same time the economic and ecological goods and services of these forests for the particular region, for the global ecological balance and also for further advances in medicine and agriculture have gained increasing esteem in recent years. Research on tropical forests as ecological systems cannot as yet be considered complete. In particular, a large potential not yet utilized lies in the rich diversity of species in the flora of tropical forests.[1]

Tropical rain forests are ecological systems which react very sensitively to external influences. Because of the heavy rainfall in tropical regions and the very thin humus layer of these forest areas, the danger of erosion becomes particularly great once the protecting treetop canopy has been disrupted by human intervention. Therefore extensive forest destruction is usually irreversible and any regrowing secondary forest formations do not achieve the complex structure of the original natural forests.

Extensive loss of forest coverage, whether in the tropics or in the temperate zone, leads to the disturbance of the regional climate through temperature increase, reduced precipitation and soil erosion with consequent reduction of agricultural yield. Tropical forest destruction also annihilates the domestic and cultural environment of native populations and leads to flooding in the populated flat lower reaches of rivers emerging out of the forests. Botanical and zoological species become exterminated, thus reducing the genetic resources of the planet Earth. Destruction of rain forests by fire and decay of residual wood release trace substances, in particular carbon dioxide (CO_2), thus contributing to the global increase of the CO_2 concentration in the atmosphere.[2]

Although the loss of tropical forest areas in the 1980s was greatest in Latin American countries on the absolute scale, Table 1 clearly shows that the rate of deforestation is greater in Asian countries characterized by an export-oriented forestry and timber industry. This suggests that measures to preserve the tropical forests should target first of all international trade and consumption of tropical timber in the industrialized countries.

---

[1]   cf. for example PANAYOTOU/ASHTON (1992).
[2]   cf. STEINLIN (1989:24ff.,55), ENQUETE-KOMMISSION (1990, 2. Bericht:536).

In recent years environmental protection organizations in many countries have therefore called for boycotts of tropical timber products. Import bans on tropical timber from unsustainable production have been suggested at various times too. Since the decision in the GATT-Panel on the „non dolphin safe tuna" dispute between USA and Mexico in September 1991, however, such a measure is generally no longer considered to be in accordance with GATT.[3] A possible way of establishing import restrictions in keeping with the GATT principles can be envisaged on the lines of a corresponding international agreement within the scope of Article XX(h) GATT (cf. ESE 1992, Vol. II:65). So far only a few species threatened by extinction, including rosewood and rio-palisander have been excluded from trading for commercial purposes by the Washington Convention on International Trade in Endangered Species (SCHIPPMANN 1994).

Table 1:   Forest Area and Deforestation in the Tropics (All Forest Formations)

	Land area	Forest area		Annual deforestation	
	1980	1980	1990	1981-90	
				Area	Loss rate
Total	Mio ha			Mio ha p.a.	% p.a.
	4 778	1 910	1 756	15.4	0.8
thereof	% of total area				% p.a.
- Africa	46.8	29.8	30.0	26.6	0.7
- Asia, Pacific	18.7	18.3	17.7	25.3	1.2
- Latin America, Carribean	34.5	51.9	52.3	48.1	0.8

Source: FAO (1993:25).

Apart from experts in the fields of science and industry, citizen's action groups and environmental protection organizations, too have become increasingly aware of the negative effects of a boycott or import ban. The tropical forest areas would be devaluated and the timber concessionaires and local population would be encouraged to clear forests by fire for livestock production and agricultural purposes. The main German environmental organizations have therefore signaled a

---

[3]   The dispute is considered to be a case of precedence for Article XX GATT. This means that unilateral trade restriction measures aimed at achieving environmental protection in third countries are not covered by the article. The USA had interpreted Art. XX(b) and XX(g) GATT to allow the hindrance of the import of Mexican tuna fish caught by methods which constitute a hazard for dolphins (ESE 1992, Vol.II:63).

possible revocation of their boycott support in the „Frankfurter Erklärung der deutschen Umweltverbände zu Kennzeichnungsinitiativen für Holz und Holzprodukte" (Frankfurt declaration of the German environmental associations on labelling and certification initiatives for timber and timber products). In principle they have made a positive assessment of a certification scheme for timber and timber products founded on an ecologically and socially compatible forestry on the basis of traceable criteria and transparent test catalogues. However, they explicitly demand that apart from tropical timber, non-tropical timber species, too should be included in a certification scheme.

A quality seal bundles multidimensional information on the features of a product or production process which the consumer himself could only collect and comparatively evaluate at huge transaction costs but nevertheless considers to be relevant for his or her choice of product. A certification scheme is a system for issuing a quality seal which guarantees certain product characteristics and/or fulfilment of certain criteria in the production and processing methods of a commodity. In connection with tropical timber, a certification scheme should guarantee certain ecological sustainability standards in the management of tropical forests. In contrast to a certificate which refers to isolated aspects of products and/or production processes, an environmental label tries to evaluate the environmental aspects of a product all the way „from the cradle to the grave" (see Chapter 5).

The establishment of a certification scheme for tropical timber products - or for non-tropical timber products, too - originating from sustainably managed natural forests entails corresponding costs, in particular the costs for setting up and maintaining institutions for issuing the quality seal and for controlling the realization of the criteria defined for awarding it.

In addition, costs arise for the producers of tropical timber from sustainable forest management (e.g. expenses for more conservative tree-felling and for any reforestation measures required). In contrast there'to, the price charged when forests are recklessly exploited - as practiced since several decades in many regions of the world - does not have to carry the costs of measures for sustainable forest management, at least not on a short- to medium-term basis. However, a certification scheme also gives the producers of tropical timber from sustainable forest management an economic benefit, provided that it can be assumed that the consumers are prepared to honour the efforts for sustainable forestry. This could express itself as increasing demand for certified tropical timber - particularly on market sectors which have been severely hit by the anti-tropical timber campaign. Furthermore, the producers could also profit from a willingness on the part of the end consumers to pay higher prices for certified timber.

For the consumers of tropical timber products, too, a certification scheme entails not only costs (through higher prices), but also benefits through the possibility of internalizing positive external effects. Through the positive discrimination in favour of sustainably produced timber, the consumer - compatible with market conditions - is able not only to consider in his purchase decision the value of the delivered timber, but also the ecological benefits of a tree growing in the tropical regions. Thus a certification scheme leads to a segmentation of the tropical timber market and may even result in complete displacement of the market for „overexploitation-tropical timber". Of course, certification should be voluntary and not flanked by an import ban for non-sustainably produced tropical timber, because otherwise, analogous to a boycott, incentives would arise to change to livestock production or agricultural usage of the land (SHAMS 1995:144).

The certification scheme enables the consumer to pay for the delivery of the previously public goods „CO_2-sink" and „diversity of species" from the natural (tropical) forests in the form of a price mark-up on (tropical) timber products. Without a certification scheme, probably no market for these public goods could develop, restricting the supply of important ecological services of the tropical forests. Therefore a certification scheme can theoretically lead to a globally more efficient allocation of resources.

The present study is specifically concerned with the reactions to a certification of tropical timber on the demand side. The certification scheme may cover non-tropical timber, too. The possible conflicts arising from this are discussed in Section 11.2. As the focus is on the demand side, an already established, functioning and credible certification scheme is taken here as a starting point. The study highlights in particular the long-term effects of certification and thereby examines not only the consequences of a certification scheme restricted to the Federal Republic of Germany, but also the effects of an OECD-wide certification scheme on the German demand for tropical timber.

By focusing attention on analysing the reaction of consumer demand the study extends the scientific discussion of certification schemes for timber, which so far has been primarily concerned with questions of standards, feasibility and costs. The central aim of this study is to estimate the expected market movements in quantities and prices which could result from a certification scheme for (tropical) timber. In particular, the quantities and prices for tropical timber products on important submarkets after the introduction of a convincing certification scheme are estimated, taking the Federal Republic of Germany, a major consumer country, as an example.

The procedure adopted is to calculate different long-term scenarios (quantity and price developments) under various assumptions about the supply of sustainably produced tropical timber and the reaction of the German tropical timber demand in response to a certification scheme. The scenarios are long-term in the sense that markets are simulated which have already absolved the necessary processes of adaptation. Therefore the assumptions made regarding the supply and demand behaviour are of long-term character, too. This means, for example, that the calculations are based on long-term substitution elasticities.

This study is sectioned in three parts with altogether twelve chapters. The first part describes the general setting of a certification scheme for tropical timber and discusses the assumptions made in this study concerning the reactions of consumers and suppliers of tropical timber to a certification scheme. The second part qualitatively and quantitatively analyses the distribution and utilization trends for tropical timber in the Federal Republic of Germany, deriving basic scenarios for certification of tropical timber in Germany. These basic scenarios constitute an initial quantity structure without taking price effects into consideration. The third part includes price effects and calculates extended scenarios of tropical timber certification for the German market founded on the basic scenarios with various assumptions regarding supply and demand.

The *first part* consists of altogether four chapters. Chapter 2 presents first of all a brief overview of the concept of sustainability and of the general design of a certification scheme. The third chapter investigates the extent to which a certification scheme for sustainably produced tropical timber is theoretically suitable for contributing to the protection of tropical rain forests and whether it is also efficient compared with alternative measures. The fourth chapter explains the assumptions made in the study concerning the long-term supply of sustainably produced tropical timber in the presence of an established certification scheme. Chapter 5 evaluates experience gathered with existing product labelling schemes in order to draw conclusions regarding the possible reactions of consumer demand to a certification scheme for tropical timber.

The *second part* of the study commences with the establishment of definitions and an explanation of the situation regarding available data (Chapter 6). The seventh chapter reviews German tropical timber imports as well as the processing and consumption structure for the year 1984 (distribution analysis). Chapter 8 examines first of all the basic product attributes of the raw material tropical timber and of the chief competing products. An analysis of developments in the substitution relationships to other timbers and to non-timber materials since 1984 for the seven major utilization fields of tropical timber in the Federal Republic of Germany (trend analysis) follows. The results of the trend analyses in five of the seven market segments are rough estimates of the consumed quantities which could be achieved (without considering price effects) in the case of a credible certification scheme and under the given substitution trends (basic scenarios).

In the *third part* the basic scenarios are extended by taking price effects into consideration. Price effects result through the costs of a certification scheme, of a change to sustainable forest management, through possible acceptance of higher prices on the part of consumers and through the extension of the certification scheme to all OECD countries. Chapter 9 explains the theoretical foundations and the adopted method for making the calculations. Chapter 10 contains the scenario calculations for the individual submarkets and Chapter 11 reviews the scenarios for the aggregate German tropical and non-tropical timber market. Finally, Chapter 12 summarizes the results and draws pertinent conclusions.

Part I

General Conditions for
Tropical Timber Certification

2 Concepts of Sustainability and the Design of a Certification Scheme for Tropical Timber

The calculated scenarios for certification assume the existence of a functioning certification scheme. Therefore only brief consideration is given here to the concept of sustainability and the conditions for designing a functioning certification scheme for tropical timber.

It will take producers several years to adapt to changes brought about by a certification scheme demanding sustainable forestry. This is partly due to the fact that less than one per thousand of the remaining tropical forests is being managed sustainably (REPETTO 1990:123, FAO 1993:50). It also takes some time to set up the necessary institutional structures and to implement the presently evolving schemes comprehensively and in a large scale.[4] Furthermore, reliable verification of sustainable forest management is possible only after the elapse of one or two rotation cycles (PRABHU/ WEIDELT/LEINERT 1993:13).

The tropical timber producing countries, as members of the International Tropical Timber Organization (ITTO), have pledged by the year 2000 to market internationally only tropical timber extracted from sustainable and environmentally compatible forest management (ANONYMOUS 1994g). Such an action marks the first step in the right direction. However, in order to increase the efficiency of the certification scheme, this goal should be extended according to the theoretical considerations of the third chapter, to the tropical timber products sold in the domestic markets by the tropical timber producing countries.

With regard to the ITTO pledge, Malaysia has been one of the first countries to show progress on fulfilling promises outlined in the ITTO pledge. A representative of the Malaysian Timber Council recently said at a conference in Antwerp that great efforts are being made to achieve the goals of sustainable forestry set by the ITTO before the deadline which was set at the year 2000. For this purpose legislation punishing illegal timber logging with fines of up to US$ 200,000 or 20 years imprisonment has been introduced (ANONYMOUS 1994c). Effects of these new regulations are already evident. In Sarawak/Malaysia the roundwood produc-

---

[4] Institutional structures for a certification scheme in tropical countries are already either being set up or in the planning stage in Africa, Brazil, Indonesia and Malaysia (SCHARDT 1994).

tion has dropped by 3.0 Mio m³ to 9.5 Mio m³ as a result of the restrictions (ANONYMOUS 1994d), but it must not be overlooked that Malaysia is characterized by a strongly export-oriented forestry and timber industry. For a country like Brazil which in comparison is less dependent on export markets, there is naturally less pressure to make adaptations according to the ITTO decision.

A controversial debate is currently raging over the **sustainable management of natural tropical forests**.[5] This involves both the technical and forestry-based discussion regarding the possibility of long-term preservation of both the tree stock and the diversity of species in a natural tropical forest area used for timber production, and the fundamental question - going beyond the consideration of the forestry sector - asking what possibilities exist at all for sustainable management in a multi-sector economy.

At the *forestry* level there are two fundamentally opposite standpoints. One side contends that forest management methods familiar in latitudes with temperate climate can be transposed to tropical forests. The other side rejects this notion as unrealistic in view of the greater complexity of tropical forests.

Bruenig, favouring the first view, is of the opinion that sustainable forest management is theoretically conceivable, and realisable in practice too, in tropical forests which are very complex compared with temperate forests. The methods of selective logging conceived for this purpose are well known.[6] According to Bruenig, isolated examples already exist in Queensland/Australia, in Malaysia, in the Congo and in Indonesia among other places. The teak and mahogany plantations maintained in Java are cited by the German Federal Environmental Agency (Umweltbundesamt, UBA 1994:242) as examples of sustainable tropical timber production. However, Bruenig concedes that de facto, due to the pressure exerted by expanding commercial logging, mainly only pure exploitational systems are being used, and that on the whole the conditions for sustainable forest management have not yet been fulfilled in South East Asia, West Africa and Latin America. He sees a basic need for investments to improve knowledge and the training quality of forestry administrations and to cope with the difficult social and political conditions in the countries involved (BRUENIG 1990a:95ff.).

Critics of Bruenig's opinion point out that methods of forest management employed in the Northern hemisphere can only be applied to a limited extent in natural tropical forests, due to their more complex nature. OBERNDÖRFER (1989:104) argued against the examples cited above by pointing out that the soil is relatively fertile in Australian Queensland, rendering a comparison with typical tropical forest areas hardly legitimate. In the Congo, where sustainable forest management in the tropics has been exemplified, the rain forests were of comparatively small

---

5   A theoretical overview of the sustainability principle from the viewpoint of forest management without special reference to particular forest formations is given by SPEIDEL (1984).

6   BRUENIG (1990b:85ff). cf. also PRABHU/WEIDELT/LEINERT (1993) and the case studies discussed there.

complexity. This reservation is also valid for the plantations on Java referred to by the UBA.

From the perspective of the *multi-sector economy*, BOJÖ/MÄLER/UNEMO (1990:14) are of the opinion that, in principle, even the logging tropical forests entirely for the purpose of export revenue would be compatible with the concept of sustainable development. However, they assert that this is only on the condition that part or all of the revenue is invested in activities which create more export revenue or which reduce imports, sustaining the welfare of future generations. This approach corresponds to the idea of replacing natural capital by man-made capital in order to guarantee sustainable development in an economy. The assumption made by Bojö, Mäler and Unemo that natural and man-made capital are completely substitutable is also called the „weak" sustainability concept. In contrast, the concept of „strong" sustainability is based on the assumption that natural and man-made capital are substitutable only to a limited degree, particularly in the case of central ecological services such as climatic stability (VICTOR/HANNA/ KUBURSI 1994).

PEARCE and TURNER (1990:24) define sustainable development as follows: „It involves maximising the net benefits of economic development, subject to maintaining the services and quality of natural resources over time". Within the tropical forest subject complex they interpret sustainability going beyond the mere preservation of a country's export capacity and therefore along the lines of the concept of „strong sustainability". They justifiably point out (ibid:49) that on account of its multi-functionality (productive and protective functions), the renewable resource „tropical forest" permits only limited substitution of man-made capital for tropical forests. The argument of Pearce and Turner concerns on the one hand sustainability of a national economy, because for example it is hardly conceivable to prevent soil erosion and flooding other than by preserving the forests in the local region. On the other hand, the argument is just as much concerned with sustainability of the global economy, because alternative possibilities for absorption or for reduced emission of CO_2 can be created only with the aid of large investments. It is immediately evident that the diversity of species in the flora and fauna cannot be preserved by human achievements, but rather by the tropical forest's intact functioning. The FAO (1993:31) estimates that between 1.6% and 4.3% of the plant species annually became extinct through deforestation of tropical rain forests in the 1980s.

A widely disseminated concept of sustainable forest management which attempts to take into consideration the various ecological and economic services of the forests, is given by the ITTO. Sustainable forest management is considered to be the process of cultivating permanent forest areas with one or several clearly defined production goals and the intention to achieve a continuous supply of the desired products and services of the forest without entailing unreasonable depreciation of the value of these areas and future productivity or undesirable environmental effects.[7] This clearly shows how difficult it is to strike a proper balance between the conflicting economical and ecological interests.

Therefore a basic **consent on the structure and weighting of the intended goals** should negotiated first when developing a certification scheme for tropical timber. The most frequently mentioned goals „preserving the diversity of species" and „protection of the global atmosphere" are already in mutual competition while only two of numerous conceivable goals such as protection of indigenous populations, protection against soil erosion, and flooding as well as the conservation of natural reserves for the population.

The competition between tree stock and diversity of species can be explained as follows. It arises in a tropical rain forest area used for forestry through the differing requirements imposed on the complexity of the rain forest as an ecological system. Old rain forests are unproductive because regeneration and production of timber mass are balanced there. Their CO_2 balance is neutral, preservation of the diversity of species is ensured. Natural forests logged for the first time can manifest a positive CO_2 balance if the tropical timber removed is used for products, the life expectancy of which exceeds the life expectancy of the tree which was logged; with the harvesting methods commonly employed at present, the balance is negative for the diversity of species. Forests utilized sustainably over long periods of time can have a greater regrowth per acre, depending on the choice of measures accompanying the logging, enabling them to bind more CO_2 than a natural forest logged for the first time (BRUENIG 1994). In the case of long-term binding of the timber - beyond the expected remaining lifetime of the logged tree - the CO_2 balance will be more positive than in a natural forest area logged for the first time.[8] However, the diversity of species will be impaired to a relatively greater extent because it can be assumed that the structure of the tree stock will be shifted in favour of commercial timber species so that the complexity of the forest will decline.[9]

The definition of the goals of a certification scheme directly affects the **design of a certification scheme**. A certification scheme for sustainably produced tropical timber must contain two core elements: Firstly, a certificate of origin verifying the source as a forestry unit which is managed in accordance with the chosen criteria and indicators of sustainability and controlled by independent inspection. Secondly, a comprehensive monitoring system documenting the course of the timber carrying a certificate of origin from the trader and processing stage right through to the end consumer (ITW 1994:6).

---

[7] ITTO (1991, according to PRABHU/WEIDELT/LEINERT 1993:11).

[8] The FAO therefore comes to the conclusion that an increase of production of timber products from sustainably managed natural forests and in particular from plantations would be the most effective means to use forests for CO_2 absorption (FAO-Aktuell Nr. 11/91 dated 15.3.1991).

[9] cf. for this and for possible preventive measures for the protection of the diversity of species PRABHU/WEIDELT/LEINERT (1993:158ff.).

We cannot go into the details of the design and implementation of a certification scheme fur sustainably produced tropical timber.[10] Whatever the outcome, the basic principles for sustainable management of natural tropical forests devised by the ITTO (1990) will play an important role in the design of a certification scheme.

In connection with the control and sanctioning mechanisms necessary for the credibility and survival of a certification scheme, a suggestion arising from a study commissioned by the European Community (EC) must be mentioned. This envisages that international monitoring organizations such as the Société Générale de Surveillance as well as the association of companies involved in tropical timber trade and further processing should be linked for improved supervision of the distribution of certified tropical timber (ESE 1992, Vol. I:10).

Structures have already appeared on the end consumer side which could facilitate the quantity flow control after import of tropical timber products from the tropical countries. Apart from the „Blue Angel" in the Federal Republic of Germany explained in Chapter 5, some brief references now follow for Switzerland and the German „Bundesland" Baden-Wuerttemberg. In Switzerland preliminary work has begun on developing a declaration scheme for building materials which takes into account a comprehensive catalogue of ecological aspects. Since environmental advantages constitute a market profile opportunity, such a scheme is intended to improve the competitive position of wood with respect to other raw materials such as plastics. The features contained cover ecological aspects of production, processing, utilization and disposal. The introduction of a related environmental label is planned. For wooden building materials, details of the timber species used, including tropical timber, are interrogated with respect to the manufacturing process (cf. LEUKENS 1993). Once such an environmental label is established, it can be used to assist a certification scheme for tropical timber by interrogation of additional information concerning the origin of the tropical timber.

The state producer association for timber and plastics (Landesverband Holz+Kunststoff) in Baden-Wuerttemberg plans to devise an environmental label for joinery products. The controls will be carried out by a recognized and independent institution. A label signifies that a product has fulfilled advisory and customer service criteria and also that the timber came from a sustainably managed forest. The labelling program's aim is to respond offensively to the consumer need for environmentally relevant information in view of the persistent trend

---

[10]   An introduction to the conditions required for a functioning and credible certification scheme is given by NEUGEBAUER (undated). JOHNSON/CABARLE (1993) and PRABHU/WEIDELT/LEINERT (1993) give an overview of the problems encountered when setting up a catalogue of criteria and indicators for sustainable forest management. According to this the long-term acceptance of the management system by the local population appears to be of importance. The important driving forces for implementing tropical timber certification schemes are the Tropical Forest Initiative (ITW) on the German side and the Forest Stewardship Council at the international level (cf. SCHARDT 1994 and GHAZALI/SIMULA 1994).

towards natural materials for furniture and the increased environmental awareness of consumers (ANONYMOUS 1994a).

The present study assumes that a credible certification scheme has been established - either for tropical timber alone or for both, tropical as well as non-tropical timber. The credibility of the scheme is a fundamental condition for the willingness of the consumers assumed in the scenarios, to accept a higher price for sustainably produced tropical timber.[11] The assumed credibility implies that after the introduction of such a scheme the market for uncertified tropical timber will, in the long run, be displaced completely. The reasons which speak for this market displacement are explained below.

(Legally) importing and utilizing uncertified tropical timber could result, in the short term, in the imports of sustainably produced tropical timber (according certification scheme statistics) being small compared with total imports of tropical timber (according to foreign trade statistics). If this share is too small, the consumer will not attach particular significance to the environmental label. Therefore it will lie in the interests of the adherents and organizations supporting a certification scheme for tropical timber, to reveal the consumption of uncertified tropical timber. In particular the environmental protection organizations will keep a critical eye on manufacturers who use uncertified tropical timber.

A certification scheme will not be able to trace *every* cubic metre of tropical timber from the tropical forest to the point of sale. Instead, an integral part of a complete and credible flow control will be a balance between the quantities of sustainably produced roundwood in the producer countries and the import of raw, half-finished and finished wood products in the consumer countries. The „free riders" of a certification scheme who falsely declare non-sustainably produced tropical timber as „sustainably produced" with the intention of profiting from the price and image advantages of the scheme, will present be a problem. However, it is expected that the established tropical timber importers and processing companies in alliance with their corresponding associations, who naturally hope for an upturn of the tropical timber sector compared with the present boycott situation, will exert pressure on the „free riders".[12] Furthermore, any company importing or processing tropical timber which conceals or falsely declares the utilization of uncertified tropical timber, is taking a great risk. A company in Germany can hardly afford to be reputed for causing systematic or deliberate environmental damage.

---

[11] SHAMS (1995) investigated the conditions required for establishing credible environmental labels and the arising information problems. He thereby took into consideration the viewpoint of the developing countries and the specific interests of the stakeholders affected by the labelling scheme.

[12] In this connection the fact pointed out by ENVIRONMENT WATCH (2.6.1995) is of interest, that large timber purchasers from three countries including the Swedish IKEA Group, the German Springer Verlag and the British do-it-yourself chain B&O are exerting strong pressure on the Swedish forestry sector to set up a certification scheme for Swedish timber as soon as possible.

3 Effectiveness and Efficiency of a Certification Scheme Aimed at Protecting Tropical Rain Forests

A certification scheme for tropical (and non-tropcal) timber from sustainable production can be called **effective** only if efforts to suppress the production of tropical timber by „reckless exploitation" succeed with the aid of this instrument. As MATTOO/SINGH (1994) have shown theoretically, an environmental label leads to the desired reduction of the „environmentally damaging" substitute only when - before introduction of the environmental label - the latent demand for the environmentally friendly commodity is greater than the available supply. In view of the increasing concern in industrialized countries over global warming and the small quantities of sustainably produced tropical timber, we can assume this condition is fulfilled.[13]

However, it is necessary to bear in mind that in the case of certification of the tropical timber markets in industrialized countries - as the first realistically executable step before certification of the tropical timber markets in the tropical countries - only a relatively small production volume will be converted to sustainable forest management. This conversion would bring protection for only about 8% of the natural tropical forest areas threatened by destruction.[14] This figure becomes

---

[13] At most one part in a thousand of all tropical forest areas are at present being cultivated sustainably (FAO 1993:50). About a third of the tropical roundwood production is exported raw or processed to industrial countries. The condition is fulfilled even if the tropical timber consumers there are latent consumers of *sustainably* produced tropical timber only to the extent of 5%. Surveys indicate that actual percentages are much greater (see Section 5.5).

[14] The share of industrial roundwood logged in the closed forests of tropical countries which is exported in raw or processed state to non-tropical countries, is about one third of the total quantity produced (AMELUNG/DIEHL 1992:19; another source, VARANGIS/BRAGA/TAKEUCHI 1993:8, states that at most 20% of the production is exported to non-tropical *and tropical* countries). After possible further processing in another tropical country almost all exports enter industrialised countries. Since forestry can be held responsible for at most about 25% of rain forest destruction and deterioration (cf. the studies cited by AMELUNG/DIEHL 1992:17), complete certification of internationally traded tropical timber products will reach only about 8% of the

even less significant with respect to the greenhouse problem, because destruction of the tropical forests contributes only 15% of all the anthropogenic factors.[15]

According to considerations of **efficiency**, a certification scheme for sustainably produced tropical timber is in principle only a second best instrument for preserving natural tropical forests, because other instruments can achieve comparable effects with lower costs. This is so because a certification scheme for the protection of tropical forests does not act directly at the source of the market failure and therefore causes market distortion in other places, imposing additional costs on the economy.

An efficient measure devised to correct a market failure should act as close as possible to the source (cf. BHAGWATI 1971:76ff.). A measure acting on the trade, as in the case of a certification scheme for tropical timber products, would therefore represent the best solution only if a distortion of the market structure for tropical timber products exists. Here this is not the case. Instead, a distortion is given because there are no markets for CO_2 and diversity of natural species. The owners or concessionaries of natural tropical forest areas are not paid for a productive service rendered to the world population (absorption of CO_2 and preservation of the diversity of species). On theoretical considerations the first best solution would therefore be a bonus payment for preserved or reforested tree stock.[16]

A certification scheme does cancel one market distortion - by inciting sustainable forest management in some tropical forest areas - but it produces another distortion. Tropical timber producers who shun the conversion and the initial costs for establishing a sustainable forest management are enticed to divert more timber to uncertified markets in the developing countries or to industrialized countries not affiliated to the certification scheme. A concerted procedure is therefore essential for all end consumer markets in the industrialized countries as well as in the developing countries, above all in China and South Korea, in order to establish the efficiency of a certification scheme.

If the costs for sustainable forest management and the certification scheme cannot be handed down to the consumers without a loss of demand, even a worldwide certification scheme would still produce distortion and therefore be second best. In this case other - also destructive - forms of utilization of the areas such as clearing forests by fire for cattle rearing or agriculture would become relatively

---

areas threatened by destruction. This does not take into consideration that timber producers would then look for new customers for non-sustainably produced tropical timber on the domestic markets, and forestry workers without a job looking for land to cultivate might exert additional pressure on the rain forest (DIEHL 1991:216).

[15] Burning and decay of tropical forests including increased emissions from the soil contribute about 15% to the world-wide additional greenhouse effect which is of anthropogenic origin; 10 percentage points as CO_2 and 5 percentage points as other trace gases, in particular nitrous oxide N_2O, methane CH_4 and carbon monoxide CO (ENQUETE-KOMMISSION 1991, 3. Bericht, Teilband I:45).

[16] ESE (1992, Vol.I:6ff.) sketch the institutional design of a scheme of subsidies for sustainable forest management in developing countries.

attractive. This distortion also arises under the instrument of import boycott presently practiced in many places.

Several reasons exist in favour of establishing a certification scheme, in spite of both the fact that theoretically bonus payments for preservation would be more efficient and that the significance of the international tropical timber trade in the context of tropical forest destruction is relatively small.

First of all it must be pointed out that the export share of tropical timber products lies far above the aforementioned average of one third in some countries so that in these regions a certification scheme could contribute correspondingly more towards tropical forest protection. Secondly, those parts of the control system of an international certification scheme which are intended and required for ensuring that the standards set for sustainable forest management are fulfilled, are also necessary for the theoretically preferable procedure of making preservation bonus payments. Therefore a certification scheme would be an important first step towards setting up necessary institutional structures.

As viewed from the political economic perspective, a certification scheme would have a certain advantage over a compensation system with preservation bonus payments. Namely, it is easier to enforce on account of the indirect financing method. A bonus payment system would be a burden on national budgets or on budgets of international institutions. A certification scheme, however, places only slight burdens on existing budgets because most of the costs are carried by the tropical timber producers or by the consumers through a certification fee. In this connection it is interesting to note that within the framework of the new ITTO-Agreement a fund is to be set up to support the developing countries in establishing sustainable management of their forests (ANONYMOUS 1994g).

Considered on the whole, a certification scheme for the German tropical timber market can constitute an important German contribution within the scope of the global community for establishing an effective set of measures to preserve the tropical rain forests. The Federal Republic of Germany can play an important pioneer role on this issue, for example in cooperation with the Netherlands.[17]

A certification scheme, aimed international trading, is also a sensible flanking measure for the self-set goal of the Federal Republic of Germany to reduce the CO_2 emissions in its territory by 25% of emissions in the year 1990 by the year 2005.

---

[17]   At first it was the intention in the Netherlands since 1993 to impose an import ban for tropical timber from unsustainable production, in a „tropical timber agreement" between the timber trade, the timber industry, trade unions, environmental protection organizations and the authorities. After some problems encountered with the implementation, it is now the intention to introduce step by step in 1996 an internationally harmonized sustainability labelling for *all* timber species, assisted by temporary aid for the producer countries (ENVIRONMENT WATCH 16.12.1994).

4 Certification and Tropical Timber Supply

This study is not concerned with drafting transitional scenarios. Instead, it assesses the long-term effects of a certification scheme, whereby the focus of interest lies in the reactions on the demand side. For this reason it is assumed with regard to the **quantities supplied** to the market, that sustainable forest management will, in the long term, compensate the production losses which could arise on a short- to medium-term basis due to the change from previously predominant reckless exploitation to sustainable management. Therefore we assume that total supply of tropical timber can kept at the present day level.[18] This should be possible primarily through conservative methods of forest management in which harvesting minimizes damage suffered by the remaining stock, but it can also be achieved by extending the transport infrastructure to production forests which have so far not been used, that is by opening up new forests within the areas already declared by legislation today as production forests.

In view of Table 2 which presents information found in the literature on sustainable growth and harvesting quantities in natural tropical forests this assumption is seen as plausible. These figures give only a rough picture of the situation because the regional differences in the stock structure, the conditions of growth and the accessibility of the forest regions are very large. In general, it is true that additional growth of commercial timber depends greatly on the harvesting methods, because the extent of damage suffered by the remaining young trees after a logging operation is decisive for their long-term growth. It has also been found that additional forest development measures lead to a considerable increase of the growth rates per hectare (PRABHU/WEIDELT/LEINERT 1993:157,260).

The FAO (1993:48) assessed the total area of non-coniferous forests in the tropics declared as production forests in the year 1990 to be 309,4 Mio ha.[19] At present (1992) the world-wide production of saw- and veneer logs from tropical non-coniferous timber amounts to about 180 Mio m³. This is the relevant raw

---

[18] In the scenarios this is the quantity offered on the market in the reference year 1993. See also the remarks at the end of the second chapter with regard to the displacement of non-certified tropical timber by consumer demand behaviour.

[19] Thereof 58.3 ha in Africa, 151.2 ha in Asia/Pacific and 99.9 ha in Latin America/Carribean.

product associated with the export of tropical timber products to industrialized countries in all stages of processing.

Table 2:   Sustainable Growth and Harvest of Commercial Timber in Natural Tropical Forests

Region	Details	[m³/ha/year]	Source
Indonesia	Conservative estimate	1.1	ATLANTA (1987, Main Report:20,21)
Indonesia	With improved reforesting and more cautious felling	5.0	ATLANTA (1987, Vol. III:33)
Indonesia	Cautious estimate	2.0	SOETOPO (1978:1)
Asia and Africa	Bandwidth for sustainable, partly plantation-like management	2.5 - 5.0	GOODLAND/ASIBEY/POST/ DYSON (1990, cited by JOHNSON/CABARLE 1993:23)
Indonesia	Average growth rate in natural forests	1.1	IBRD (1990:7)
Worldwide		0.5 - 2.0	UNIDO (1983:22)
Malaysia	Average dipterocarpaceae forest with rotation cycle of 70 years of 30 years	7.0 2.4 - 3.5	BRUENIG (1990b:87)
Philippines	Average dipterocarpaceae forest with rotation cycle of 70 years of 30 years	7.0 3.8	BRUENIG (1990b:87)

These quantities can also be produced on a long-term basis under sustainable forest management. According to Table 2, a conservative estimate of sustainable harvest volume is 1,1 m³ per hectare and year and for the given structure of timber species. Thus, assuming a maximum cultivated area of 309 Mio hectare, it is possible to harvest approx. 340 Mio m³ per year on a long-term basis. However, taking into account that, according to information provided by the FAO (1993:52), so far logging is taking place in - per year - only 3% of the production forest areas and that wide forest areas have not yet been opened up, the medium- to long-term production potential for sustainably produced tropical timber is smaller. On the other hand, the figure of 340 Mio m³ per year does not incorporate the fact that previously unknown timber species could become marketable and that the structure of timber species can be influenced by suitable forest management intervention in favour of commercial species in order to increase the sustainable harvesting volume above the figure of 1.1 m³/ha/year specified above. However, it should be kept in mind that increases of the yield per hectare in a sustainable forest management unit take effect only after considerable delay because of the long ripening time of the trees in natural tropical forests.

In the long run it is therefore certainly possible to increase the global production volume or, alternatively, to extend the protection forest areas by changing the declared status of some present production forests while maintaining the same volume of timber production. All in all, the assumption made in this study within the scope of long-term scenarios, that a complete conversion to sustainable tropical timber production is possible, seems to be justified.

Not only the credibility of the scheme, but also the **price** for which certified tropical timber can be made available to the end consumer determines the effectiveness of a certification scheme. A distinction must be made here between:

- the costs for sustainable forest management,
- the costs for inspections of forest management units with regard to the sustainability criteria defined by the certification scheme and
- the costs for monitoring the flow of tropical timber from the sustainably managed and inspected forest management unit via the further processing stages right through to the end consumer.

Some research is still needed for properly assessing the costs of. A first impression indicates that the higher costs per cultivated hectare *sustainable forest management* compared with the reckless exploitation so far practised in large regions could in the long run be over-compensated by the greater yields per hectare mentioned above - in particular through more conservative harvesting methods and opening the canopy (BRUENIG 1994).[20] Therefore in general the additional assumption is made that an established sustainable forest management will not cause additional costs. Without going into further details of this subject, it suffices to point out that in a sustainably managed forest area in joint-product production further income can be achieved through secondary timber products, that is with non-timber products originating from the flora and fauna.[21]

The assumption that sustainable forest management does not induce additional costs will be altered in Chapter 11.1, where the effects of an increase in logging costs of 5 DM/m^3 are estimated for the aggregate German tropical timber market.

GRAY/HADI (1990:118) evaluated logging costs for the year 1990 in one of the most important tropical timber producing countries, namely Indonesia. The costs for harvest, transport, 20% return on investment and depreciation for logging Meranti roundwood in a moderate to difficult terrain amounted to 32.2 US$/m^3(r). Calculating with a long-term increase in production costs by 10% after changing to a sustainable production and assuming an exchange rate of 1.5 DM/US$, the production price per cubic metre of roundwood would rise by 5 DM/m^3(r). In

---

[20]   For example it was found in an experimental forest management unit in a tropical wetland forest of Surinam that a conservative and efficient timber harvesting method is more priceworthy than the conventional method of reckless exploitation. The direct costs of 0.1 to 0.3 US$/m^3 for environmental protection measures were relatively small (PRABHU/WEIDELT/LEINERT 1993:146).

[21]   cf. DEUTSCHER FORSTVEREIN (1986:43ff.) and PLOTKIN/FAMOLARE (1992) who also consider questions of international marketing in detail.

relation to the average German import unit value for tropical timber this equals an increase of 0.8%.

The second block consists of the costs for an initial *inspection* and for further ongoing inspections. The costs for a first inspection which might even require expensive satellite photographs are estimated as amounting to approx. 1 US$/ha. Follow-up inspections are considerably cheaper at approx. 0.4 US$/ha (BRUENIG 1994). For the further course of events it is therefore assumed that the inspection costs including the initial inspection will average out to an annual amount of 0.43 US$/ha. For the set yield of 1.1 m^3/ha/year for sustainable timber production this is equivalent to about 0,4 US$/m^3.

The costs per m^3 for the *flow control system*, according to data provided by Bruenig, depend strongly on the volume because of the large fixed costs component. For controlled import quantities of logs, sawnwood, etc. in quantities of up to 1.1 to 1.3 Mio m^3 - a volume typical for the Federal Republic of Germany - the costs lie around 1.0 US$/m^3. Figures of 0.3 to 0.6 US$/m^3 or less could be achieved by virtue of the incorporation of non-tropical timber and the greater total volume within the scope of an EC solution. Both aspects must be taken into consideration anyway on account of the international discussion of timber certification and the given competence of the EC for the foreign trade regime. As this figure contains only the costs for quantity flow control within Europe, it is furthermore assumed here that *all* inspection and monitoring costs from the initial source to the end consumer averaged over all imported raw, half-finished and tropical timber products, will amount to 1.6 US$ or 2.4 DM per m^3 roundwood equivalent.[22]

At the present stage of the discussion of certification for tropical timber it is appropriate to trace several versions in the scenarios to be calculated with respect to the range and also the costs of a certification scheme. The following variations will be considered: *Version A I*: The specified certification costs will be charged only on tropical timber whereas timber from northern latitudes will not be certified. However, there is an increasing trend towards extending a certification scheme for timber to the temperate climate latitudes too.[23] For this reason a second version is considered in the scenarios, whereby certification costs will be charged on all timber species (*Version A II*). Finally, a model will be considered in which in addition to a certification scheme for all timber species, the prices for the chief substitute materials for timber (aluminium, plastics and steel) will be increased by an energy tax or by other measures presently being discussed in connection with the reduction of CO_2 emissions (*Version A III*).

---

[22]   Here as in the following an exchange rate of 1.50 DM/US$ is assumed.

[23]   cf. GRAMMEL/KARMANN (1994) and SCHOLZ/KYNAST (1994). Within the scope of the new International Tropical Timber Agreement it was agreed to start consultations for extending the sustainability requirement to all timber species (ANONYMOUS 1994g). The German social democratic party SPD has submitted a petition in the German Federal Parliament which envisages obligatory labelling for timber and timber products from all species and all countries of origin. An analogous ruling is to be prepared at the EC level (ANONYMOUS 1994h).

A rough calculation for window frames shows that an envisaged German energy tax of 7% proposed and calculated by the German Institute for Economic Research (Deutsches Institut für Wirtschaftsforschung, DIW) would increase the prices for aluminium and plastic windows to a greater extent than a certification scheme for tropical and non-tropical timber would increase the prices for wooden windows. Assuming a once-only increase of the energy prices by 7%, the prices for plastic products will rise by 0.3% and the prices for non-ferrous metals and non-ferrous semi-finished products will increase by 0,6% according to calculations made by the DIW (BACH et al. 1994:138). On the other hand, the present price of 540 DM for a wooden window using approx. 0.1 m^3 sawnwood will increase by only 0.24%, taking into account the certification costs specified above and the price increase of 0.2% for wood products due to the energy tax.

5 Environmental Labels and Consumer Behaviour

The ecological aspects of products are becoming increasingly important. Many companies now advertise the environmental compatibility of their products. This is accomplished partly through internal declarations of single companies or associations choosing their own criteria. A survey carried out by IPOS (1993) showed that the credibility of such declarations on the part of consumers is generally slight. Self-declarations of this kind are possible because terms such as „environmentally compatible" and „bio" are not protected by law.

Apart from this, environmental labels exist which are issued by governmental organizations such as the German Institute for Quality Control and Labelling (RAL, Deutsches Institut für Gütesicherung und Kennzeichnungen e.V.) on the basis of scientifically reproducible criteria. These labels are widely accepted by the general population.

Refering to the experience gathered with government controlled environmental labels the following discussion attempts to draw conclusions concerning the effectiveness of a certification scheme for tropical timber originating from sustainable production.

5.1 The Distribution of Environmental Labels

Environmental labels inform consumers about the positive environmental aspects of a product. This is intended to motivate both, consumers to purchase environmentally compatible products and industry to produce them (RAL 1993:3).

Serious environmental labels are issued as quality marks for products which have been tested according to selected criteria to verify their environmental compatibility. It is attempted to take the entire course of a product into consideration. However, the overall assessment of a product is often difficult due to methodical problems in devising „ecological balance sheets" among other reasons, or on account of the geographic distance between the testing institute and the place of production. Often the assessment also depends on social priorities (STAUPE 1990).

Environmentally related product labels are to be found not only in the Federal Republic of Germany, but also - inter alia - in Japan, in the USA and in France. Laundry and dishwashing machines were the first product group to receive the environmental label „European Flower" from the European Union in 1993 (UBA 1993:124).

The environmental label „the Blue Angel" has been issued in the Federal Republic of Germany since 1977 by the German Institute for Quality Control and Labelling. In principle, all consumer goods can apply for the Blue Angel label on the condition that the respective products are environmentally relatively compatible *within their product group*. The criteria are defined by an independent jury consisting inter alia of experts from industry, environmental protection organizations and consumer associations.

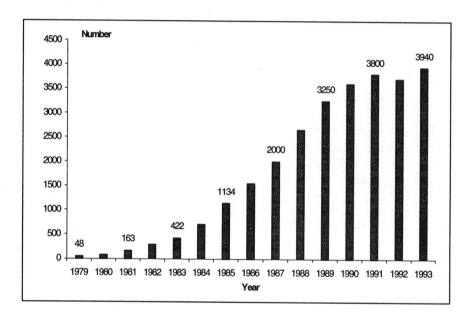

Figure 1:   Products Labelled with a „Blue Angel" in Germany

Source: UBA (1993).

In addition to or as supplement to environmental labels such as the Blue Angel, which can be assigned to any kind of product, product-specific government-controlled information instruments are recommended - for example from the Federal Environmental Agency - such as environmentally related certification of textiles or tropical timber, as a further development of environmental information for the consumer (UBA 1994:54).

The success of the German Blue Angel is evident from the demand by manufacturers for this label. In the meantime a greatly increased number of products are designated with the Blue Angel (see Fig. 1). Only 80 products carried this environmental label in 1980. The number had already risen to 2 650 in 1988, and in 1993 altogether 3 940 products in 77 product groups were entitled to carry this environmental label. Positive developments are seen particularly for central heating systems, paints and paper production (ibid:53).

The market share development of a certified product depends not only on the consumer behaviour but also on the competitive situation in the market. For example, the Blue Angel was unable to establish itself at the end of the 1970s in the German market for paper containing waste paper. Federal German suppliers followed suit only after a foreign company used the Blue Angel when advertising recycling paper. Since then the share of recycled paper products on this market has increased continually (cf. TÖPFER 1990 and OECD 1991:30).

Because of the increased use of environmental labels, the OECD (1991:30f.) is optimistic about their effect on consumer behaviour: „ ... environmental labels can effectively stimulate latent consumer concern in a number of product categories". However, empirical confirmation of this assessment is still lacking because all analyses of the effect of environmental labels known so far ignore the *actual* effects on purchasing behaviour (MATTOO/SINGH 1994:63). Instead, they are based on questioning consumers about their environmental awareness and their resulting consumption preferences. So these analyses are only conditionally suitable for assessing the sales success of products bearing an environmental label because it cannot be assumed that the environmental consciousness declared when questioned automatically reflects corresponding consumer behaviour. This was confirmed by the conversations with specialists held in the course of this study.[24]

A comprehensive empirical investigation of the effects of environmental labels on a market would have to take into account other factors of influence apart from the certificate. Furthermore, it would have to consider the effect of the environmental label on both, on consumer as well as on producer behaviour. As this study concentrates on the effect of tropical timber certification on demand, the following sections focus attention on the effect of environmental labels on consumer behaviour.

The general factors influencing environmentally conscious consumer behaviour are analysed in Section 5.2. Thereafter follows an overview of investigations concerning the Blue Angel (Section 5.3). An empirical analysis of the actual effect of the Blue Angel on consumer behaviour is made in Section 5.4 for low-pollution emulsion paints. Section 5.5 summarizes the results obtained with reference to the product tropical timber.

---

[24]   cf. also UBA (1994:5).

5.2   Factors Influencing Environmentally Conscious Consumer Behaviour

The purpose of an environmental label is to draw the attention of the consumer to a product which is relatively environment-friendly all the way „from the cradle to the grave". The environmental label as visual symbol on the product or its packing material is thereby an information aid ensuring that certain criteria are fulfilled and that the given product is relatively environment-friendly compared with competing products. Therefore the Blue Angel can open up a buyer market of persons controlling their purchasing behaviour in accordance with their environmental consciousness. Furthermore, the room for the pricing policy of producers becomes larger, the more a product can distinguish itself from its competitors through the Blue Angel (MEFFERT/KIRCHGEORG 1993:224).

The effect of an environmental label depends, finally, on the extent to which its information content is consciously noted and accepted by consumers, directing their behaviour accordingly. Therefore the basic condition for success of environmental labels is the existence of environmental awareness of the consumers.

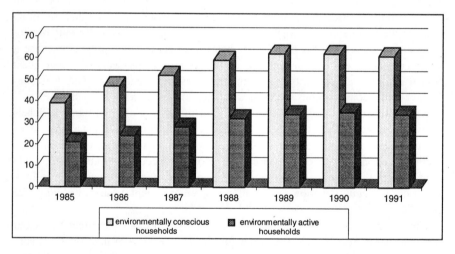

Figure 2:   Divergence Between Environmental Consciousness and Environmental Behaviour in German Households [% of persons questioned]

Source: G&I (1990, cited by MEFFERT/KIRCHGEORG 1993:89).

The environmental consciousness of domestic households in the Federal Republic of Germany has increased distinctly in recent years. Environmental consciousness can be understood as „...knowledge and understanding of the ecological consequences (for example pollution, waste heap, health hazard) of personal consumer behaviour (purchase, consumption, usage and disposal of products) and willingness to adopt consumption behaviour directed towards solving environmental problems" (ibid:91; translation by the authors).

However, social sciences studies have shown that increased environmental awareness has not adequately led to corresponding purchasing behaviour.[25] A market examination by G&I made in 1990 showed that more than half of the German households consider themselves to be environmentally conscious, but only one third manifest this environmental consciousness in corresponding consumer behaviour (see Fig. 2). For example, WENKE (1993:66) points out that in spite of the increased environmental consciousness, the consumption of household chemicals endangering the environment has not decreased. Also, the production of plastic shopping bags and plastic household utensils has increased over the period from 1975 to 1989. On the other hand, the compact washing powders with good environmental assessment have become well established in Germany (UBA 1994:40). Environmentally conscious behaviour must therefore be considered for individual cases.

Numerous personal and exogenous factors affect the relationship between environmental consciousness and consumer behaviour. Some of these factors are:

- *Consumer satisfaction*: The environmental consciousness of consumers is partly in competition with other personal needs and desires. This can have an effect on purchasing behaviour if for example environmentally conscious behaviour would conflict with consumer satisfaction (cf. HERKER 1993).
- *Effectiveness*: Apart from awareness of ecological relationships, awareness of the effectiveness of one's own behaviour on mitigation of environmental problems had a positive effect (ibid). The more complex the relationships are, the less apparent the effectiveness of one's own behaviour is and therefore the weaker the reflection of environmental consciousness in corresponding behaviour will be.
- *Values*: Compliance with environmentally related social values can produce environmentally conscious behaviour if this is coupled with prestige or recognition. At the same time compliance with social values can also have a damaging effect on the environment (cf. HERKNER 1981).
- *Identification*: The greater the extent to which environment-related product features are directly perceivable, the more likely environmentally conscious consumer behaviour becomes. Thus products with little environmental reference produce less environmentally positive purchasing behaviour than ones with greater environmental reference. So because the environmental effects in the production and disposal phases are largely concealed from the consumer, they have little effect on his or her buying decisions (cf. MEF-FERT/KIRCHGEORG 1993:97).
- *Costs:* The environmental compatibility of products may entail additional costs for the consumer which he or she must weigh-up against the advantages of en-

---

[25]   In addition to the studies named, see also STENDER-MONHEMIUS (1995).

vironmentally conservative behaviour (cf. HÜSER 1993). Apart from the actual product price, transaction costs for information on environmentally compatible products, their procurement, utilization and disposal are also involved in the assessment. This factor plays an important role especially for commercial and industrial consumers.

- *Personal benefit:* The greater the personal benefit of environmentally compatible product characteristics, the more likely a consumer is willing to adapt his or her buying behaviour accordingly within the scope of his or her personal assessment of costs and benefits (cf. UBA 1994).

- *Availability:* The transfer of environmental consciousness of consumers into corresponding behaviour is facilitated if the environmentally compatible products are listed in the product range of important retailers.

5.3   Studies Concerning the Blue Angel

So far no quantitative investigations of the effects of an environmental label on the actual buying behaviour have been made.[26] This is also true for Blue Angel products, in spite of the fact that the data available in Germany (for example for modular washing powders and paints) is still the best compared with the international situation.[27]

The existing investigations concerning the Blue Angel in Germany ask instead, among other questions, whether private end consumers pay attention to products bearing the Blue Angel when out shopping. This question was answered in the affirmative by altogether 43% of the consumers questioned (see Table 3).

According to this study, 62% of the persons questioned named the Blue Angel as the attribute which indicates that a product is environmentally compatible. In contrast thereto, terms such as „Bio" or „Eco" are recognized as indicators for environmental compatibility by only 8% of the persons questioned (IPOS 1993). This makes it clear that primarily the environmental labels issued by neutral institutions are perceived as convincing. For certification of tropical timber this means that only an independent institute comes into question for issuing and controlling such a label.

Somewhat less than half of the interrogated consumers expressed willingness to pay a higher price for products with an environmental label (see Table 4). 36% of the persons interrogated in the IPOS study were willing to pay a surcharge of 5%,

---

[26]   A starting point for quantitative effect analysis is given by an investigation made by the German Federal Environmental Agency in relation to environmental behaviour of consumers using data on energy or water consumption covering the entire federal territory (cf. UBA 1994).

[27]   According to a judgement made by the OECD (1991:28f.).

12% a surcharge of 6% to 10% and 2.5% of all persons questioned were even prepared to pay prices increased by 11% to 15%. Only 0.8% of the questioned persons stated that they would pay a price increase of more than 15% for environmentally compatible products. Nearly half of all persons interrogated were not prepared to accept any price increase at all.[28] As quantitative indicator of the willingness to pay higher prices, these figures give a weighted average of 2% for the whole of Germany and 2.6% for the former federal states.

Table 3: Who Pays Attention to the Blue Angel When Shopping?

[% of persons questioned]	*Germany*	*West*	*East*
yes	43	57	29
no	34	30	38
Blue Angel unknown	23	12	33

Source: IPOS (1993).

Table 4: Willingness of Consumers to Pay: Who is Prepared to Pay More for Blue Angel Products?

[% of persons questioned]	*Germany*	*West*	*East*
yes	45	60	28
no	30	19	38
do not know	2	3	1
Blue Angel unknown	23	12	33

Source: IPOS (1993).

Conversations with representatives of industrial associations and companies held within the scope of this investigation made it clear that in general no significant willingness to pay more for environmentally compatible products is actually observable among private or commercial end consumers. According to these conversations, price disadvantages of certified compared with uncertified products are above all hardly accepted by commercial end consumers so that a certified product is given preference over an uncertified product only if the prices are the same. For example, it was not possible to enforce higher prices for saw chain oils made from plant oils and labelled with the Blue Angel against the competition of oils without Blue Angel produced from fossil raw materials. Experience with photo-

---

[28] Data from AXEL BILLIG & PARTNER (1992) and „Daten zur Umwelt 1992/93" (cited by UBA 1994:37). Similar results were also obtained from surveys carried out in USA and Canada (cf. OECD 1991:12 and ROPER ORGANIZATION 1990, cited by MATTOO/SINGH 1994).

copy units showed, too that only price arguments play a role, and that price disadvantages of certified products are not accepted by commercial end consumers.

These examples point out the problematic aspect of environmental labels for manufacturing supplies and for raw materials which are not contained in the final product in a directly perceivable manner. Besides, in advertising their utilization can only be made clear to the customer with great difficulty.

This is different in submarkets where tropical timber is visibly contained in the final product. Conversations with representatives of the association of the paint industry showed that labelling of emulsion lacquer paints with the Blue Angel is an effective marketing instrument especially in the do-it- yourself field, permitting product differentiation with respect to competing products.

5.4   Case Study: Low Pollution Emulsion Lacquer Paints

For lack of corresponding primary surveys on consumer behaviour, the market development of a product - emulsion lacquer paints, which are mostly labelled with the Blue Angel - has been taken within the scope of this study to quantify the effect which an environmental label can have on consumer behaviour.

The possibility of awarding the Blue Angel to low-pollution paints has existed since 1988.[29] In the official production statistics, paints with low or no solvent content and paints with solvents are classified in different product groups. The distinction chosen here between paints with low or no solvent content and paints containing solvent is based on the distinction given by the association of the paint industry (VERBAND DER LACKINDUSTRIE e.V. 1993). Examples of paints containing solvents are alkyde resin paints, cellulose paints and polyester resin paints. Examples of paints containing little or no solvent are powder paints, emulsion paints, emulsion lacquer paints and electrophoretic paints.

According to statements made by experts[30] it can be assumed that the majority of the emulsion lacquer paints for buildings listed in the production statistics under the registration number 4641-81 as containing little or no solvent, are labelled today with the Blue Angel. Direct substitution relationships with regard to emulsion lacquer paints exist primarily with respect to solvent-containing alkyde resin paints.

The following discussion investigates the effect of the Blue Angel on the basis of a comparative analysis of the production and consumption development of

---

[29]   The environmental label RAL-UZ 12a has been awarded to low-pollution paints and the label RAL-UZ 12b to powder paints.

[30]   Representatives of the Association of the Paint Industry and of a research institute for pigments and paints (Forschungsinstitut für Pigmente und Lacke e.V.).

emulsion lacquer paints, other paints containing little or no solvent and the sol-vent-containing paints (see also Appendix A2).[31]

It is thereby not possible within the scope of this study to examine the extent to which factors other than award of the Blue Angel affect the production develop-ment. It is therefore assumed that all paints are subject to the same general eco-nomic setting so that the Blue Angel and the product characteristics directly con-nected therewith (for example, lower solvent emission) constitute the only distin-guishing feature. Effects on the total sales of paints and lacquers are eliminated from the analysis by considering the development of the respective shares in the total production.

Table 5:   Share of Paints Containing Little or No Solvent and Paints Containing Solvents in Total West German Production

[%]	1986	1987	1988	1989	1990	1991	1992	1993
Share of paints containing solvents in the total production,	85.9	84.5	83.9	82.4	81.4	79.1	78.2	77.2
thereof share of alkyde resin paints in the total production	---	28.1	26.5	26.5	24.4	25.7	24.2	22.2
Share of paints containing little or no solvent in the total production,	14.1	15.5	16.1	17.6	18.6	20.9	21.8	22.8
thereof share of emulsion lacquer paints in the total production	2.4	2.7	3.1	3.7	4.1	4.0	4.3	4.9
Notes: --- No information available. Market shares calculated on the basis of quantities.								

Source: Federal Statistical Office (STATISTISCHES BUNDESAMT, Fachserie 4, Reihe 3.1, various years); VERBAND DER LACKINDUSTRIE (1993). Own calculations.

It is evident from Table 5 that the share of paints containing little or no solvent in the total production has steadily increased in the course of time. In 1986 the share of these paints was only about 14%, but by 1993 it had increased to more than 22% of the total paint production in Germany. On the other hand, the pro-duction share of paints containing solvent dropped from 86% to 77% during the period from 1986 to 1993. Alkyde resin paints and emulsion lacquer paints have both shown a behaviour corresponding to the trend of their product groups. The share of alkyde resin paints in the total production dropped from 28% in 1987 to 22% in 1993. The substitutes for alkyde resin paints labelled with the Blue Angel, the emulsion lacquer paints, increased from 2.7% to nearly 5% during the same period. The production share of emulsion lacquer paints has thereby increased to a

---

[31]   It must thereby be borne in mind that apart from emulsion lacquer paints, also powder paints can be awarded the Blue Angel. However, before 1993 no Blue Angel has been awarded to a powder paint (RAL 1993:35f.).

much greater extent than that of all paints with little or no solvent content considered together. In a parallel fashion, the share of alkyde resin paints dropped more than the production share of all paints containing solvents considered together.

Thus it is evident from the *production development* that the significance of paints containing little or no solvent has increased on the whole. In particular, emulsion lacquer paints mainly labelled with the Blue Angel were able to extend their market share in Germany to an above average extent. Therefore it is reasonably plausible to conclude that the Blue Angel was the decisive factor for this market development. This is confirmed by the fact that their direct substitute, the alkyde resin paints, reported above average market losses.

The successful transposition of environmental consciousness of the private consumer to corresponding buying behaviour is assisted in this example by the personal concern about the toxic emissions involved when using paints containing solvents. Solvent-free paints labelled with the Blue Angel have only slight significance for the professional user, in which case the purchaser is usually not exposed to the fumes him- or herself. Selection of materials by these users is determined less by environmental considerations and more by product characteristics and prices (OECD 1991:29).

Table 6:   Development of Production Unit Values for Paints Containing Little or No Solvent and Paints Containing Solvents

[DM/kg]	1987	1988	1989	1990	1991	1992	1993
Total paint market	6.7	6.8	6.9	7.1	---	---	7.4
Paints containing solvent	7.9	7.6	7.9	8.5	---	---	8.5
thereof alkyde resin paints	6.4	6.6	6.6	6.8	6.7	6.7	6.8
Paints containing little or no solvent	6.4	6.4	6.5	6.7	---	---	7.0
thereof emulsion lacquer paints	4.7	4.7	5.2	5.6	6.7	7.0	8.0

Notes: --- : No information available.
The essentially solvent-free emulsion paints and artificial resin bound plasters are not included among the paints containing little or no solvent.

Source: See Table 5. Own calculations.

The *price development* in Table 6 shows that the average production unit value per ton of emulsion lacquer paints predominantly labelled with the Blue Angel enjoyed an above average increase. The value almost doubled during the period from 1987 to 1993. A cautious interpretation of this - and of the rising market share - would be that consumers are willing to pay more for environmentally compatible products.

The evaluations have so far considered only the development of inland production. For a correct analysis it is necessary to take *foreign trade effects* into consideration, too, because foreign consumers of these products exist, and domestic consumers also use like imported products.

Two items relevant to this investigation are covered by the foreign trade statistics of the Federal Statistical Office (STATISTISCHES BUNDESAMT, Fachserie 7, Reihe 2): „Paints and lacquers based on synthetic polymers or chemically modified natural polymers dispersed or dissolved in a non-aqueous medium" and „Paints and lacquers based on synthetic polymers or chemically modified natural polymers dispersed or dissolved in an aqueous medium". Paints in a „non-aqueous medium" are predominantly solvent-containing paints and lacquers. Paints with an „aqueous medium" are chiefly ones with little or no solvent content. However, in contrast to the production statistics, emulsion lacquer paints and alkyde resin paints are not treated separately in the foreign trade statistics.

Table 7: Domestic Market Shares of Paints Containing Little or No Solvent and Paints Containing Solvents

[%]	*1989*	*1990*	*1991*	*1992*	*1993*
Share of paints containing solvents in the total domestic market	83.6	82.8	---	---	79.5
Share of paints containing little or no solvent in the total domestic market	16.4	17.2	---	---	20.5
Notes: ---: No information available. Market shares calculated on the basis of quantities (inland production minus net export).					

Source: See Table 5 and STATISTISCHES BUNDESAMT (Fachserie 7, Reihe 2, various years). Own calculations.

Supplementing the analysis of the production development of paints and lacquers, the foreign trade data (exports and imports) permit conclusions concerning the development of the domestic market for paints and lacquers containing little or no solvent on the one hand and containing solvents on the other hand.

It becomes clear that there is a trend towards paints containing little or no solvent (see Table 7) in the inland consumption too. The share of paints containing little or no solvent in domestic consumption increased from 16% to more than 20% during the period from 1989 to 1993, whereas during the same time the market share of paints containing solvents dropped from 84% to 80%. It is also clearly evident that foreign trade with paints and lacquers follows the trend towards paints containing little or no solvent. The contribution to exports and imports made by paints containing little or no solvent increased, too during the period from 1988 to 1993, whereas the contribution made by paints containing solvents fell during the same time (see Table 8).

Table 8:   Shares of Paints Containing Little or No Solvent and Paints Containing
Solvents, in the Export and Import of All Paints

[%]	1988	1989	1990	1991	1992	1993
Import share of paints containing solvents	36.9	37.0	37.7	38.4	---	39.7
Import share of paints containing little or no solvent	63.1	63.0	62.3	61.6	---	60.3
Export share of paints containing solvents	27.7	26.8	28.6	30.9	---	34.0
Export share of paints containing little or no solvents	72.3	73.2	71.4	69.1	---	66.0
Notes: ---: No information available. Market shares calculated on the basis of quantities.						

Source: See Table 7. Own calculations.

In summary it can be said that that there is a definite trend in Germany towards the use of paints containing little or no solvent. This is borne out by the development of paint production in Germany as well as by the consumption development. In particular, the production of emulsion lacquer paints labelled with the Blue Angel has increased to an extent which is above average. The extent to which the use of emulsion lacquer paints in domestic consumption has increased cannot be determined unambiguously because corresponding sectioning of the foreign trade statistics does not exist. However, since the consumption development for paints containing little or no solvent is comparable to the tendency shown by the production development of these paints, it can be assumed that the development of inland consumption of emulsion lacquer paints corresponds to the production development in general.

The extent to which the positive development of paints containing little or no solvent is *solely* attributable to the effect of the Blue Angel cannot be assessed with certainty from the available statistical information. For this purpose it would be necessary to distinguish between products with and without Blue Angel within the paints containing little or no solvent in all relevant statistics.

The association of the paint industry considers the Blue Angel to be an effective marketing instrument and draws a positive balance as follows: „ ... the industry and consumers have both gathered good experience with the Blue Angel as criterion facilitating comparative purchasing decisions ... ".[32]

---

[32]   VERBAND DER LACKINDUSTRIE (1993:8); translation by the authors.

5.5   Implications for a Certification of Tropical Timber

From the case example of emulsion lacquer paints labelled with the Blue Angel, it can be concluded that an environmental label can support a product's market penetration effectively. This result cannot be applied to the case example of tropical timber without reservation: The negative effects of reckless forest exploitation do not affect consumers as directly as exposure to the toxic fumes emitted by paints containing solvents, making direct analogy to the sales and price dynamics unrealistic.

Conversations with representatives of the association of the paint industry revealed that above all there exists a market potential on the do-it-yourself sector for emulsion lacquer paints labelled with the Blue Angel. Analogously, it is predicted that consumers will react positively to a tropical timber certification for the sale of mouldings and building material in the hobby and building market.

The general factors described in Section 5.2 influencing environmentally considerate behaviour of consumers, are also of significance with respect to consumer demand for certified tropical timber. In this case it is appropriate to consider not only private end consumers of tropical timber, but also to include domestic processing consumers of tropical timber and tropical timber products, because in many cases the end consumer is not aware of the utilization of tropical timber in a final product.

In the following discussion the possible reactions of consumers to a certification scheme for tropical timber will be examined theoretically and polarized into two typical scenarios of the demand. The demand scenarios will be linked into the calculations performed in Part III. The basis for these scenarios consists of the available results of surveys, statements made by representatives of industrial and consumer associations on the effects of the Blue Angel, as well as the case example of low-pollution paints, in addition to the discussion of the factors influencing environmentally considerate consumer behaviour given in Section 5.2.

The utilization fields for tropical timber can be fundamentally differentiated in terms of the immediate perception and decision range for the private end consumer (visible uses) and uses for tropical timber which are recognisable for the processing consumer but do not normally reach the private end consumer (invisible uses). The addressee of the information an environmental label contains is different for these two cases. In the case of visible uses, end consumers, that is households purchasing for example furniture or windows made of tropical timber, can be addressed directly. In contrast, the reaction of the tropical timber processing industry is decisive in the case of invisible uses (for example concrete formwork).

The following *basic assumptions* are made for both demand scenarios: It is assumed that in the course of introducing the certification scheme, the discussion on tropical forest problems will be carried out in a more differentiated manner and that the purchase of certified tropical timber will find positive recognition in society (factor „values"). It is furthermore assumed that consumers will find the certification scheme credible and that former consumer preference for tropical timber, which existed before substitution due to social pressure exerted by the campaign against tropical timber, will be effective again.

On some submarkets there was until recently a fashion trend towards lighter timber to the disadvantage of some of the relatively dark decorative tropical timbers. It is assumed that a certification scheme - in the course of the already manifest fashion reorientation in favour of darker timber -[33] can set positive accents for tropical timber in competition with non-tropical non-coniferous timber. This means that it is assumed that a certification scheme can help to reverse the negative effect of the past fashion trend on the demand for tropical timber.

At present many potential suppliers of tropical timber products, for example building material markets, have removed these products from their product line. It is therefore assumed that in the course of the introduction of a certification scheme, the willingness of the trade to stock certified tropical timber products will again increase accordingly. This will make tropical timber products available again to the consumer (factor „availability").

For visible uses it is assumed that certified tropical timber will establish itself relatively quickly, completely replacing uncertified tropical timber in the course of time. For invisible uses, where the utilization of tropical timber is only partially or not at all evident for the end consumer, certified tropical timber will first of all recover former markets on which tropical timber has technical advantages which could compensate for possible price disadvantages. In the long run tropical timber will assert itself in other utilization fields too, because advertising with the certificate is possible and the use of uncertified tropical timber entails the danger of loss of image (in this respect, see the remarks made at the end of Chapter 2). Furthermore, companies can include the use of certified tropical timber as a positive aspect in their environmental declaration within the scope of the EC environmental audit regulations.

Both of the following demand scenarios therefore assume that a certification scheme can reverse the effects of the campaign against tropical timber and the shift of fashion in recent years, so that the demand for tropical timber will increase in any case. However, the demand scenarios differ with regard to the extent to which consumers are prepared to pay a higher price for certified tropical timber products.

The experience of private and commercial consumers with products labelled with the Blue Angel as described in Section 5.3 lead to the conclusion that craftsmen and industry are only willing to pay more for certified tropical timber (see the example given above for saw chain oils and photocopy units) when the tropical timber products are passed-on to the end consumers after processing (windows, doors). They will not if the tropical timber is consumed in the production process (concrete formwork, packaging). It is to be expected that among the handed-over tropical timber products, primarily the visible uses will meet increased consumer

---

[33]   cf. among others KAMM (1991), ANONYMOUS (1994e) and NAUMANN (2.8.1994).

willingness to accept higher prices (see the analogous example of low-pollution emulsion lacquer paints given above), because here the consumer can clearly identify the use of tropical timber. Therefore the commercial processing consumer of tropical timber will regard the certificate as an efficient marketing instrument for placing his products in certain groups of buyers, primarily where visible uses are involved.

Awareness of the environmental aspects of tropical timber trade is very distinctive through public discussion of the climate change (factor „identification"). Nevertheless, the different environmental consequences resulting from reckless exploitation of tropical timber on the one hand and sustainable forest management on the other hand, can hardly be perceived directly by the consumers on account of their great geographical distance from the producer countries. Therefore it is difficult for consumers to verify the results of their own behaviour (factor „effectiveness"). Furthermore, the climatic effects of tropical forest destruction are long term so that the personal advantage is not immediately evident as in the case of paints. So the individual consumer can hardly expect a immediate positive advantage from the purchase of certified tropical timber (factor „personal utility"). All these considerations lead to the expectation that a possible willingness to pay higher prices for certified tropical timber is unlikely to be strongly pronounced.

Two consumer demand scenarios will be calculated in Part III of this study:

Consumer demand scenario with willingness to pay higher prices:
    „Due to their concern about conservation of tropical rain forests, *consumers* are willing to pay higher prices for certified tropical timber especially in visible uses of tropical timber, but also in the case of properly declared invisible uses. For *inland processing consumers* of tropical timber, certified tropical timber has no quality advantages over „recklessly" produced tropical timber, so these consumers refrain from expressing any preference. However, when processing certified tropical timber, the company has the possibility of passing-on the higher prices for certified tropical timber to the consumers on account of their increased willingness to pay. In this situation, processing consumers, too will accept additional costs incurring to them when using certified tropical timber."

More detailed information regarding willingness to pay higher prices is contained in the figures obtained from the investigations concerning the Blue Angel (IPOS 1993). These figures showed that consumers in the former federal German states are prepared to pay 2.6% more for products labelled with the Blue Angel, calculated as a weighted average. Varangis et al. (cited in MATTOO/SINGH 1994:62) found that European consumers are willing to pay 5% to 15% more for sustainably produced tropical timber. A representative survey of British consumers commissioned by the World Wide Fund for Nature found willingness to pay 13.3% more for tropical timber from sustainable forestry (ESE 1992, Vol.II:92).

Within the scope of this study, a lower value lying at the bottom end of the spectrum is chosen on account of the restrictions mentioned above. It is assumed that consumers in all submarkets as well as in the total market are willing to pay 5% more.

Consumer demand scenario without any willingness to pay higher prices:

„The environmental consciousness of *consumers* does not reflect any willingness to pay higher prices for certified tropical timber in visible or invisible uses. The reasons for this are that positive effects of sustainable forest management are not directly perceived by the consumers, and the utilitarian value for the individual is slight. However, certified tropical timber will be given preference if prices are comparable. *Producers* do not pay attention to the certificate when consuming tropical timber. They use certified tropical timber for further processing only if the price is the same as for substitutes or if any superiorities in quality justify the higher price."

Part II

Basic Scenarios for a
Certified Tropical Timber Market
in the Federal Republic of Germany

The purpose of this part of the study is to calculate basic scenarios for the main German end consumer areas of tropical timber under simplified assumptions for the case that this timber will be certified, in order to estimate the amounts of tropical timber consumed. These basic scenarios are then used in Part III as the basis for calculating extended scenarios taking into consideration all adaptations on the supply and on the demand side resulting from the costs of a certification scheme and of sustainable forest management, from the willingness of consumers to pay more for a commodity produced with due consideration for the environment and from the price-boosting effect of an OECD-wide certification scheme.

First of all (Chapter 6) some terms will be defined and the database will be described. In the chapters which follow, the distribution of tropical timber will be examined starting with the imports (Section 7.1) and continuing via the processing industries (Section 7.2) to the end consumers (Section 7.3). A complete distribution is then derived (Section 7.4) for a typical year (1984) before the onset of the campaign against tropical timber. A specification of the basic scenarios for the main end consumer areas then follows in Chapter 8.

6 Definitions, Database and Data Processing

It is first of all necessary to provide a formal **definition** for the term „tropical timber" compatible with this research subject, because this term can be used in rather different manners. Strictly speaking, tropical timber is the designation applied to timber growing in more or less closed tropical forests between the Tropic of Capricorn and the Tropic of Cancer. The most recent estimates made by the United Nations (UN) indicate that these forests constitute 43% of the world-wide timber stock (UN/ECE /FAO 1992:1). The species structure of natural tropical forests is dominated by non-coniferous trees. Coniferous species such as agathis or pinus merkusii are found only to a limited extent.[34] Because of the dominance of non-coniferous timber species, the term „tropical timber" is often used as if it applies only to non-coniferous tropical timber.

Non-coniferous timber is often called hardwood, because compared with coniferous timber it is generally characterized by shorter fibres and a greater density. However, there are exceptions to this general rule. For example, the widely distributed African abachi (also called obéché) is lighter than many domestic German timbers such as poplar or spruce (VDH, Blatt 57, 58).

The study contributes to the discussion of sustainable development. The fact that non-sustainable exploitation of tropical forests has far-reaching consequences for the global climate and the diversity of species in the flora and fauna forms the basis for the study. It is therefore appropriate that this study focuses as much attention as possible on tropical timber from natural forests, excluding timber from plantations.

Coniferous roundwood constitutes only a small part of exported roundwood from natural tropical forests. This primarily reflects the stock structure of natural forests. In contrast, in tropical plantations both coniferous timber species such as pinus caribea and different species of non-coniferous timber such as eucalyptus and teak are cultivated (STEINLIN 1987:51). However, the volume of tropical timber obtained from plantations is small compared with the amount logged in the natural forests. The foreign trade statistics do not give any information on the geographical location of the tropical timber, so the auxiliary assumption is made

---

[34] Non-coniferous timber is timber from non-coniferous trees which are classified botanically as Angiospermae. Coniferous timber (softwood) comes from pine trees classified botanically as Gymnospermae.

here, supported by similar delimitation methods found in the literature, that all exported non-coniferous tropical timber comes from natural forests and all coniferous tropical timber originates from plantations. Therefore, unless specified otherwise, in this study tropical timber is understood to mean non-coniferous timber originating from natural forests.

The year 1989 is taken for Germany as the start of a publicly effective **anti-tropical timber campaign (ATC)**. The German Federal Environmental Agency (UBA 1994:234) listed in 1989 altogether 73 non-governmental organizations calling for a general boycott of tropical timber. In January 1989 the German association of councils and municipalities (DEUTSCHER STÄDTE- UND GE-MEINDEBUND) declared in a press statement (No. 1/89) that it intended to work toward a more intensified use of domestic timber in public building projects. An important German non-governmental environment organization (Deutscher Natur-schutzring - Bundesverband für Umweltschutz) started a campaign in June 1989 to entice German cities, rural districts and communities not to use tropical timber any more. Until then only 25 cities and communities had agreed to such a waiver, among them Göttingen, Hannover, Kassel, Münster, Wuppertal and parts of Berlin. By 1994 the UBA (ibid) had counted roughly 3000 communities and many units of public administration who had made such decisions.

The **database** for the distribution analysis for the year 1984 shown in Section 7.4 was established primarily through the results of the extensive research and calculations of MÜLLER (1987) concerning the utilization, processing and final consumption of timber of all species and regions of origin, in the Federal Republic of Germany.[35] A similarly comprehensive distribution analysis for the 1990s was not possible for lack of data. Additionally, the data from Müller had to be supplemented with own calculations because they were not specifically related to tropical timber. A distribution analysis solely confined to tropical timber was impossible too, because consistent data concerning the use of tropical timber in the German timber industry can be obtained only by continually making comparisons with the quantities of other home-grown and imported non-coniferous and coniferous timber species.

For this study, the authors were unable to collect their own primary data on the distribution of tropical timber in the 1990s in the German timber industry, due to the large number of producers. With relatively few companies processing tropical timber, the only possibility which might have provided a starting point was the German veneer industry. However, following this end was superfluous because at the same time a Dutch institute commissioned by the ITTO carried out, among other tasks, a survey in the German veneer industry.[36] As with its predecessor in

---

[35]   The data from MANTEL/SCHNEIDER (1967) and KRAFT (1975) are considered in the meantime obsolete.

[36]   Independently of this it appears to be appropriate, as the authors found in the course of the study, to exercise moderation or to bundle data requests made to the industry. RESSEL (1986:11) too found in the course of his interrogation of the German timber industry various complaints about too frequent interrogation by various institutions.

1993, the response to this survey was limited in the Germany veneer industry, so that reliable extrapolations were not possible (DE BOER 13.12.1994).

The trend analyses for certain end consumer sectors in Chapter 8 were based on official statistics, on data from various producer associations and commercial branch information services and on information gathered from the published literature and discussions with experts. The evaluated statistical material is very diverse in its disaggregation into coniferous and non-coniferous timber from the tropics and from temperate and boreal zones. The next section summarizes the details of data processing for the trend analyses.

The German foreign trade statistics contain only for a small number of half-finished and finished tropical timber products explicit data on *imports and exports*. For other products the utilization of tropical timber must be inferred from the country of origin (see Appendix A1 for the procedure). In official German statistics on *production* a distinction between non-coniferous and coniferous timber is made in only a few instances. The extent to which timber from tropical or temperate latitudes is involved, is not specified. The „timber statistics" provided by the Federal Statistical Office (STATISTISCHES BUNDESAMT, Fachserie 4, Reihe 8.3) do not document the quantities of tropical roundwood taken-in by German veneer factories on commission order. Only roundwood issued by the veneer factories themselves on commission order is listed. Considerable quantities are thereby not considered because the large German veneer factories mostly produce on commission order, for example for the veneer dealers (OLLMANN 31.8.1994). For this reason, the tropical timber consumption of the German timber processing industry is, according to these statistics, less than the amount of tropical timber imported during the same period.

The *linkages* of the individual sectors of German forestry and timber processing industry cannot be discerned from input/output tables regularly published by the Federal Statistical Office, due to the rather high degree of aggregation. Special excerpts of the input/output calculations kindly provided by the Federal Statistical Office gave better starting points, even though it was again not possible to distinguish between tropical and non-tropical timber.

The database on the *end consumer* side is of varying quality.[37] In addition to the input/output tables which do not consider tropical timber separately from other timber, official statistics provide a rough orientation on domestic wood consumption through the statistics on material and merchandise received in mining and in the processing industry (STATISTISCHES BUNDESAMT, Fachserie 4, Reihe 4.2.4). These statistics too do not distinguish tropical timber from other species.

For some timber products designated as „tropical timber", the foreign trade statistics shows consumption abroad. However for most exports of tropical timber products such a category does not exist, so that here too, as for all half-finished and finished tropical timber products consumed in the domestic market, it was

---

[37]   cf. also MÜLLER (1987:Summary, 29-30) with regard to the inadequacy of available data on production and utilization of timber products of all timber species in the Federal Republic of Germany.

necessary to resort to questionnaires and statistics of the corresponding producer associations, branch information services and leading manufacturers. In many cases full time series are therefore not available, or they are still being constructed and therefore in a rudimentary state due to the fact that the demand for information arose only recently in connection with the campaign against tropical timber. Explicitly this means that in some branches only data on percentages of timber used which is tropical timber are available.

In the building sector too, which is important for tropical timber, the qualitiy of the data with regard to the utilization of all timber species in general and tropical timber in particular, varies. The official statistics contain no detailed information on tropical timber. For example, the series „selected figures for the building industry“ from the Federal Statistical Office contains only data on wooden particle boards and coniferous sawnwood. Even the analysis by Müller which is fundamental for every investigation of timber consumption in the Federal Republic of Germany, can only roughly estimate timber consumption in the building industry. Among the more recently collected data, the study made by KROTH/ KOLLERT/FILIPPI (1991) is of special significance. These authors analysed and quantified timber utilization in important fields of civil engineering and building construction for the period from 1986 to 1988 on commission by the German Federal Department of Food, Agriculture and Forestry.

For the window, outer door, inner door and staircases markets, detailed figures concerning material utilization for domestic production sold in the domestic market are available from the branch information service Detail-Marketing-Dienste Baumarktforschung in Essen (DMD 1995a,b,c,d). The data covers the consumption of aluminium, plastic, glass, tropical and non-tropical timber, respectively.

Important details and background information were also obtained through conversations with Prof. Dr. Heiner Ollmann of the Federal Research Centre for Forestry and Forest Products in Hamburg.

7 Distribution of Tropical Timber in the Federal Republic of Germany

For evaluating the consequences of a certification scheme for the German tropical timber market it is necessary to determine imports, further processing and final utilization of tropical timber in the German timber industry.

The next section documents the development of foreign trade of tropical timber products in all stages of processing since 1984. Then follows a selection of raw timber categories, half-finished and finished timber products in which inland processing of tropical timber is known to be involved (Sections 7.2 and 7.3). Finally, Section 7.4 brings an analysis of the distribution of tropical timber in the Federal Republic of Germany for the year 1984.

7.1 Tropical Timber Imports and Exports

As explained in the previous chapter, the amount of statistical information available on production, import and export of tropical timber products in Germany is limited. The foreign trade statistics indicate that Germany exports few tropical roundwood and half-finished goods made of tropical timber. Finished products too, in as far as they are listed with a separate itemisation for „tropical timber", show no significant export volumes. For some important half-finished and finished tropical timber products, only aggregate export figures covering all timber species are available from the foreign trade statistics. For example, these statistics show that for windows, wall and ceiling coverings and furniture made of *all timber species*, imports exceeded exports in recent years and that the volume of goods either imported or exported was far less than those traded domestically (cf. also MÜLLER 1987:89,94,118). Since there are no indications that the share of domestic consumption of windows, wall and ceiling coverings and furniture made of *tropical timber* is smaller than the average for all timber species, it is assumed in the further discussion that their import development is an accurate indicator of the development of domestic consumption.

Fig. 3 shows the results of the evaluation of the foreign trade statistics. The gross imports, expressed as roundwood equivalents, are depicted here.[38] It is clearly evident that the import structure has shifted away from roundwood, sawn-wood and mouldings towards processed products such as plywood and building material.[39] This is a development which is primarily due to export restrictions on unprocessed tropical timber in important export countries.

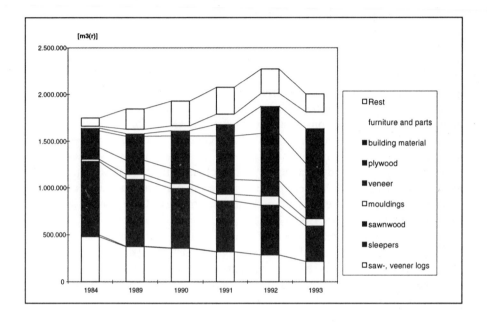

Figure 3:   Structure of Tropical Timber Imports in the Federal Republic of Germany

Source: STATISTISCHES BUNDESAMT, Fachserie 7, Reihe 2, various years. Own calculations.
Note: Instead of the actual timber content of the imports, the roundwood volume used to produce them is shown here, expressed in roundwood equivalents [m³(r)].

The volume of tropical timber imports, expressed as roundwood equivalents, increased until 1992 in spite of the campaign against tropical timber. This is a clear indication that an analysis of the German tropical timber market and of the possible effects of certification, must start by considering the individual tropical timber products and markets.

---

[38] Exports and re-exports are not taken into consideration, see Appendix A4 in connection therewith.

[39] Such as windows, doors, parquet flooring and parts thereof, see also Fig. 5 in Section 7.3.

It cannot be conclusively assessed at the present time whether the import de-cline in 1993 introduces a reversal of the long-term rising trend. It may even be the case that statistical problems lie at the root of this conspicuous development. Although the initial version of the foreign trade statistics for 1993 has already been revised, errors are evidently still present in the latest version for some timber products. The price of tropical timber has recently increased so that the indicated trend may partly be a normal adaptation to the price development.

The diagram shows that furniture and furniture parts, building material and plywood are chiefly responsible for the import increase. The increased plywood imports are also traceable to the fact that plywood formerly produced in Germany from imported tropical roundwood has been replaced with imported finished products (OLLMANN 16.12.1994). The recovery rates are usually lower in the plywood factories of tropical countries, so that this substitution process boosts the entire import volume expressed as roundwood equivalents without necessarily implying increased final consumption of plywood in Germany.

For tropical timber veneers, several major German companies reacted to the massive export restrictions of many tropical timber exporting countries at the beginning of the 1980s by erecting new production facilities in these countries or moving old ones there. Therefore the increased imports of tropical veneers are largely substitutes for veneers formerly manufactured in Germany by the same companies (GREFERMANN 1988:119).

Among the building materials, the booming parquet branch and the increasing imports of window parts stand out. The parquet branch is expanding especially in the field of finished floors, as veneer sheets are preferentially used as carriers to give the required flat underfloors. This may also be a reason for the increasing volume of plywood imports. Underfloors are a typical invisible use of tropical timber. The consumer is not aware of the utilization of tropical timber so that the campaign against tropical timber does have an effect, resulting possibly in in-creased consumption.

OLLMANN (16.12.1994) suspects that other areas which are remote from the consumer and which showed increased consumption in spite of the campaign against tropical timber include coach and vehicle interior materials, as well as individually produced furniture and fitted furnishings in shops, hotels, banks and insurance company offices. Ollmann also assumes that altogether approximately 50 000 m^3 of tropical timber are consumed as mouldings not sold through building material markets (picture frames, sauna, etc.). This area too was hardly affected by the campaign against tropical timber.

7.2   Processing of Tropical Timber in the German Timber Industry

Before analysing the final consumption of tropical timber products in the Federal Republic of Germany, the general structure of inland further processing of raw timber, half-finished timber products and finished timber products made of tropical timber will first be considered. A discussion of those products in which tropical timber dominates in relative or absolute magnitude is presented, thus evaluating the scope for a distribution analysis.

In the Federal Republic of Germany the inland consumption of timber is dominated by coniferous timber,[40] 80% of which originated from inland forests. Tropical non-coniferous timber amounts to only about 5% of the domestic timber consumption (not including cellulose, paper and paperboard) and is therefore of less significance (OLLMANN 1994:3). Among timber imports in all production stages, tropical timber plays only a subsidiary role, representing approx. 3% of all imports.[41] For the German timber industry as a whole, the tropical timber used as a raw material consequently plays only a small role. However, in certain sectors, for example in the production of windows, peak values of 28% of the total timber consumption in that particular sector can be reached.

The German timber industry is sectioned into the wood processing industry, the timber working industry, the pulp and cellulose industry, the timber trade and the timber craft. Timber processing comprises cutting, slicing, planing and bonding processes (GREFERMANN 1988:24). The products are half-finished wood products such as veneers, sawnwood and mouldings. In the production statistics of the Federal Statistical Office, wood processing (commodity group „wood products"), like the commodity group „pulp, paper and paperboard", is assigned to the basic and producer goods sector.[42] The wood working industry, on the other hand, falls under the consumer goods sector. Products of this sector are timber items such as doors, windows and furniture made of veneers, sawnwood and mouldings intended for the end consumer.

---

[40]   About 77% of the total imported and inland timber (not including timber residue materials) in 1984 consisted of coniferous timber (cf. MÜLLER 1987, summary:10-25).

[41]   Own calculations according to BML (1993:389) and OLLMANN (1993a: Table 1).

[42]   In some places this assignment is questionable. For example, increasing amounts of the goods of the wood processing industry reach private end consumers directly through the building material markets. Strictly speaking, some products of the wood processing industry should be assigned to the wood working industry for technical production reasons. For example, mouldings are sawnwood which have been subject to further processing, namely planing in a second step. The same argument applies to impregnated products such as masts, railway sleepers and poles (GREFERMANN 1988:23).

To introduce the structure of the German tropical timber industry we can start with the grading system for raw timber as shown in Fig. 4. We will see in the course of the further examination that it is not necessary to consider all of the itmes listed when considering non-coniferous timber from natural forests.

Raw timber:
- Stacked timber
- Roundwood
     - Saw- and veneer logs
     - Rods and laths
- Timber for special uses
     - Sleepers
     - Industrial roundwood
          - Mechanical breakup (for the production of particle boards and fibreboards)
          - Mechanical and chemical breakup (for the production of paper and paperboard or hardboard)
          - Chemical disintegration (for the production of cellulose)
     - Fuelwood
     - Charcoal

Figure 4:   Raw Timber Grading According to German Forestry Grading System

Source: KROTH/BARTELHEIMER (1993:28) and HOLZ-LEXIKON (1988).

For example, the raw timber categories stacked timber and industrial round-wood are irrelevant for tropical timber. For stacked timber (wood in the rough cut to lengths of one to three metres and stacked in piles) there is no commodity designation in the foreign trade statistics. Industrial roundwood is roundwood for disintegration for specific purposes. Neither the German cellulose industry[43] nor the German particle board and fibreboard industry[44] import natural tropical forest

---

43   MÜLLER (1987:63) points out that at the beginning of the 1980s considerable amounts of eucalyptus timber from plantations were imported for German cellulose and pulp production, whereas in the mid-80s mainly home-produced timber was used. In recent times too, no tropical timber has been used for inland cellulose production. Two factors are chiefly responsible for this. Firstly, homogeneity within the timber species is necessary for fibre materials. Natural forest tropical timber often cannot fulfil this requirement on account of the many sub-species. Secondly, non-coniferous timbers in general, on account of their shorter fibres, are less suitable than the long-fibre coniferous timbers (LORENZ 2.8.1994).

44   RESSEL (1986:56) found in 1984 by questioning 15 particle board factories representing 52% of German production, that only 18% of the raw material used consists of industrial non-coniferous timber. Its origin is unknown, but he assumes that chiefly residual wood from the processing of German non-coniferous timber is involved. Ac-

timber for processing, so industrial roundwood is not considered in the distribution analysis.

Telegraph poles and line masts erected inland are usually made of pine or spruce timber so that they are not interesting for the present study. No inland processing of tropical timber to make piles (posts) is known, as well.[45] Also the small volume of imports of fuelwood and charcoal from tropical countries, whose origin (plantation or natural forest) is usually not traceable, are not included in the analysis.

The timber categories roundwood and sleepers are of particular interest on account of the considerable amounts of tropical timber from natural forests which they represent. Sleepers are considered in Section 7.3 because they are transfered directly to the end consumer.

Saw- and veneer logs consist of the logged tree as sent to the sawmill and plywood factory for further processing. The logs may already have been squared or roughly shaped.[46] In the wood processing industry, logs are first of all processed into half-finished products (sawnwood, veneer, veneer plywood and blockboard).

Sawnwood is understood to mean laths, deals, rectangular timber, quarter timber and beams which usually have a thickness of more than 5 mm. (GREFERMANN 1988:88). Mouldings is a collective term used to describe both smooth-edged sawnwood (doles, profile sawnwood, shelfboards, and balcony boards) and sawnwood planed on both sides and usually provided with groove and tongue or other device for lateral connection (cf. MÜLLER 1987:43). Among other uses, sawnwood and mouldings are used to make i.a. furniture, doors and windows and artistic objects. They are also used directly as dole or balcony timber. In Germany tropical timber may be used for all of these purposes, making it necessary to include its foreign trade and domestic production in the analysis.

Veneers are made by slicing or peeling logs and usually have a thickness of less than 5 mm.[47] Although peeled veneers from normal-quality timber are used chiefly in the production of plywood or blockboard, they are sometimes also used directly in packing items such as tea crates (TAKEUCHI 1983:319). Sliced veneers (luxury veneers) from tropical high-quality timbers, on account of their attractive

---

cording to MÜLLER (1987:52), the German particle board industry in 1984 used mainly logs from pine, spruce, beech and oak. It can be assumed that the structure of demand has not changed dramatically since then, at least not as far as tropical timber is concerned and that today no natural tropical forest timber is used in the German particle and fibreboard industry (OLLMANN 16.12.1994).

[45] In 1984 almost exclusively coniferous timber was used in inland production as well as in imports to make telegraph poles and line masts (MÜLLER 1987:49). For posts and stakes too (winegrowing, hop developments, palisades and other stakes, fence posts, wooden stakes for gardens, pergolas, playground facilities and other such constructions), it can be assumed, according to a survey by the CMA (1983:96, cited by MÜLLER 1987:51) that only coniferous timber is used.

[46] FAO (Yearbook of Forest Products, 1994, Introduction, p.x).

[47] When slicing, the veneers are cut individually by a knife moving along the fixed log, whereas peeled veneers are made by continuous peeling of a rotating log.

grain and colouration, are used, for example, to cover furniture and for indoor decoration of buildings (ANONYMOUS 1989:1).

Because natural solid timber can have some undesirable features, wood-based panels with improved features have been developed which in some cases have superior characteristics. Plywood, fibreboard and particle board are three examples.[48] These goods are made by splintering solid timber and then reassembling it together with glue or other substances. Sometimes the timber is combined with other materials such as plastic sheets. Such timber materials can have improved strength and better resistance against the weather, changing atmospheric humidity and attack by pests. Compared with solid timber they are also more homogeneous, contain fewer flaws and can be produced in any required sizes and quantities (GREFERMANN 1988:23-24).

With plywood a distinction is made between veneer plywood and blockboard. Veneer plywood consists of at least three layers of cross-bonded veneers. Blockboard consists of two outer veneer layers between which lies a centre layer of solid timber strips (HÄBER 1990:14). In the widest sense, the term „plywood" covers veneer plywood and blockboard, but in the strictest sense it is often applied only to veneer plywood, a convention which we will not follow here. Veneers as well as plywood and blockboard made of tropical timber or containing some tropical timber, are imported and produced in the Federal Republic of Germany. They constitute important elements in a distribution analysis for tropical timber.

As already mentioned above in connection with raw timber imports, no tropical timber from natural forests is used in German particle and fibreboard production, so it is only necessary to consider the imports of finished goods. The extent of imports of particle boards from tropical countries is very small. Fibreboard imports from tropical countries (chiefly from Brazil) have fallen considerably in recent years, amounting to only about 10 000 $m^3(r)$ in 1993. Since the origin of the utilized timber (plantation or natural forest) cannot be determined, particle boards and fibreboards will not be included in the analysis.

Apart from veneer plywood, blockboard, particle board and fibreboard, wood-based panels also include form pieces made of veneer, fibre or chip material.[49] Since form pieces made of or containing timber appear only in small quantities in the production statistics, and the foreign trade statistics do not contain a corresponding item, and no adequate information from other sources is available on the relevance of tropical timber, this class of timber products will also not be considered in the analysis.

Finally, a decision must be made regarding imported wood pulp, cellulose, paper and paperboard. Imports of wood pulp from tropical countries are negligible

---

[48] Similar boards can be made from other materials of plant origin, so to be more precise we should use the terms „wood fibreboard", „wood particle board" etc. However, as this study is concerned with timber products unless explicitly otherwise stated, the prefix „wood" in these terms will be omitted.

[49] Plywood form pieces are special products required, for example, for seating furniture, casings and containers (HÄBER 1988, Teil 2:1281).

and their raw material basis is largely coniferous timber from plantations. For imported cellulose from tropical countries as well, it can usually be assumed that the utilized solid timber originates from plantations and not from natural forests.[50] For paper and paperboard imports too, no information on the origin of the consumed timber is available, but we can reasonably assume that it is not originating from natural tropical forests. Consequently, these production lines drop right out of the analysis because, as already shown above, no precursor products made of tropical timber are used for domestic production of wood pulp, cellulose, paper and paperboard.

Sawnwood, mouldings, veneers and plywood made from tropical timber are thus the core of a distribution analysis for tropical timber on the import and production side, because tropical timber is used for domestic production and similar products made from tropical timber are imported into the Federal Republic of Germany.

7.3   Final Consumption of Tropical Timber

Products made from sawnwood, mouldings, veneer and plywood consisting of or containing tropical timber are found among consumer goods, consumer durables and capital goods.

Examples of short-term consumables in the private sector are wooden plates and boards for household use. Concerning volume, industrial consumption of tropical timber for railway sleepers, packing and above all for concrete formwork, is more significant.

Consumer durables in private households mainly comprise furniture, works of art, household utensils and picture frames as well as building materials, such as doors, windows, wall elements and floors.

Building material dominates among the investment goods too. These include windows and floors, shop furniture and individually manufactured furnishings for hotels, banks and insurance company offices. Most of the tropical timber consumed belongs to this sector, not only in the Federal Republic of Germany but also in other important consumer countries.[51]

Fig. 5 gives an overview of the various common end uses for tropical timber in the Federal Republic of Germany. This list does not claim to be complete, but it

---

50 Small amounts of cellulose usually originates from eucalyptus plantations are imported from Latin America (THOMAS 2.8.1994; cf. also MÜLLER 1987:68). However, in recent times reports are giving rise to considerable concern, that large amounts of natural forest coniferous timber are being logged in Chile to make cellulose for export to Japan. Pine and eucalyptus plantations are then being cultivated on the cleared areas with up to 75% state subvention for the planting costs (PINZLER 1994).
51 Further details are given in Tables 18 and 19 in the introduction to Part III.

does cover the chief sectors. We start considering utilization fields in which either tropical timber consumption is relatively small compared with total German tropical timber consumption or, the percentage share of tropical timber in the entire timber consumed by the particular field is so insignificant that reliable conclusions regarding the utilization trend cannot be drawn. The most important end uses of tropical timber are considered later.

```
- Outdoor uses (excluding building)
        - Sleepers
        - Timber used in hydraulic engineering
        - Garden furniture
- Building
        - Building material in structural engineering
                - Windows
                - Outer doors, gates
                - Floors, underfloors
                - Staircases
                - Wall and ceiling panels
                - Inner doors
                - Shutters, blinds, rollers
                - Sauna
        - Temporary site uses
- Other interior uses
        - Household utensils and other objects
        - Furniture
        - Furniture parts
- Packing
```

Figure 5:   Main End Consumer Uses for Tropical Timber
in the Federal Republic of Germany

Source: Based on MÜLLER (1987:15).

Among other fields, tropical timber finds few if any utilization in wooden facades, masts for electric power and telecommunication lines, telegraph poles, stakes, fuelwood, palettes or coffins (see Appendix A9).

In *sauna construction* only reclining seats and seating benches utilize tropical timber. In the Federal Republic of Germany about 80% tropical timber and 20% domestic poplar timber is used here. The campaign against tropical timber has had only a slight effect in this field (OBERLE 28.7.1994). About 5% of the timber content of a sauna is tropical timber. Referred to the production for the year 1993 (according to the production statistics), this is a comparatively small annual amount of only 1300 m^3.

Broom handles and other utensil handles consist about 90% of tropical timber, formerly chiefly brazil pine. Today these items are imported almost exclusively as round rods. Substitution on account of the campaign against tropical timber took place only to an extent of less than 1% (VORMANN 2.8.1994).

The production of *railway sleepers* was previously a typical field for utilizing tropical timber. However, since the railway network in the Federal Republic of Germany (and world-wide) is expanding at a reduced pace and at the same time steel and concrete substitutes are gaining ground, domestic production as well as import of impregnated and non-impregnated wooden sleepers has fallen strongly (GREFERMANN 1988:92). German imports of wooden railway sleepers from tropical countries have now fallen to zero. No inland further processing of tropical roundwood into railway sleepers is known, so it can be assumed that no tropical timber at all is still being used in Germany for railway sleepers. However, it was not possible to discern any effect of the campaign against tropical timber in this field.

Building operations are the chief field of use for tropical timber. A basic distinction must thereby be made between timber used in civil engineering and timber used in building construction.

On the whole, civil engineering is a comparatively insignificant field of utilization for timber. MÜLLER (1987:103,104) assigns for 1994 about 5% of sawnwood consumption and a quarter of the timber consumed for concrete formwork to civil engineering. Tropical timber used in civil engineering is mainly found in concrete formwork.[52] Utilization of tropical timber for concrete formwork either in civil engineereing or in building construction is considered further below. Wooden bridges are products of civil engineering, but their annual consumption of sawn tropical timber is on the decline, due to the anti-tropical timber campaign, and now only amounts to about 175 m³ per year (KREIS/FILIPPI 1991). No tropical timber is used for bridges in glue-laminated structures.

Conventionally buildings are erected on site. Pure timber constructions[53] thereby compete with massive building methods (brick, concrete, metal or glass) whereby timber is used almost exclusively in roof construction and interior furnishings. For prefabricated buildings, prefabricated components with high timber content are prepared for internal and external walls. Building operations on existing buildings are subdivided into conservation and extension projects. A lot of timber is used in both of these fields (KROTH/KOLLERT/FILIPPI 1991:7ff.).

Tropical timber plays no role in the *constructional field* (OLLMANN 16.12.1994). MÜLLER (1987:80,86) found for 1984 a share of 6% in prefabricated houses and only 1% in building without timber skeleton, for tropical timber in the

---

[52] Pine, spruce and beech timber is chiefly used for pits and piles.

[53] Timber constructions are understood to mean all constructions „in which the constructional features of the block, stand, wooden frame, wood panel or timber skeleton constructional method or their combination with massive building methods are implemented predominantly through the utilization of timber building elements" (KROTH/KOLLERT/FILIPPI 1991:33; translation by the authors).

solid wood consumption. Because it has a rather large shrinkage, tropical timber is hardly suitable for constructional uses, as rather unsuccessful experiments in England have shown. More consumption of tropical timber in the constructional field would only be conceivable for hydraulic engineering, for winter gardens and for pedestrian bridges (OLLMANN 16.12.1994).

Insufficient quantity and species information is available for *timber in temporary* site uses (scaffolding, concrete formwork, building site fences, etc.). Scaffolding is made predominantly from coniferous timber (MÜLLER 1987:105). Tropical timber veneer plywood is usually employed as formwork for casting concrete when non-standardized casting locations are involved. They are cut to size on site and therefore usually cannot be re-used (lost utilization). Concrete formwork systems use coniferous timber veneer plywood.

Important utilization fields for tropical timber in building operations are its utilization in *building materials*. This chiefly comprises doors, windows, wall and ceiling coverings, staircases and flooring. In 1984 altogether 5% of the utilized mouldings and 23% of the utilized sawnwood were tropical timber (MÜLLER 1987:101).

The chief alternatives for *wooden floors* in the German market are textile, plastic and ceramic linings whereby the latter are particularly suitable for floor heating systems.[54] Among the wooden floors, floorboards compete with parquet flooring. However, floorboards and their underfloors do not employ any tropical timber. American softwoods are chiefly used instead (WEGELT 28.7.1994; cf. also MÜLLER 1987:91). There is significant economic activity in the parquet market indicating a good chance for prefabricated parquet with timber veneer as well as for laminated floors to develop (ANONYMOUS 1994b). According to the CMA (1983, cited by MÜLLER 1987:90), the sawnwood used in Germany for parquet production at the beginning of the 1980s consisted of 92% oak and 5% tropical timber. At the present time only about 1.1% tropical timber is still used here (WEGELT 28.7.1994). With an average parquet thickness of 1 cm, this gives a volume of only about 570 m³ for the entire German production in 1993.

7.4   Distribution of Tropical Timber in 1984

Fig. 6 shows the flow of tropical timber via import, wood processing and wood working industry to the end consumer for the Federal Republic of Germany in 1984, according to MÜLLER (1987) and own calculations. Apart from domestic processing of the primary commodity tropical timber, imports of similar goods

---

[54]   MORSCHHÄUSER (1988:220). KROTH/KOLLERT/FILIPPI (1991:152,154) calculated at the end of the 1980s market shares of altogether 60% to 80% for non-timber building materials in floor linings of residential and non- residential buildings.

from the tropical countries and the (partly estimated) exports of German producers, are thereby taken into consideration too. Some of the tropical timber final products appearing in Fig. 5 are not included in the analysis, due to negligible quantities and/or missing data, so that they fall into the category „unknown". It was not possible to make a more topical distribution analysis because data as comprehensive as those of Müller for 1984 were not available.

The import, export, production, stock and sold quantities are specified in various different units of measurement in the respective sources. They have been converted to the common unit of measurement „timber volume" [m^3] in Fig. 6. This means that - other than in the case of a representation with „roundwood equivalent" [m^3(r)] as unit of measurement - for the imported half-finished and finished timber products, the waste quantities incurred in the tropical countries are not contained in the values shown in Fig. 6. However, the percentages given for the individual utilization forms and fields in the last column and last row have been calculated on the basis of roundwood equivalent to permit comparisons.

It is evident from Fig. 6 that approx. 80% of all tropical timber uses can be covered by confining the trend analysis in Chapter 8 and the subsequent scenario calculations to the seven product ranges windows, panels and cassettes, inner doors, furniture, staircases, outer doors and gates as well as the do-it- yourself sales via the building market.

These seven product ranges for tropical timber are primarily assignable to the visible uses area of the private end consumer. Some restriction is necessary regarding furniture construction, because apart from the visible utilization of tropical timber veneers on the surface of furniture, there are some concealed uses of tropical timber too, for example as rear panels of wardrobes and for the side parts of drawers.[55] The remaining product areas which are not considered in the trend analysis and scenario calculations, chiefly concern invisible uses of tropical timber (for example concrete formwork in building construction). It is quite certain that the reduction of demand through the campaign against tropical timber and the change in fashion was relatively slight in these areas.[56] So the chosen delimitation corresponds well to the areas where the campaign against tropical timber and the change in fashion were effective or not effective.

---

[55]   It is fairly certain that the actual consumption volume for furniture production is greater than shown in Fig. 6. MÜLLER (1987:33) suspects that some of the relatively large amount of plywood which went to destinations he was unable to discern in his study, must have actually been assigned to furniture construction.

[56]   An exception can be found in certain public building projects (for example wooden bridges and park benches) where the strong pressure of the campaign had its effect on local authorities and public administration.

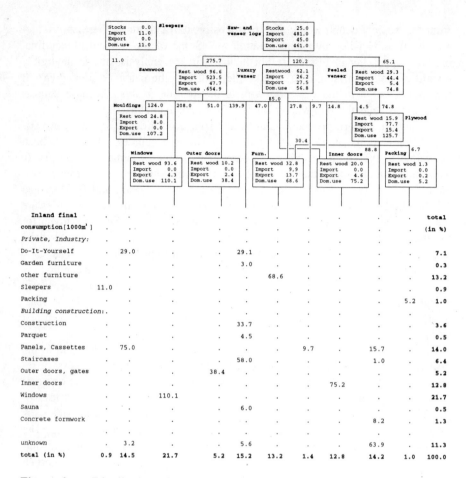

Inland final consumption [1000m³]											total (in %)
Private, Industry:											
Do-It-Yourself	29.0			29.1							7.1
Garden furniture				3.0							0.3
other furniture					68.6						13.2
Sleepers	11.0										0.9
Packing										5.2	1.0
Building construction:											
Construction				33.7							3.6
Parquet				4.5							0.5
Panels, Cassettes	75.0					9.7		15.7			14.0
Staircases				58.0				1.0			6.4
Outer doors, gates			38.4								5.2
Inner doors							75.2				12.8
Windows		110.1									21.7
Sauna				6.0							0.5
Concrete formwork								8.2			1.3
unknown	3.2			5.6				63.9			11.3
total (in %)	0.9 14.5	21.7	5.2	15.2	13.2	1.4	12.8	14.2	1.0		100.0

Figure 6:   Distribution of Tropical Timber in the Federal Republic of Germany in 1984

Notes: The values of the quantity of tropical timber distribution in the Federal Republic of Germany are stated as timber volume [1000 m³], but the percentage figures have been calculated on the basis of roundwood equivalents so that they take into account the waste wood involved in further processing in the exporting countries. The resulting total final consumption of tropical timber is 654 100 m³ plus inland waste wood of more than 386 600 m³ tropical timber used in energy generation, particle board and fibreboard production as well as wood pulp and cellulose production. Because some goods are imported in the processed state, there is an additional waste wood volume of approx. 379 000 m³ tropical timber - for recovery rates see below - which remained in the exporting countries. Thus altogether a total volume of 1 419 700 m³(r) of tropical timber was logged for final consumption in the Federal Republic of Germany. The difference with respect to the net import volume of tropical timber shown in Appendix A4 amounting to 1 594 211 m³(r), is chiefly due to export estimates and partly due to slightly different recovery rates.

Assumptions: For lack of export information, for some products the export structure for all timber species in general, as specified by MÜLLER (1987), was assumed for tropical timber in particular. Therefore the share of exports in the domestic production plus imports, was taken to be 16.7% for furniture, 5.8% for inner and outer doors, 2.0% for windows and 4.0% for packing. The entire utilization structure was taken over for plywood: 10.9% export, 21.5% furniture, 11.1% panels, 4.7% packing, 0.7% staircases, 5.8% concrete formwork, etc., and 45.3% unknown. The inland utilization structure was taken over for (sliced) luxury veneers: 4 500 m³ straight off for plywood production, 26.0% for inner doors, 17.0% for panels and the rest for furniture.

The recovery rates were assumed to be as follows, according to statements by MÜLLER (1987), DE BOER (1994) and KROTH/KOLLERT/FILIPPI (1991): Logwood to sawnwood 65%, to sliced veneer 50% and to peeled veneer 55%. Sawnwood to mouldings, outer doors and inner doors in each case 80%, to windows and furniture in each case 55%. Peeled veneer to furniture, inner doors and plywood in each case 80%. The assumed recovery rates of peeled veneer for plywood (80%) and of plywood to furniture and packing systems (80%) are based on own estimates.

Source: Own calculations with the stated assumptions based on MÜLLER (1987) and data taken from the foreign trade statistics.

8 Trend Analysis and Basic Scenarios

The present chapter analyses the utilization and substitution trends for tropical timber after 1984 on the basis established in the previous two chapters. Information from the previous years is generally not carried forward because it is considered obsolete.

The procedure adopted is explained and theoretically justified in Section 8.1. Section 8.2 examines utilization and substitution trends for the raw material tropical timber in general. Following thereafter (Section 8.3), the trends found after 1984 are examined qualitatively and quantitatively for the seven chief end consumer categories for tropical timber in Germany. Using the results of this analysis and the procedure described in Section 8.1, the consumed quantities which could be achieved by setting up a credible certification scheme, are calculated to a first approximation for five submarkets (basic scenarios).

In the first instance the basic scenarios just represent quantity trends, that must be modified in order to be able to consider price effects too. The modifications are made in Part III and involve several effects on the supply and on the demand side (extended scenarios).

8.1 Procedure for Determining the Basic Scenarios

This study is characterized by two essential methodical aspects. Firstly, several important submarkets for tropical timber are examined with regard to their reaction to a certification scheme. This approach was given preference over a highly aggregated analysis of the total German demand for tropical timber because very different conditions prevail on some of the submarkets, for example with regard to possible substitutions for tropical timber or with regard to the effects of the campaign against tropical timber.

Secondly, a method was chosen for indirectly estimating the increased demand which a credible certification scheme could produce in the respective end consumer areas. The two chief factors of influence which have in recent years acted against the utilization of tropical timber in the individual submarkets, were the campaign against tropical timber and a change of fashion in favour of lighter-coloured timbers thus discriminating against the often relatively dark tropical timber species. Instead of assessing in bulk the increased demand which could result in the submarkets through a certification scheme, for example by estimating or setting a certain percentage increase of demand, this study is guided by the market losses suffered by tropical timber in the individual end consumer categories through the campaign against tropical timber and/or the change of fashion in recent years (trend analysis). Building on the results of the trend analysis, the possible increase of demand in the course of establishing a credible certification scheme is defined on the assumption that the certification scheme will restore the consumption of tropical timber in the affected submarkets from the present low level to the long-term trend level which existed before the campaign against tropical timber and the change of fashion.

The detailed procedure is explained below. The seven chief end consumer categories for tropical timber products are known from the distribution analysis. For five end consumer areas it was possible to calculate two trend quantities as basic scenarios:

The *Basic Scenario T I* describes for the year 1993 the quantity which would have been demanded according to the historic trend without the campaign against tropical timber.

The *Basic Scenario T II* describes for the year 1993 the quantity which would have been demanded according to the historic trend without the campaign against tropical timber *and* without the change of fashion towards lighter-coloured timber species in recent years.

Consequently the basic scenarios determine the quantities which could be consumed today in the respective segments, if the effects of the two chief negative factors operating against the utilization of tropical timber in recent years, can be cancelled again by a certification scheme. It is assumed that this is 100% possible with a credible certification scheme.

Fig. 7 shows graphically the price and quantities development on introduction of a certification scheme confined to the Federal Republic of Germany. If the consumers who have withdrawn from the market on account of the campaign against tropical timber and/or the change of fashion can be recovered by a certification scheme, the quantities T I and T II respectively would have been achieved for the reference year 1993, taking into consideration the growth rate on these markets between 1984 and 1993. These are the basic scenarios calculated in Section 8.3 for important submarkets.[57]

Ideally a complete market model should have been specified and estimated econometrically for each submarket, instead of just calculating trend quantities. As chief components, the model would have contained dummy variables for the campaign against tropical timber and for the change of fashion. Estimates made with the model and simulations derived from it with/without the campaign against

---

[57]   For the construction of the trend quantities T I and T II, see for example Fig. 11 in Section 8.3.1 and the associated explanation.

tropical timber and with/without a change of fashion would have produced, at least theoretically, more accurate results. Unfortunately it was impossible to implement such a procedure with the available data. Instead, the adopted procedure projects future trends based on observed historic market equilibria in the basic scenarios. Based on these basic scenarios of a certification of tropical timber extended scenarios with modified supply and demand behaviour are calculated.

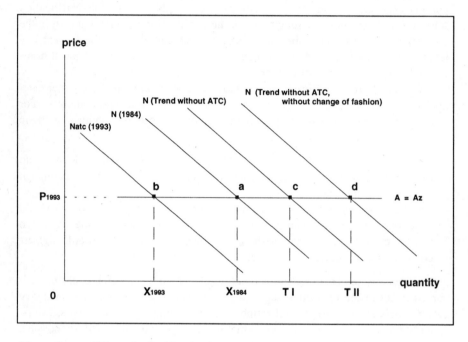

Figure 7:   Effect of a Certification Scheme for Sustainably Produced Tropical Timber Confined to the Federal Republic of Germany

Legend: Demand function before the anti-tropical timber campaign(ATC) and before the change of fashion: N(1984); thereafter: Natc(1993).
With a certification scheme which cancels the effects of the campaign against tropical timber: N(trend without ATC), which also cancels the effects of the change of fashion: N(trend without ATC, without change of fashion).
X1993 and X1984 designate the consumed amounts actually realized in these years in the considered market.
A = Az: Supply (offer) function before and after introduction of a certification scheme (assumed to be equal).

It is assumed that the campaign against tropical timber and the change of fashion affected the volume of German demand for tropical timber (shift from **a** to **b**). However, it is also assumed that no pressure was exerted on the world market

price. Therefore the calculations are based on an unchanged world market price
(P_{1993}). This assumption is justified, as Table 9 shows. The average German import
unit value for tropical logs has been stable since 1989, and the average import unit
value for sawn tropical timber has actually risen. Vice versa, Fig. 7 illustrates the
assumption made, that the expansion of the German demand for tropical timber
caused by a certification scheme limited to the Federal Republic of Germany will
not increase the world market price (shift from **b** to **c** or **d**).

Table 9:   Price Development for Saw- and Veneer Logs and Sawnwood from
Various Supply Categories [1989 = 100]

	Saw- and Veneer Logs				Sawnwood			
	World	FRG	FRG		World	FRG	FRG	
	Ø Export unit value	Ø Import unit value	Producer price		Ø Export unit value	Ø Import unit value	Producer price	
	non-conif. timber	non-conif. tropical timber	beech	spruce	non-conif. timber	non-conif. tropical timber	non-conif. timber	coniferous timber
1980	106	102	83	111	87	136	88	105
1981	90	106	---	---	79	143	---	---
1982	88	104	---	---	75	147	---	---
1983	86	105	---	---	76	153	---	---
1984	73	116	---	---	72	158	---	---
1985	71	115	88	86	70	150	93	93
1986	75	112	---	---	81	127	---	---
1987	89	96	94	86	85	125	96	90
1988	94	90	95	87	87	108	96	89
1989	100	100	100	100	100	100	100	100
1990	104	100	112	113	109	158	108	114
1991	101	95	91	64	115	151	108	99
1992	101	99	111	82	118	157	109	95

Notes: --- no information available; Ø: average.
All index values are calculated on the basis of non-deflated prices.

Source: Own calculations on the basis of: Column 1,5 from FAO (Yearbook of Forest
Products, various years); column 2,6 from OLLMANN (1993a); column 3,4,7,8 from BML
(1993).

Without modification the basic scenarios T I and T II carry only limited weight
because they represent only quantity trends without any consideration of price
effects resulting from the increased demand in the case of a common certification
scheme throughout the OECD, from a possible willingness of buyers to pay more

or from the costs of the certification scheme and a sustainable forest management. These effects will be taken into consideration in the extended scenarios in Part III.

On each submarket T I and T II span a range within which the expansion of demand after introduction of a certification scheme will probably develop. In the worst case a certification scheme should - in view of the technical advantages sketched in Section 8.2, the price competitiveness of tropical timber and the positive image of the material timber - be able to cancel the effects of the negative campaign. In the best case a credible certification scheme can not only cancel the effects of the campaign against tropical timber, but will also give tropical timber an additional image gain helping to compensate for the fashion shift in recent years towards lighter coloured timber thus giving dark tropical timber species a competitive advantage over dark non-tropical timber species. Without a certification scheme and taking into consideration the presently observable return of fashion trend towards darker timber species, a persisting campaign against tropical timber would give the competitive advantage chiefly to non-tropical coloured non-coniferous timber species or stained coniferous timber.

The fact that the seven submarkets which were investigated cover only 80% of German tropical timber imports could mean that the scenarios calculated in this study are more likely to represent the bottom limit of possible increased demand through certification. The remaining 20% of the market could as well turn out to be responding to a certification scheme with expanding consumer demand so that the demand situation modelled here with T I and T II for tropical timber could in fact be even greater.

In order to exclude long-term growth effects in future years (after 1993) from the analysis so that only the effects of the certification scheme are assessed, 1993 is chosen in each case as reference year. The actual facts of the conditions in 1993 are taken as a reference situation. The scenarios calculate hypothetical conditions for 1993. This procedure permits assessment of the long-term effects of a certification scheme for tropical timber on the development of prices and quantities of tropical timber products in the considered markets, separated from growth and structural effects.

The absolute values are not decisive for the interpretation of the results, but rather the differences between the quantities and prices actually achieved in the reference year and the hypothetical quantities and prices forecast in the scenarios T I and T II. The calculated *increases* are likely to be relatively reliable estimates for the developments induced in the Federal German market for tropical timber by a certification scheme.

For calculating the trend quantities for the simulated situations with a certification scheme, the observed competitive and displacement dynamics between the material groups timber (all kinds) on the one hand and all non-timber materials on the other hand, are assumed to continue in the long-term development of the respective markets. For example, this means that in the windows market the trend of plastics replacing all other materials is taken as given. On each submarket, exclusively the market share shifts *within* the timber group will be examined with regard to the influences of the campaign against tropical timber and the change of fashion.

It is necessary to consider right away the question of whether the changes in demand within the timber group which arose in particular after 1989 could also have been caused by changes in the relative prices, unrelated to the change of fashion and the campaign against tropical timber. Table 9 shows various index values for prices and average import/export unit values in the world market and in the German market for tropical timber. A comparison permits assessments regarding the development of prices for tropical timber relative to two important competing timber species, non-coniferous timber and coniferous timber from German production and origin.

The average export unit value for non-coniferous saw- and veneer logs in the world market fell continuously until 1985. However, this loss was at least nominally recovered by 1989 through the tightening of export restrictions from the beginning to the middle of the 1980s in many tropical countries. Since then the nominal export unit value is stable. From 1980 to 1992 the average import unit value for tropical timber in Germany remained approximately on the same level. This means that its relative price dropped in comparison with beech as chief competing timber which became more expensive during the same period.

The market for tropical sawnwood presents a differentiated picture. Here the development of log prices made itself felt in the world market so that analogously prices fell until 1985 and then recovered completely. The average German import unit value dropped until 1989. At the same time non-coniferous sawnwood from German production became more expensive whereas the price for German coniferous sawnwood remained stable. Therefore, the relative price of tropical sawnwood has fallen until 1989, compared with non-coniferous and coniferous sawnwood from German production. However, after 1989 the average import unit value for tropical sawnwood increased strongly and has since then persisted on a higher level. But this increase does not imply any increase of the relative price for imported tropical sawnwood in comparison with 1980 and 1985, because the domestic producer price for non-coniferous sawnwood has rosen even more strongly during the period from 1980 to 1992 as well as during the period from 1985 to 1992. Compared with coniferous sawnwood from domestic production, imported tropical sawnwood showed a relative increase of the average import unit value during the period from 1980 to 1992, but the relative price remained stable compared to the years 1985 and 1992.

The facit of these considerations of the price and import unit value developments in the log and sawnwood market is that the relative price of tropical timber has not risen in long-term comparison with home grown timber as chief competitor. So it may be assumed that shifts in the relative price of tropical timber can hardly be taken as a determining factor for any reduced demand.

Comparing current absolute prices in the submarkets for windows and outer doors with those of competing products made of plastics, coniferous timber, or non-tropical non-coniferous reveals that corresponding tropical timber products are still cheaper or available for the same price.

8.2   General Development in the German Tropical Timber Market

The chief determining factors for the market chances of tropical timber in the German market are:

- the material qualities of tropical timber,
- the image of timber on the whole and tropical timber in particular,
- fashion trends favouring lighter or darker timber species,
- competition from
    - non-timber materials,
    - particle boards and fibreboards (usually not containing tropical timber),
    - coniferous timber (usually non-tropical) and non-tropical non-coniferous timber.

This section explains the chief tendencies observed with regard to these factors.

The diversity of tropical timber species is enormous and the potential of timber species not yet traded on national or international markets is large. FAO studies assume that world-wide there are 950 regularly utilized tropical timber species and 840 more used occasionally. Only 40 to 50 species are traded internationally.[58] For Indonesia it is estimated that of 3000 known species 400 are exploited commercially, but only 127 of them are traded regularly (KARGER 1978:16).

Before the 1940s the world trade with tropical timber chiefly consisted of export of unprocessed luxury decorative kinds such as mahogany from Central America, teak from Southeast Asia and ebony from Africa. The timber industry of industrialized countries used this timber predominantly in furniture production. During the years thereafter the demand for general purpose timber increased strongly, where the supply of cheap mass quantities is decisive, not the decorative aspects (PANAYOTOU/ASHTON 1992:29). At the end of the 1960s the supply of many African timber species diminished after years of logging without adequate reforestation, and the prices rose accordingly. The shortage of African luxury timber species and the shift in demand towards mass quantity timber had the consequence that keruing, meranti and ramin offered by export-willing concessionaries in Malaysia and Indonesia, conquered the world market (KUMAR 1982:181).

---

[58] TAKEUCHI (1983:318). See also Appendix 3 which lists the various tropical timber species exported to Germany and their typical uses.

ave a positive attitude towards the relatively easy to handle material
hermore, the campaign against tropical timber was still in its first
9.

imes there has been **a trend** for the Federal Republic of Germany,
he long-standing preference for lighter timbers and back to medium
lours (cf. KAMM 1991, ANONYMOUS 1994e, OLSEN 2.8.1994). At
ly non-coniferous timber from temperate climatic regions are profi-
s trend, chiefly beech (ANONYMOUS 1994b). Walnut and beech are
darker (HERRMANN 1.2.1995). Many darker tropical timbers could
:oo from this recent change of fashion, under a credible certification

ral years tropical timber products compete increasingly in the Federal
Germany with products made from temperate non-coniferous timber,
nber products and non-timber products. On some market segments
titution movements towards non-timber products are evident.
: the substitution of plastics for furniture construction or aluminium
or windows (see also Appendix A8).

lds in which special timber species with specific technical characte-
nployed, such as shipbuilding and hydraulic engineering, tropical
: replaced primarily with non-timber materials such as concrete and
'MOUS 1989:2). For boat construction tropical timber has been re-
nt years by polyester or epoxy resin reinforced with glass or carbon
NN 16.12.1994). Some tropical timbers will keep for an unlimited
rotection when in contact with the soil (three examples are bongos-
nd basralokus). Such timbers are often used for fences, noise shiel-
d bridges. Increasing substitution with steel, concrete and plastics is
sector. Impregnated domestic timber which has already had a tradi-
share in this sector, is gaining ground in this area too. It has thereby
at the keeping qualities of non-tropical timber in outdoor uses can be
mproved timber building methods (ESE 1992, Vol.II:58).

nly a few areas in which substitution for tropical timber hardly
:. One of these areas is the construction of musical instruments for
range of different kinds of tropical timbers has always been used
R 1989). In certain uses in shipbuilding, for staircases and for tool
substitution for tropical timber with other timber species or non-
als impairs the technical quality of the products (ESE 1992,

tion pressure on timber as a whole exerted by the advance of pla-
ombated by the timber industry with marketing campaigns. Danzer,
an producer of veneers, recently launched an advertising campaign
large furniture manufacturer, to boost the image of timber veneers.
o Badenia in the Federal Association of the German Timber Trade
uced the initiative project „pro timber window" in order to strengt-

By virtue of its high density, tropical timbe
resistance to negative ambient influences. Apa
terial characteristics, there are also many
tropical non-coniferous timer kinds by virtu
Some kinds decay quite quickly, others rema
ease of sawing, peeling or slicing differs great
grain is also very large (TAKEUCHI 1983:318).

The technical constructional properties of
of tropical or non-tropical origin - were mos
the results of a survey carried out by KROTH/
man architects and manufacturers of prefabri
ticular emphasis was placed on the good proc
insulation performance and the good ratio of
Timber is a timeless building material wi
known undesired side effects. However, som
tioned too. One disadvantage is the often la
timber entailing the need to use chemicals
required for protecting timber in exterior u
from using timber. Both aspects apply to nc
ber. On the economic side, according to the
timber is usually more expensive than usin
performance ratio is correct only for woo
merous legal statutes and regulations ofter
timber (ibid: 114,124).

As far as demand is concerned, timber sti
terials, in spite of the setbacks suffered tl
timber and the formaldehyde debate.[59] In
sessment of various building materials, tir
brickwork, metal, plastics and concrete (AN

Basically, the survey made by KROTH/KC
that the utilization of timber in building co
gent and often highly subjective factors. Er
example, it was said that timber confers a v
random sample interrogation of end consu
home worker markets also showed clearly
ber are „nature", „forest", „warmth" and „
stioned persons asserted that their attitude
result of the tropical forest discussion (PET
ver, in connection with these opinions it r
concerned, as visitors of a building mater
lected group in the sense that they are e

inclined to
timber. Fu
stages in 19

In recent
away from
and dark c
present mai
ting from t
often staine
profit again
scheme.

Since sev
Republic of
coniferous
strong sub:
Examples a
and plastics

In other fi
ristics are e
timber can b
steel (ANON
placed in rec
fibre (OLLM
time without
si, bangkirai
ding walls ar
found in this
tional market
been found t
increased by

There are
seems possib
which a wid
(TRÜBSWETT
handles, etc.,
timber mate
Vol. II:58-59)

The substit
stics is being
a leading Ger
together with
The state gro
last year intro

59   With regard to the subject complex of
Federal Republic of Germany (wood du
GREFERMANN (1988:72ff.) and the compr

hen the market position for timber windows which is threatened by strong competition from plastics (ANONYMOUS 1994b).

The following discussion investigates how the solid timber products sawnwood, veneers, veneer plywood and blockboard, which, in the German market, contain tropical timber species, **compete with particle boards and fibreboards** which do not contain any tropical timber (see also Appendix A8).

In the 1960s a large part of the tropical roundwood imported into the Federal Republic of Germany was still processed into plywood (OLLMANN 31.8.1994). At the current time other areas dominate. This change is primarily due to the fact that particle board has taken over many of the former functions of plywood (DAHMS 1980:525). Particle board produced in Germany features diversity of possible uses and convenient processing. Very extensive uses lie chiefly in interior furnishing and refurbishing (HÄBER 1990:13). Fibreboards have penetrated into utilization areas formerly covered by plywood, especially in furniture manufacture and building operations. Hardboard panels are used today as rear panels of boxes and floors of drawers, and also as panels for interior furnishings (TÖTSCH/DUBE 1990:1). Plywood is currently used in furniture manufacture where greater mechanical strength is required, for example cupboards and drawers.

Blockboards are a typical product of the German market and were developed here. They are taken for uses whose requirements cannot be fulfilled with particle boards and simple veneer boards, for example large area shell boards, bases for high quality furniture, shelves which can support heavy loads and piano manufacturing (HÄBER 1988, Teil 2).

The advance of fibreboards and particle boards is also connected with the aforementioned favourable price/performance ratio which is due to the greater flexibility of the raw material for fibreboards and particle boards compared with sawn timber or veneer and blockboards, because all sizes and qualities of timber can be used (SARTORIUS/HENLE 1968:10).

In the meantime domestic consumption of hardboard panels in Germany is under pressure through the environmental protection legislation, above all due to the waste water pollution during production (DEPPE 1988:28). Compared with other timber materials, medium density fibreboard has nevertheless still gained ground, at least as far as its share in the total German production of timber materials is concerned (BML 1993). In terms of output volume, particle board is at present the leading product among timber materials by a long stretch. Fibreboard and blockboard follow with a close tie. The latter are in the meantime even more important than veneer plywood and other kinds of plywood.[60]

How **tropical timber competes with coniferous timber and non-tropical non-coniferous timber** is the chief aspect to be taken into consideration for the trend analysis in addition to non-timber substitutes. In general, coniferous timber

---

[60]   With regard to the sale production in 1993 according to the Federal Statistical Office (STATISTISCHES BUNDESAMT) (Fachserie 4, Reihe 3.1., 1993): All kinds of particle boards 7 571 000 m^3, unprocessed fibreboards 250 000 m^3, blockboard 205 000 m^3, other plywood kinds 99 000 m^3 and veneer plywood 87 000 m^3.

is used preferentially for building elements as well as for wood fibre and paper production, whereas non-coniferous timber species are chiefly used for furniture manufacture and building carpentry (TAKEUCHI 1983:321).

One can get a good overview of the mutual advantages and disadvantages of the various timber species by considering the decision process which an industrial consumer undertakes when selecting a new (tropical) timber. He or she considers primarily the following aspects (DAHMS 1980:523):

- Economic efficiency
    - Availability in adequate quantities and qualities
    - Political and economic guarantees of supply
    - Stability of prices and freight rates
    - Storage and transportation capability
- Quality
    - Interesting growth structure, grain and possible recovery rates
    - Colours in accordance with fashion trends, adequate colour stability in processing
    - Flaws due to splits, branches, decay and discolouration
- Dimension
    - Minimum log diameter
    - Constant average
- Technical characteristics
    - Density
    - Organic and inorganic substances contained

The aspects of quality, dimension and technical characteristics speak in favour of tropical timber for many uses. Many tropical timber species have large log diameters and can be processed with a higher yield compared with temperate timber because of the usually straight trunks with almost no branches. On account of its generally higher density compared with temperate non-coniferous timber, tropical timber has longer life, excellent keeping qualities, good resistance to ambient influences and it entails lower costs for chemical pre-treatment (NEISSER/BOTZEM 1992). However, competitive advantages through grain and colour depend greatly on the current fashion trend.

Nevertheless - here the question of economic efficiency dominates - it is stressed time and again that tropical timber often is chosen on price considerations and not on account of its specific properties (OLLMANN 31.8.1994, UBA 1994:237). Some exceptions to this are windows, staircases, some outer doors and musical instruments. All these are areas in which tropical timber is technically superior to other materials.

For areas in which large quantities of timber are required, the use of tropical timber can be prevented if there is concern about the long-term dependability of delivery on account of political and economic risks. Due to the log shortage in Malaysia and Indonesia, the question of availability has become increasingly acute. On the other hand it is also becoming necessary to doubt adequate availability of non-coniferous timber species from temperate latitudes. Branch-free sawn timber assortments matching tropical timber in this respect are relatively rare in Northern latitudes. Since there is now a shortage of walnut, cherry and oak from the classical European source countries in the German market, USA and Canada are taking over a greater role (GREFERMANN 1988:103). But even in USA, a shortage with rising prices is to be expected for oak, ash and cherry veneers on account of the already persistently increased demand (EHRENTREICH 11.1.1995).

Chiefly the mass production timbers such as meranti and ramin (earmarked for processing into sawnwood and plywood) are exposed to substitution pressure by coniferous timber. The possibilities of substituting tropical luxury timbers such as mahogany and teak with coniferous timbers are slight, and by non-tropical non-coniferous timbers limited. The demand for tropical luxury timbers is based on attractive colour, structure and grain which are found only in limited variety or not at all in coniferous timbers and non-tropical non-coniferous timbers (ANONYMOUS 1989:1).

The competitive potential of coniferous timber is great. The world-wide annual production quantities of coniferous roundwood lie around 710 Mio m^3. This is about two and a half times as much as the non-coniferous timber production in the tropics and in temperate latitudes. The dynamics of increasing competition have expressed themselves in that the world market for coniferous roundwood was still relatively small in 1978 with a volume of 29.4 Mio m^3 corresponding to 61% of the world trade quantities of non-coniferous roundwood which is in the meantime exceeded by 9% with a volume of 31.9 Mio m^3. The competitive potential of coniferous timber is also reflected in the world market for sawnwood. The world-wide annual production of coniferous sawnwood was about 370 Mio m^3 and thus about three times that of non-coniferous sawnwood. The world-wide trade with coniferous sawnwood is also much greater than the world-wide traded amount of non-coniferous sawnwood (73.9 against 14.5 Mio m^3).[60]

8.3   Trend Analysis and Basic Scenarios in Individual Submarkets

The following discussion begins with the distribution analysis for 1984 and examines the seven chief end consumer areas with regard to general trends and the use of tropical timber during the years up to 1993 in greater detail. It is the aim of this chapter to investigate the substitution relationships of tropical timber to other materials and, in the case of any diminishing consumption quantities of tropical timber, to isolate the effect of technological trends from the effects of the cam-

---

[61]   This was the situation in 1990 (own calculations based on FAO, Yearbook of Forest Products, various years).

paign against tropical timber and of the change of fashion. At the end of the individual market analyses, basic scenarios for T I and T II can be determined for five of the seven areas. This means that those quantities are determined which could be achieved - as a first approximation not considering price effects - under a credible certification scheme by reversal of the campaign against tropical timber (T I) and by additional reversal of the change of fashion effects (T II).

On account of the heterogeneous structure of the available data described in Chapter 6, the basic scenarios for T I and T II are set up by a procedure combining different sources. For each examined utilization area this:

- takes or estimates import and export of tropical timber products from the foreign trade statistics,
- approximates the processed amounts of tropical timber from information given by the Federal Statistical Office with regard to timber consumption of the timber processing industry (timber statistics) and with regard to the production of timber products for all timber species (production statistics),
- draws up as realistically as possible an overview of the final consumption of tropical timber products by evaluating the statistical information obtained from the producer associations and from the branch information services and from conversations with associations and leading manufacturers and unifies these three sectors consistently.

In Sections 8.3.1 to 8.3.7 the utilization trends will be investigated in the seven chief end consumer areas for tropical timber, and in five cases basic scenarios for a certification scheme will be calculated therefrom. In Section 8.3.8 a summary of the individual basic scenarios of a certification scheme for tropical timber for the trend quantities T I and T II follows.

As a rule, data are available for the years until 1990 only for the former federal states. Combining this data with data from 1991 on which also cover the new federal states, when calculating the trends in the submarkets considered, has two consequences. Firstly, the consumer patterns of the former federal states receive undue statistical weight. However, severe distortion of the calculations is not expected as a result, because log-term mutual adaptation of the consumption patterns is expected. Secondly, the trend lines underestimate the hypothetical consumed quantities for the reference year 1993. The calculation of the trend lines is largely based on the market volume of the former federal states, whreas the reference situation, that is the actual consumption in the year 1993, is based on the full market volume of the former and new federal states. Therefore a systematic underestimate of the increased consumption which a certification scheme can induce results in the comparison of actual and hypothetical tropical timber consumption. This is in keeping with the intention of making a cautious estimate of the effects of a certification scheme.

8.3.1   Windows

The German market for windows is the largest in Europe. Including the new federal states it is twice as big as the British and three times as big as the French market. At present the new building submarket is the driving force in the West German window market. In the meantime this sector has caught up with the formerly
leading but now stagnating refurbishing sector for old buildings. Itemized for
1994 in Western Germany according to the kind of buildings, about 64% of all
window units were incorporated in modernized or newly erected residential buildings and the remaining 36% in modernized or newly erected non-residential
buildings.

In the new federal states, a boom in the construction of new buildings is starting
in addition to the strong increase of modernisation activities after German reunification. This has a positive effect on the sale of windows and other fittings and
furnishings (cf. DMD 1995d:25ff.). As Table 10 shows, refurbishing of existing
buildings still dominates in the new federal states.

Roof and cellar windows as well as windows in separating walls inside buildings, are not included in these and the subsequent statistics from the Detail-
Marketing-Dienste Baumarktforschung (DMD) in Essen. The share of tropical
timber in these types of windows is very small. Spruce is chiefly used for roof
windows, whereas mainly steel and plastics are used for cellar windows.

Table 10:   German Market for Windows According to Building Types

[Mio WU]	1991			1995[1]		
	New buildings	Old buildings	Total	New buildings	Old buildings	Total
former federal states	7.9	9.8	17.8	10.3	9.6	19.9
new federal states	0.5	1.5	2.0	2.5	4.2	6.7
FRG	8.4	11.3	19.7	12.8	13.8	26.6
[1] Estimate by the Detail-Marketing-Dienste Baumarktforschung, Essen						
Note: WU: Window units.						

Source: DMD (1995d:28).

The data from the DMD essentially constitute the basis of the analyses for windows. The distinction according to different tropical timber species which the
foreign trade statistics make for roundwood and sawnwood provides little information which can be used as a basis for categorising the final consumption into
special fields of utilization (see Appendix A3).

In the former federal states timber is the dominant window frame material used
in new residential buildings. Plastics dominate here for the modernisation of residential buildings, and aluminium as well as wooden windows with aluminium
shell the new construction and modernisation of non-residential buildings. In the

new federal states, plastic-coated timber windows as well as pine or spruce wooden windows, were the most common types until 1989. The production of plastic-
coated windows has ceased in the meantime because it was found that this type
has only a short life. Since 1989, primarily plastic windows have filled the market
gap. These windows find a high degree of acceptance in the new federal states in
spite of the critical discussion on the utilization of polyvinyl chloride (PVC). With
61.2% (1991) they have an even higher market share there than in the former
federal states (50.7% in 1991). This is surprising, because the plastic-coated windows displaced from the market due to their qualitative deficiencies formerly only
had a market share of about 30% (DMD 1995d:47-57). On current price considerations, plastic, tropical timber and spruce windows lie close together, so that
there is no explanation for the preference for plastic windows on this score.[62]

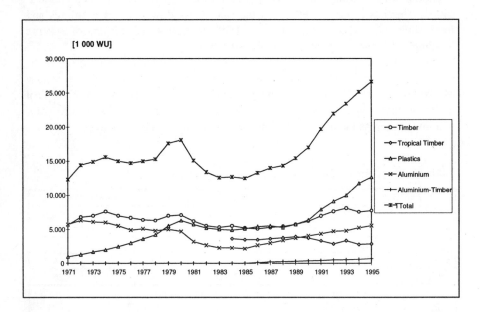

Figure 8:   Frame Materials in German Production of Windows

Source: DMD (1995d) and VERBAND DER FENSTER- UND FASSADENHERSTELLER (1994).
Notes: WU: Window units. No information is available for tropical timber shares before
1984. As from 1991 including the new federal states.

In the meantime the market share of plastic windows is rising too in the traditional preference regions for wooden windows in Southern and Southwestern

---

[62]   Current prices for a single wing window, 1000 mm x 1000 mm, according to the
EDITION AUM (3.3.1995): Tropical timber approx. 513 DM, spruce approx. 523 DM,
oak approx. 690 DM, plastics approx. 520 DM, aluminium approx. 960 DM.

Germany. Considered according to building types, the importance of plastics is increasing especially in new buildings and in particular in houses for several families. On the whole these trends lead to the expectation that without special marketing measures for wooden windows (made of tropical or non-tropical timber), the market share of plastic windows will continue to increase. Fig. 8 shows the considerable expansion of German window production since the end of the 1980s and in particular the share of plastic windows in this market. Aluminium windows are again approaching the high production quantities of the 1970s.

An analysis of market shares (see Fig. 9) indicates that plastics are the material showing the greatest dynamic development in recent years. This is at the expense of timber, especially tropical timber. Aluminium windows too are losing ground which cannot be recovered by aluminium/timber windows. Fig. 9 raises the question whether the tropical timber share in the windows market, which has in the meantime reached a historic low, will continue to fall.

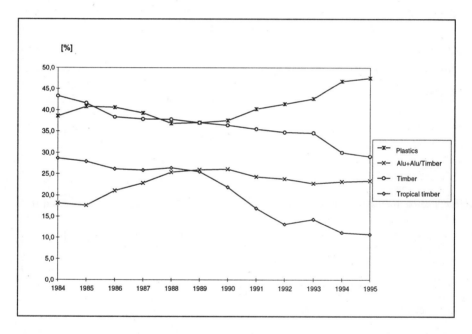

Figure 9:   Market Shares of Materials Used in German Production of Windows

Source: Own calculations on the basis of data from the DMD (1995d).
Note: Including the new federal states as from 1991.

This possibility certainly exists on the *supply side*. According to estimates by the DMD (1995d:57), even a further strong rejection of tropical timber on the part of consumers can be counteracted within a short time because adequate supplies of alternative timber are available from Sweden and Canada. However, it is necessary to reckon with increasing prices which are already becoming evident for Swedish timber. On the other hand, tropical timber is in many aspects the technically superior material. When using coniferous timber, processing industries have to contend with additional work to ensure continuous and proper fulfilment of the quality regulations (ANONYMOUS 1991).

Rejection of timber in general on the *demand side*, with a change to aluminium and plastics, is not favoured by German architects, as the survey by KROTH/KOLLERT/FILIPPI (1991:111) mentioned above has shown. On the contrary, timber is considered to be particularly suitable for window construction on account of the possibilities for individual colouration, the good steam diffusion characteristics and uncomplicated repair.

Table 11:   Environmental Effects of Various Window Materials

	Energy content	Raw material availability	Raw material procure- ment	Proces- sing	Dura- bility	Waste dispo- sal
untreated timber from temperate latitudes	1.0	0.0	2.0	1.0	2.0	1.0
treated timber from temperate latitudes	1.0	0.0	2.0	2.0	1.0	2.5
Aluminium	3.0	2.0	2.0	3.0	0.0	1.0
PVC	3.0	3.0	3.0	3.0	0.0	3.0
untreated tropical timber	1.0	3.0	3.0	1.5	1.0	1.0
treated tropical timber	1.0	3.0	3.0	2.0	0.0	2.5
untreated tropical timber from sustainable production	1.0	0.0	2.0	1.5	1.0	1.0
treated tropical timber from sustainable production	1.0	0.0	2.0	2.0	0.0	2.5
Notes for ranking system: 0.0: no environmental effect, 1.0: slight environmental effect, 2.0: distinct environmental effect, 3.0: very damaging to the environment.						

Source: UNIVERSITEIT VAN AMSTERDAM (cited in ESE 1992, Vol. II:60).

Further reduction in the use of tropical timber would also aggravate the already existing environmental problems in Germany on account of the need for chemical treatment of non-tropical timber. The increasingly employed coniferous timber species - European spruce and pine, but also North American spruce, fir, pine, hemlock and douglas - are not sufficiently weather resistant compared with tropical window timbers such as meranti, so increased amounts of paint have to be applied. More important is the need to use primers with blueing substances (TRÜBSWETTER 1989). Environmental pollution problems arise in the production of the paints and primers as well as in the waste disposal of old windows.

A study carried out by the University of Amsterdam to establish a systematic overview of materials used in window construction revealed that tropical timber from sustainable forest management should be given preference over other materials (see Table 11).

The stated advantages of using tropical timber for making windows, the generally positive assessment of the material timber and the evident fashion trend towards coloured and darker timber species give reason to presume that the decline of the share of tropical timber in the window sector has reached rock bottom. Temporarily there is still some substitution pressure exerted by plastic windows in the new federal states, but on a medium-term basis the share of tropical timber is likely to stabilize or even expand. A certification scheme for tropical timber, if introduced within the next few years, would therefore find a generally favourable market development for tropical timber and could - possibly extended to non-tropical timber too - in this market environment efficiently fulfil its intended role as marketing instrument for the 'natural' product timber produced from a renewable raw material (KROTH/KOLLERT/FILIPPI 1991:110).

For exact quantitative analysis of the material input for German window manufacture, it is first of all necessary to define the conversion rates. MÜLLER (1987:89) assumes a sawnwood input of 0.1 m^3 per window. The DMD (1995d:25,59) calculate 0.07 m^3 per window *unit*, corresponding to about 0.11 m^3 per window.[63] This value is taken as basis also by the German Tropical Forest Initiative (Initiative Tropenwald, ITW 1994:4) and seems to be a realistic quantity. It can also be assumed that the data determined by the DMD concerning the total production and material consumption in the German window production, obtained within the scope of a survey in cooperation with the registered German Association of Window and Facade Manufacturers (Verband der Fenster- und Fassadenhersteller), is closer to the real situation than the figures assumed by Müller.[64]

Table 12 indicates that, according to the association, the tropical timber share of all timber used in 1984 was 66.2%, giving a total consumption of tropical sawnwood of 254 000 m^3 for windows. In the meantime the share has dropped to about 40% of all wooden windows or 15% of all window materials. Müller had assumed a tropical timber share of 40% of all timber for 1984, but he also based

---

[63] The data from the DMD in Table 12 as also in Fig. 8 are stated in the statistical window units (WU). A window unit is a standardized square window with dimensions 1.3 m x 1.3 m. The specified material consumption for a window unit includes the wing frame and the fixed frame.

[64] The survey made by the association covered about 70% of all German window manufacturers and received answers in about 50% of all contacts made. In the opinion of the association, this survey gives a representative picture of this business branch (ANONYMOUS 1991).

his figures on a greater total production of timber windows and therefore calculated a tropical timber consumption of only 208 000 m³. Therefore part of the undeclared final consumption of tropical timber appearing in his distribution analysis (see Fig. 6) can thus be attributed to window production.

Table 12:   Trends in the German Market for Windows

	Material	1984	1989	1990	1991	1992	1993
Dom. production [Mio WU]	all	12.7	15.4	17.0	19.7	22.0	23.4
- from plastics [%]		38.6	37.0	37.5	40.2	41.4	42.7
- from aluminium [%]		18.1	24.0	23.9	22.1	21.5	20.5
- from alu/timber [%]	(TT+nTT)	0.0	1.9	2.2	2.2	2.3	2.3
- from timber [%]	TT+nTT	43.3	37.0	36.4	35.5	34.8	34.6
Sawnwood consumption for domestic window production [1000 m³]	TT+nTT	384	418	446	504	553	586
thereof tropical timber [1000 m³]	TT	254	288	268	240	209	242
[%]	TT	66.2	68.9	60.1	47.6	37.9	41.2
thereof imports [1000 m³]	TT	0.0	0.6	0.8	4.0	0.6	0.7

Imports of windows from tropical countries, converted to sawnwood. Exports of
windows made from tropical timber cannot be discerned from the foreign trade statistics.
The imports for 1991 are evidently a unique special movement.
Notes: As from 1991 including the new federal states.
TT: Tropical timber. nTT: Non-tropical timber. WU: Window units.

Source: VERBAND DER FENSTER- UND FASSADENHERSTELLER (1994) and DMD (1995d).

Table 12 also shows that non-tropical timber was not able to take up the losses
of tropical timber completely, so that all kinds of wooden windows had a slightly
declining market share after the onset of the campaign against tropical timber in
1989. However, it can be assumed that the recession of tropical timber utilization
in German window production is not only due to the campaign against tropical
timber, even though this recession intensified in 1989 after the campaign against
tropical timber started. The fashion trend towards lighter coloured timbers persisting since several years can also play only a subordinate role in the windows
sector. Further research is needed to elucidate the possible influencing factors. For
example, as already mentioned above, it is conspicuous that in the meantime in-
stallation of plastic windows is increasing even in the traditional timber-preferring
regions, in spite of the absence of price advantages (see footnote 61) and in spite
of quality advantages of using tropical timber for windows. Nevertheless, part of
the reduced demand is assigned to the scenario with reversal of the effects of the
change of fashion (T II). So the scenario T II also contains reversal of other, not
specifically known effects in the windows field.

Fig. 10 clearly shows that the use of plastics has, since German reunification, received an additional boost with negative consequences for all other materials. This special movement is not considered further in the calculations for the scenarios of a certification scheme, because long-term effects are of more importance. The calculated basic scenarios are oriented on the long-term trend for plastic windows (upper trend line) and on the long-term trend for all kinds of wooden windows (middle trend line). The basic scenarios simulate various tropical timber shares in the trend of the market volume for all timber species. Therefore the distribution between the timber species is decisive for defining the trend quantities T I and T II.

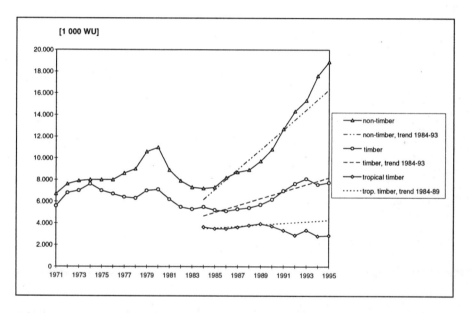

Figure 10:   Trends in Material Utilization in the German Production of Windows

Source: See Figure 9.

Fig. 11 is an enlarged section of the trends for timber, taken from the previous diagram for the years as of 1984. Data reaching further back are not available. The upper trend line corresponds to the middle one in the previous diagram. The bottom trend line is calculated from the tropical timber consumption during the years 1984 to 1989. The difference with respect to the actual consumption is interpreted as the effect of the campaign against tropical timber. The middle trend line shows how the consumption of tropical timber would have developed with a constant share of 69% (as in the mid-1980s) in the total timber consumption. As explained above, the difference with respect to the bottom trend line is interpreted as an effect of the change of fashion and other structural developments.In the reference year 1993 the average import unit value of imported tropical sawnwood amounted to 923 DM/m^3 or, converted to the roundwood input, 600 DM/m^3(r). The tropical sawnwood consumption realized in 1993 for window production, deviating from the figures shown in Table 12, is taken to be 210 000 m^3 sawnwood (323 000 m^3(r) converted to roundwood equivalents), because it is suspected that a special movement took place in that year.[65]

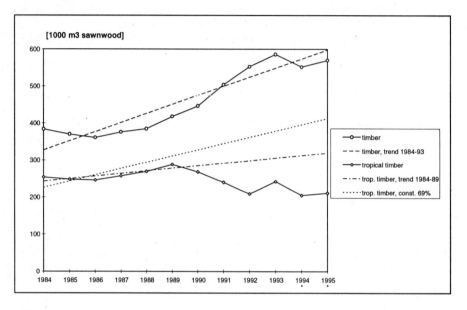

Figure 11:   Trends in the Utilization of Timber in the German Production of Windows

Source: See Figure 9.

The bottom trend line in Fig. 11 simulates the reversal of the campaign against tropical timber, produced by a certification scheme (basic scenario for T I) and gives for the year 1993 a consumption of 306 000 m^3 sawnwood (or 471 000 m^3(r)). This is 96 000 m^3 sawnwood (148 000 m^3(r)) more than in the reference situation, the actually realized consumption in 1993.

The middle trend line in Fig. 11 simulates both reversal of the campaign against tropical timber and reversal of the change of fashion effects and other structural developments, by a certification scheme (basic scenario for T II). In the reference year 1993 an increased consumption of 169 000 m^3 or 260 000 m^3(r) above the actual consumption is reached.

So a certification scheme would lead to a considerable increase of consumption in these basic scenarios (45.8% and 80.5% respectively). Little more than half of

---

[65]   See bottom line in Fig. 11.

the fall in tropical timber consumption for window production in recent years can consequently be attributed to the campaign against tropical timber.

8.3.2   Outer Doors

In the Federal Republic of Germany the market for outer doors enjoyed a lively increase during the past ten years, chiefly due to extensive refurbishing activities. In the meantime the degree of saturation for high quality outer doors is increasing, so that gradual flattening of the growth rate is expected at least in the former federal states. Impulses are still coming from the new federal states, for example because the insurance companies are insisting on outer doors conforming to the latest state of technology (DMD 1995b:36). Classified according to type of buildings, in particular residential housing construction is strongly increasing in the former and new federal states (see Table 13).

Table 13:   German Market for Outer Doors According to Building Types

[1000 pcs]	1991			1995 [1]		
	Residential	Non-Residential	Total	Residential	Non-Residential	Total
former federal states	729.5	380.8	1110.3	791.7	342.2	1133.9
new federal states	142.8	18.7	161.5	289.6	69.9	359.5
FRG	872.3	399.5	1271.8	1081.3	412.1	1493.4
[1] Estimate made by the Detail-Marketing-Dienste Baumarktforschung, Essen.						

Source: DMD (1995b:55).

Table 14 clearly depicts the continuous growth of domestic consumption of outer doors from German production in recent years. This is primarily attributable to increased demand from the new federal states. Thereby plastic and aluminium windows have lost market shares whereas glass has gained. Development of the outer door shows an upward trend in the absolute sense as well as in the market share (see also Fig. 12 and Fig. 13).

At the end of the period, tropical timber doors no longer participated in the positive trend for wooden doors. In 1987 tropical timber still had a share of 62.2% in the utilized timber. This share rose to 71% by 1992. Since then there has again been a continuous decline down to an estimated 60.2% for 1995.[66]

Within tropical timbers, displacements are observed discriminating against meranti. In 1991 meranti still had a share of 85% among all tropical timbers. This

---

[66]   The magnitudes indicated by the DMD data are confirmed by KROTH/KOLLERT/ FILIPPI (1991:71). They state 70% as the share of tropical timber outer doors for prefabricated houses at the end of the 1980s, with respect to all wooden outer doors.

share has dropped to an estimated 57% for 1995. This is probably connected with the large price increase for meranti sawnwood. According to the foreign trade statistics, German imports of meranti sawnwood fell continuously with rising prices until 1992 and then suffered a further sharp reduction of about 40% in 1993.

Table 14:   Trends in the German Market for Outer Doors

	Material	*1984*	*1991*	*1992*	*1993*
Domestic production [1000 pcs]	all	----	1.272	1.328	1.370
- from plastics [%]		----	7.1	7.4	6.6
- from aluminium [%]		----	41.8	39.5	38.5
- from glass [%]		----	4.8	5.6	6.9
- from timber [%]	TT+nTT	----	46.3	47.5	48.0
Domestic consumption of sawn-wood for outer doors [1000m³]	TT+nTT	125	174	186	194
thereof trop. timber [1000 m³]	TT	approx. 51	117	132	126
- [%]	TT	approx. 40.8	67.5	70.9	64.9
thereof from net import [1000 m³]	TH	2.9	-0.3	6.6	4.3

¹ Imports minus exports of tropical timber doors from tropical countries, converted to sawnwood. Inner and outer doors cannot be distinguished in the foreign trade statistics, so the volume was subdivided in 1:1 ratio.
Notes: nTT:non-tropical timber; TT:tropical timber; ---: no information available.
As from 1991 including the new federal states. The material consumption is based on door wing and frame.

Source: For 1984 MÜLLER (1987:89) and own estimates; for the other years DMD (1995b).

As Table 9 in Section 8.1 shows, the average price level for the most important raw material for tropical timber door production, tropical sawnwood, still nomi-nally lies on the level of the mid-1980s. At present a tropical timber outer door is still cheaper than other doors or only slightly more desireable than a plastic outer door.[67] Tropical timber consumption is stagnating in the absolute sense too (see Fig. 12), so the decline cannot be explained solely by different consumption pat-terns in the new federal states. One would have expected that the increasing signi-ficance of residential buildings for the outer door market (see Table 13) should have led to increased demand for tropical timber outer doors. In view of the technical advantages of tropical timber over other materials employed outdoors,[68] the discrepancy between the actual consumption and the trend must be associated with the effects of the campaign against tropical timber and/or the change of fashion.

---

[67]   Current prices for a single wing outer door with crossbeams, 1125 mm x 2125 mm, according to EDITION AUM (3.3.1995): Tropical timber approx. 3037 DM, spruce approx. 3090 DM, oak approx. 3490 DM, plastic approx. 3000 DM, aluminium approx. 5480 DM.
[68]   See also the explanations on windows given in Section 8.3.1 and valid here too.

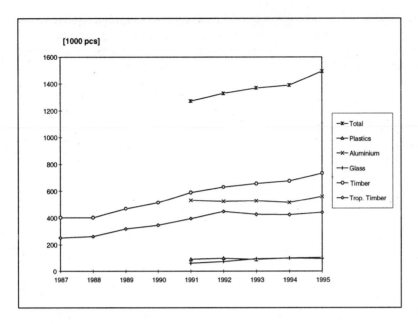

Figure 12:   Materials Used in German Production of Outer Doors

Source: DMD (1995b). 1994 and 1995 estimates made by the DMD. As from 1991 including the new federal states

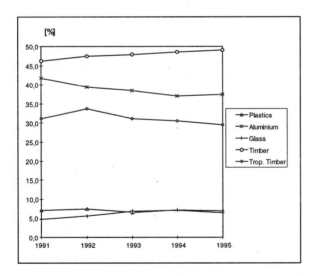

Figure 13:   Market Shares of Materials Used in German Production of Outer Doors

Source: See Figure 12.

Thereby the deviation with respect to the trend cannot be attributed solely to the campaign against tropical timber. The latter commenced in 1989 and can, as the window market shows, induce quicker consumer reactions. Furthermore, according to the data from the DMD, tropical timber reached its highest share of 71% of all timber consumption yet in 1992. Consequently a basic scenario for T I is not calculated for outer doors. The decline from 1992 to 1993 continuing in 1994 and 1995, is cautiously interpreted as the combined effect of the campaign against tropical timber and the change of fashion. It is therefore assigned to the basic scenario for T II.

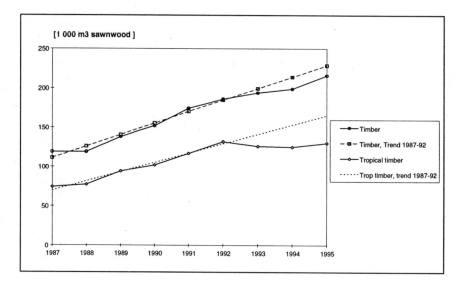

Figure 14:   Trends in the German Market for Outer Doors

Source: See Figure 12.

In 1993 the actual consumption of tropical timber for making outer doors amounted to 126 000 m³ sawnwood or, converted to roundwood, 194 000 m³(r). For consumption within the trend (see our trend line in Fig. 14), a consumption of 141 000 m³ sawnwood corresponding to 217 000 m³(r) roundwood would have been achieved in 1993. The basic scenario for TII is defined at this level.

8.3.3   Staircases

Only a few time sequences are available for the German staircase market. The DMD (1995c) has been observing inland timber utilization for staircases since 1990. There is no such item in the foreign trade statistics.

Tropical timber has technical advantages over other timbers at any rate in the high quality sector. Quality Class I of the DIN Standard 68368 stipulates for staircases that the utilized sawnwood must not have any knots on the surfaces which remain visible. It is easy to fulfil this condition with tropical timbers such as meranti, iroko or kosipo.

Table 15:   German Market for Timber Staircases

	Material	1984	1990	1991	1992	1993
Domestic production [1000 pcs]	nCT+CT	320	121	129	151	168
Domestic consumption [1000 m³ sawnwood]	nCT+CT	120	172	188	177	189
thereof trop. timber [%]	TT	50.0	30.4	29.9	29.5	28.3

¹ Timber staircases are built to fit on site, therefore the foreign trade statistics contain no corresponding goods item. The production figures given by Müller for 1984 lie far above the production according to the Federal Statistical Office amounting to 107 000 pieces. We assume that this is so because the craftsman production is included.
Notes: nCT: Non-coniferous timber; CT: Coniferous timber; TT: Tropical timber
As from 1991 including the new federal states.

Source: For 1984 MÜLLER (1987:91-92). As from 1990 domestic production according to the Federal Statistical Office (STATISTISCHES BUNDESAMT, Fachserie 4, Reihe 3.1); domestic consumption according to DMD (1995c).

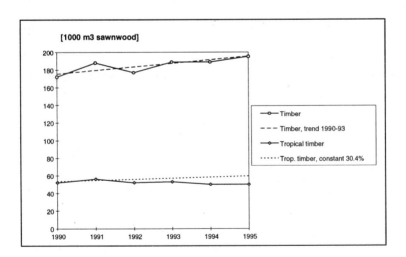

Figure 15:   Trends in the German Market for Staircases

Source DMD (1995c). 1994 and 1995 estimate made by the DMD. As from 1991 including the new federal states.

However, when using domestic timbers there is a loss of up to 50% if the requirements are to be fulfilled for Quality Class I, because of the shorter distance between branches (TRÜBSWETTER 1989:1669). Possibilities for substitution nevertheless exist. For example, recently increasing amounts of maple are being used for building staircases due to the rising prices for meranti sawnwood (ANONYMOUS 1994b).

Fig. 15 shows the development of material used in German staircase construction since 1990. Evidently the share of tropical timber is falling. It was still 30.4% in 1990 but already down to 28.3% in 1993 (see also Table 15). The DMD estimate that the share will drop further to 25.5% in 1995. No data are available for the years before 1990, so it is not possible to differentiate the long-term decrease according to the effects of the campaign against tropical timber and a change of fashion. For this reason only the basic scenario T II is defined here describing the reversal of both effects by a certification scheme (bottom trend line in Fig. 15). T II shows that tropical timber can hold the share it had in 1990 among all timbers (30.4%). This share is referred to the trend for all timbers (upper trend line).

The actual tropical timber consumption in 1993 for staircase construction was 53 000 m^3 corresponding to 81 500 m^3(r). In the basic scenario for T II it is 57 000 m^3 corresponding to 87 700 m^3(r).

8.3.4   Do-It-Yourself Mouldings

Private persons buy large amounts of sawnwood, squared timber, laths and strips on building material and hobby markets, especially for refurbishing old buildings. 90 000 m^3 of glued timber went to private persons in 1984 on this distribution route, 5% thereof tropical timber (according to information from the CMA 1986, cited by MÜLLER 1987:99). Shelves and smooth edge sawnwood bought by private persons in 1984 amounted to 582 000 m^3 and comprised 8% tropical timber according to information from the CMA (ibid). This gives a total volume of about 51 000 m^3 corresponding to about 85 000 m^3(r). This volume has dropped by about 80% due to the campaign against tropical timber (RISTAU 1.3.1995) so that the cautiously estimated volume would lie today at about 17 000 m^3 corresponding to about 30 000 m^3(r).

The market growth for the do-it-yourself sale of sawnwood, squared timber, laths and strips of all timber species since 1984 until 1993 can only be estimated roughly. According to the production statistics, the production of carpet strips increased by 38% during this period. Production of building strips and other strips increased by 85% and that of mouldings[69] by 58%. Taking a cautious value of 40% for the sales increase from 1984 to 1993, the tropical timber volume for the

---

[69]   The production of all kinds of mouldings is meant here, including that not for private use. The precursor product for the production of carpet strips, building strips and other strips is partly contained too.

do-it-yourself market in 1993 without the campaign against tropical timber could have been about 71 400 m^3 corresponding to about 126 000 m^3(r).

The reduction of sales due to the campaign against tropical timber, comparing the actual and the possible amounts sold in 1993, amounts to about 54 400 m^3 corresponding to 96 000 m^3(r) according to this rough estimate. This amount could be regained by a certification scheme. Quadrupling of the demand as response to a certification scheme seems unlikely. However the initial amount is small and, as already pointed out in Section 5.5, buyers react very positively to environmental labels in the building material and hobby markets.

Since tropical timber sales in the hobby and building material markets were affected by actions aimed directly at these markets within the campaign against tropical timber, the potential volume increase is assigned to the scenario T I. Scenario T II is not required here, because any effects of a change of fashion cannot be identified on the basis of the available information.

8.3.5   Wall and Ceiling Coverings

Tropical timber in the form of *sliced veneers* is used for surface decoration on walls and ceilings as well as for inner doors (only cover veneers) and furniture. No information is available on the consumption of tropical sliced veneers in these individual fields, so it was first of all necessary to make an analysis of the total volume in the domestic market in order to be able thereafter to make an approximate distribution between the volume in the three fields.

According to the foreign trade statistics, the net imports of sliced veneers amounted to 3700 m^3 in 1984. In addition, 58 000 m^3 sliced veneer were produced in Germany with a roundwood consumption of about 120 000 m^3 (MÜLLER 1987:26). Thus the total volume in the domestic market for 1984 was about 60 000 m^3.

Only insignificant changes of the net imports (3 800 m^3) took place before 1993. The raw African timber consumption of German veneer factories was about 14 000 m^3 in 1993 according to the official timber statistics (raw timber and half-finished timber products). This is 22 000 m^3 less than in 1984.[70]

A certain amount of sliced veneer manufactured on paid order and not covered by the statistics (see Chapter 6) must be added to these quantities for 1993. Paid orders are typical for the veneer industry. Some factories specialized in working to paid order peel or slice chiefly roundwood imported by the timber importing trade which also undertakes the distribution (GREFERMANN 1988:121). According to the production statistics, 46 000 m^3 sawed and sliced veneers were produced in 1993 from all timber species. According to HESS (19.9.1994), about 50% of these were American oak and 10% timber from neighbouring European countries. Assuming

---

[70]   The timber statistics also include a category „other foreign timber" containing small amounts of Asian timber. However, this category mainly comprises American oak (HESS 19.9.1994).

that the remainder is tropical timber chiefly processed to sliced veneers, the imports, the raw timber consumption according to the timber statistics, and the processing of tropical timber on paid order add up to an approximate total volume of sliced veneers (after deducting the exports) of about 25 000 to 30 000 m^3. Consequently there is a reduced consumption on the part of all users of tropical timber amounting to a total of about 50% compared with 1984.

The available data permits only an approximate subdivision of this volume for 1984 and for 1993. For 1984 MÜLLER (1987:29) assigned the domestic market utilization of sliced veneers for all timber species with 45% to furniture production, 26% to inner door production and 17% to panel production. Müller thereby considers the 45% for furniture as being more likely an underestimate of the actual consumption. More recent information of the distribution is not available.

Profile wood, panels and cassettes (square panels) are used for *wall and ceiling coverings* made of timber. The chief competing non-timber product in this field is wallpaper. Panels are surface-refined timber materials which have a surface made of timber veneer, plastic film, metal film or melamine-impregnated printed paper, on a carrying board made of particle board, plywood or wood fibreboard. Panels and cassettes produced in Germany may contain tropical timber in the outer layer, but as a rule not in the carrier board (OLLMANN 16.12.1994).

The competitive advantage panels have over solid timber products (profile sawnwood) has deteriorated in recent years, because higher quality and fewer health hazards are associated with (solid) sawnwood compared with veneered particle boards. Among panels, lacquer and decoratively coated surfaces have gained in the market relative to timber veneers. They are often priced lower and score with their more robust surface and more uniform visual appearance. Furthermore, even trained persons find it difficult to distinguish good prints from genuine veneers. According to BECKER (1994), on the whole there is a „loss in the middle", that is, either high quality goods - usually made of solid timber - are bought, or the price dominates the buying decision and an imitation pattern is accepted. The range between these two extremes, in which veneers have the greatest market shares, is losing volume.

Among the veneers, the most common kinds are oak, beech, birch and white ash (ANONYMOUS 1994b). The fact that „veneer cosmetics" are increasingly adopted is also important for the tropical timber market. A luxury timber grain closely imitating the genuine product is produced in a multi-step process on cheaper timbers such as tropical limba or non-tropical beechwood (DEPPE 18.1.1995).

Taken together, the described quality trends mean that the decision for or against tropical timber is strongly influenced by technical novelties on the supply side. These influences - for tropical timber competition within the timber group, especially the advance of profile wood and the trend towards luxury timber imitations - may be superimposed on the effects of the campaign against tropical timber on the effects of the change of fashion.

The available statistical information on the consumption of profile wood and on the utilization of tropical timber panels is inadequate for analysing the utilization trends,[71] so no basic scenarios can be defined for the wall and ceiling covering submarket.

8.3.6   Furniture Surfaces

Since data in the furniture market is only available for indoor furniture, therefore garden furniture and other furniture for outdoor usage will only be mentioned briefly. According to estimates made by MÜLLER (1987:77), about one third of all *wooden garden furniture* is made from tropical timber with a small total volume amounting to only 3000 m³. For other outdoor furniture, such as laths for park benches, weather-resistant   tropical timbers such as sipo and bongossi, which require no special surface treatment, were preferred for a long time. The boycott by many communities gave rise to problems here, because coniferous timber often cannot provide the desired hardness, oak, although having the required quality is very expensive, and robinia is not available in large quantities. Beech or ash must first be subjected to impregnation under pressure. Since salts soluble in water are used as protecting agents, problems arise when disposing the wood residues, sawdust and later the worn-out bench laths. Protecting materials on the basis of oil can also be used for pressurized impregnation of beechwood (TRÜBSWETTER 1989). In any case, higher costs arise in comparison with tropical timber on account of the protecting agents and additional processing steps. For garden furniture and other outdoor furniture, no statements can be made regarding consumed quantities or quantitative trends after 1984.

For *indoor furniture*, the use of timber as a whole and with respect to specific timber species is determined to a very great extent by fashion trends. For example, in the kitchen wooden surfaces are at present being displaced by lacquer and plastic surfaces, whereas luxury veneers are again gaining ground over films (KAMM 1991). This trend still persists in recent times as evident at the international office furniture trade fair held in Cologne in October 1994, and it is expected to intensify. In addition to beechwood, increasing amounts of pearwood and walnut are being used here (ANONYMOUS 1994e). For box furniture (wardrobes, inbuilt wardrobes, shelves, sideboards and other furniture in box form), there is a recent trend in the market competition of different surfaces in favour of solid timber. This goes at the expense of veneer and plastic surfaces (SEIZINGER 1995).

Tropical timber is used as sawnwood and as surface-covering material (veneer) in furniture production. MÜLLER (1987:117) estimates tropical sawnwood consumption in 1984 to be 47 000 m³. More recent information is not available. The-

---

[71]   cf. MÜLLER (1987:92ff.). In the investigation carried out by KROTH/KOLLERT/FILIPPI (1991:47ff.), a high percentage of the interrogated architects were unable to state what timber species are used in ceiling coverings. Among other reasons, this is due to the fact that wall and ceiling coverings are usually installed later by the owner of the new building.

refore in the following discussion the calculations are confined to the development of tropical timber veneers for surface design.

Tropical timber is increasingly being substituted by non-tropical timber in *furniture surfaces*. The dominating timbers are here oak and cherry as well as American walnut. The process of substitution by timber imitations (laminates) seems to have been stopped in spite of the good returns which can be achieved in production. This development can be attributed both the increasingly good image of timber as compared with plastics and to technical problems in the laminating process. The width of the pressure rollers cannot be increased indefinitely, so that over large areas pattern repetition reveals that the material is not genuine veneer (DEPPE 18.1.1995).

The tropical timber content of genuine timber veneers for furniture production is about 5% today compared with about 8% to 9% twenty years ago (ibid). This agrees with the calculations mentioned above for the development of the volume of sliced veneers in the domestic market, which has fallen by 50% since 1984. HERRMANN (1.2.1995) assumes that today about 3% of the entire veneer timber consumed in the German furniture industry is tropical timber. According to a recent survey questioning box furniture manufacturers and traders, the share of tropical timber in the surfaces of box furniture is less then 2% (SEIZINGER 1995). It is today less than 0.2% in the domestic and kitchen furniture area (NAUMANN 2.8.1994), and also in the production of functional furniture (kitchen and laboratory equipment), tropical timber and wood altogether plays no significant role (DEPPE 18.1.1995).

According to calculations by Müller (see Fig. 6), 27 800 m^3 sliced tropical timber veneers were processed for furniture production in 1984. Roughly estimated on the basis of the number of pieces of furniture manufactured, furniture production has increased by about 40% up to 1993, so that today without the negative effects of the change of fashion and the campaign against tropical timber, a tropical timber consumption around 39 000 m^3 could have been achieved. According to the information mentioned above, only about 14 000 m^3 corresponding to 28 000 m^3(r) are actually consumed today. This is at the most half of the amount consumed in 1984. So if it is successful in reversing the effect of the campaign against tropical timber and of the change of fashion, a certification scheme could altogether achieve an increase of consumed volume amounting to 25 000 m^3 for furniture surfaces.

The industry estimates that the decrease of tropical timber luxury veneers is due to the campaign against tropical timber and to the change of fashion by about equal amounts (HERRMANN 1.2.1995). Therefore the basic scenario for T I is defined with a consumption amounting to 26 500 m^3 corresponding to 53 000 m^3(r) and the basic scenario for T II is defined with a consumption of 39 000 m^3 corresponding to 78 000 m^3(r).

8.3.7   Inner Doors

For lack of information, no statements can be made for inner doors with respect to the development of tropical timber consumption for the doorframe (sawnwood) and for any covering layers underneath (such as plywood). Since this is an invisible use, it can be assumed that it was hardly affected by the campaign against tropical timber so that it can be ignored in connection with the questions which are the subject of this study. This may even be a field of use in which the consumption of tropical timber has increased in spite of the campaign against it (see Section 7.1).

Only incomplete numerical sequences exist for non-timber surface materials used in domestic production of inner doors for the domestic market. Table 16 summarizes the available information. A comparison with the data from MÜLLER (1987) for 1984 has not been made, because his data for inner doors are based on very rough estimates and he does not take non-surface covering layers into consideration. The data show that the share of luxury timber veneers is falling and that lacquered or plastic-coated inner doors are continually increasing their market share.

Table 16:   German Market for Inner Doors

	Material	1985	1987	1990
Domestic consumption [1000 pcs]	all	6080	5727	7584
Surface material				
- untreated/lacquered [%]		7.8	9.8	11.0
- Plastics [%]		8.1	8.7	9.3
- Sliced veneers [%]	TT+nTT	84.0	81.5	79.7
Domestic sliced veneer consumption for inner doors [1000 m³]	TT+nTT	---	34	50
thereof trop. timber - [1000 m³]	TT	---	14	23
- [%]	TT	---	41.8	46.4
thereof from net import [1000 m³]	TT	3.7	0.0	1.6

¹ 25% of all imports (minus the exports) of sliced veneers (<1 mm) for the particular year went to inner doors; the remaining 75% went to furniture and panels (cf. MÜLLER 1987:29). The value from 1984 was taken for 1985.
Notes: ---: no information available; TT: tropical timber; nTT: non-tropical timber. Only for the former federal states. The material consumption stated is only for the door wing.

Source: STATISTISCHES BUNDESAMT (Fachserie 7, Reihe 2), DMD (1995a).

Complete time series are available for the distribution of the timber species among the luxury veneer doors. According to this data, the share of tropical timber after the beginning of the campaign against tropical timber actually increased from 43.6% (1989) to 46.4% (1990) and still further to 46.6% (1991).[72] A decrease came only in 1993 in which year the share of tropical timber dropped to 42.3%. The DMD estimate that the share will fall further to 40.2% in 1995. Either the campaign against tropical timber took effect after a considerable delay so that it is no longer unambiguously identifiable, or the change of fashion has taken until this time to show an effect. Since the market share of tropical timber for 1993 was only slightly below the level for 1989 and still increased until 1991 in spite of the campaign against tropical timber and the change of fashion, no basic scenarios will be defined for this submarket. The available information suggests that the campaign against tropical timber and the change of fashion had no significant influence on the decision for or against tropical timber veneer for door surfaces.

8.3.8   Summary of the Basic Scenarios

Table 17 summarizes the basic scenarios defined for the five end consumer areas and compares then with the quantities actually consumed in the reference year 1993. The totalled scenarios of the submarkets give an increased consumption of 41% in the scenario T I compared with the actual consumption *in the five submarkets* in 1993. Therefore reversal of the campaign against tropical timber (T I) has a greater effect than reversal of the effect of the change of fashion on the reaction of the entire German demand for tropical timber (T II lies only 25 percentage points above the scenario T I). Relative to the *entire* German tropical timber import volume for 1993 amounting to 2 005 000 $m^3(r)$, T I corresponds to an increase of 13.4% and T II an increase of 21.7% (see also Table 33).

---

[72]   DMD (1995b). This order of magnitude is confirmed by KROTH/KOLLERT/FILIPPI (1991:152). They state a share of about 80% at the end of the 1980s for timber veneer used as cover for domestic building inner doors. Tropical timbers thereby have a share of 30% to 50% depending on the kind of living quarters.

Table 17:   Basic Scenarios in Five Important Submarkets for Tropical Timber

[1000 m³(r)]	Reference situation: actual con-sumption in 1993 R	Reversal of effects of campaign against tropical timber by a certification scheme T I	Reversal of effects of campaign against tropical timber and of a change fashion by a certification scheme T II
Consumed amount for			
Windows	323.0	471.0	583.0
Outer doors	194.0	194.0	217.0
Staircases	81.5	81.5	87.7
Do-it-yourself mouldings	30.0	126.0	126.0
Furniture surfaces	28.0	53.0	78.0
Total	656.5	925.5	1091.7
Increase against **R**			
Windows		148.0	260.0
Outer doors		0.0	23.0
Staircases		0.0	6.2
Do-it-yourself mouldings		96.0	96.0
Furniture surfaces		25.0	50.0
Total		269.0	435.2

Notes: No scenarios were calculated for inner doors because the effects of the campaign against tropical timber and of the change of fashion could not be identified clearly. No scenarios were defined for wall and ceiling coverings because of insufficient data.

Source: Own calculations.

Part III

Extended Scenarios for a Certified Tropical Timber Market under Different Supply and Demand Constellations

The third part of this study consisting of four chapters calculates extended scenarios with modified supply and demand constellations on the basis of the basic scenarios developed in part two for the five most important submarkets and for the aggregate German market for tropical timber. Fig. 16 gives a systematic overview of all the scenarios analysed here.

Two basic alternative versions are considered in all cases:

The „*small country*" assumption is based on the concept that a certification scheme for tropical timber will be set up only in the Federal Republic of Germany. The German demand for tropical timber amounts to only 2.6% of the world wide demand and is so small that changes in the German demand for tropical timber would have little or no effect on the world market price development. Therefore, the world market price is here assumed to be exogenous. Consequently, with the small country assumption, the extended scenarios consider only those market movements which arise from the certification costs, from additional costs caused by sustainable forest management and any increased willingness on the part of end consumers to pay higher prices.

The „*big country*" assumption is based on the concept that the certification scheme will be implemented simultaneously in all OECD countries. Because these countries, taken together, constitute all important end consumers of tropical timber not consumed in the tropical countries, their simultaneous demand variations will have a significant effect on the development of world market prices. Therefore in the big country version the market movements already incorporated in the small country version are expanded by the market movements induced by the increase in world market prices.

The theoretical basis and the general procedure for making the calculations are explained in Chapter 9. Chapter 10 next calculates special scenarios for the five submarkets. Chapter 11 is concerned with the aggregate German tropical timber market. Starting out from a highly aggregated supply of tropical timber and the accumulated increased demand in the five submarkets (in the basic scenarios for T I and T II), this part of the study calculates different scenarios for the big country case and the small country case.

In the big country version of the total market it is assumed that the other OECD countries will manifest the same percentage increase of demand for tropical timber in response to a certification scheme for tropical timber as is found in the Federal German tropical timber market. The world market price increase determined in these scenarios is fed into the big country scenarios of the individual submarkets in Chapter 10.

The assumed extrapolation of the reaction of the German tropical timber market to the entire OECD demand is a simplified model chosen because more detailed studies of the development of the demand for tropical timber in these countries are not available. The question of whether the calculated percentage demand expansions for the Federal Republic of Germany give realistic results when transposed to the entire OECD group essentially depends on three factors: Firstly, the potential effect of a certification scheme for tropical timber in other countries will be the same as in the Federal Republic of Germany only if the end consumer structures are similar with regard to visible uses of tropical timber and thus offer a similar potential for a certification scheme. Secondly, an OECD-wide certification scheme in these countries can have demand-expanding effects similar to those of a certification scheme confined to the Federal Republic of Germany, only if similar effects of the campaign against tropical timber and change in fashion can be found in all these countries for recent years. Finally, consumers in all countries must be willing to the same degree to pay higher prices for certified products.

Scenario:	Submarkets	Total Market
Basic scenario (no CS, without willingness to pay higher prices)	x	x
World market price increase due to OECD-wide certification (no CS costs, no willingness to pay higher prices)		x
Extended scenarios for the submarkets (Chapter 10) (with CS costs, no additional costs by sustainable forest management)		
no willingness to pay higher prices		
CS for tropical timber	x	
CS for all timber	x	
CS for all timber and energy tax	x	
willingness to pay higher prices exists		
CS for tropical timber	x	
CS for all timber	x	
CS for all timber plus energy tax	x	
Extended scenarios for the total market (Chapter 11) (with costs of the CS, CS for tropical timber) no additional costs by sustainable forest management		
no willingness to pay higher prices		x
willingness to pay higher prices exists		x
additional costs by sustainable forest management		
no willingness to pay higher prices		x
willingness to pay higher prices exists		x

Range of the certification scheme and world market price development:
The scenarios are calculated for a small country version (certification scheme only in the Federal Republic of Germany) and for a big country version (OECD-wide certification scheme).
The world market price remains unchanged in the small country version except for a possible change due to the actual costs of the certification scheme (CS).
In the big country version the world market price increase is assessed for the total market and then taken over into the submarkets.

Figure 16:   Systematic Overview of the Timber Certification Scenarios

Regarding the latter point, it is only possible to refer to the two studies mentioned at the end of Section 5.5. They strongly suggest that analogous willingness to pay higher prices exists at least within the European region. The other two factors are examined in greater detail below.

The *end consumer structures* are basically similar within the OECD countries, because not only in the Federal Republic of Germany, but also in the other large consumer countries tropical timber is used chiefly in the building industry and for furniture production. On the building sector tropical timber is used mainly for joinery (doors, windows, staircases, etc.), but also formouldings, floors and ceilings. Only a small portion of the tropical timber consumption is used for constructional purposes. In addition to the building sector and furniture production, several other uses exist, such as in engineering projects (for example hydraulic engineering), transportation packing, interior fitting of vehicles, musical instruments and toys (see Appendix A3 and A8).

Several factors are responsible for differences in consumer habits: Historical development (particularly trading relationships with former colonies), the level of economic development and cultural differences (house building and furniture manufacturing technologies) (cf. NECTOUX/DUDLEY 1987:35). Relationships to former colonies also determine the regional structure of tropical timber imports.

Table 18:   Consumption Structure for Tropical Sawnwood in Selected Countries

[%]	FRG	Japan	USA	Europe	Great Britain	France	Nether- lands	Italy	Por- tugal	Switzer- land	Poland
Timber type	TT	TT	nCT	TT	TT	nCT	TT	nCT	nCT	TT	nCT
Ref. year	1984	1986	1981	1986	1984	1979	1981-84	1979	1980	1971	1980
Building	89.4	50.4	7.0	63.0	58.0	37.2	67.0	20.0	73.0	66.0	60.0
Furniture	7.1	21.3	30.0	27.0	33.0	31.3	3.0	40.0	22.0	24.0	15.0
Packing	0.0	18.3	51.0	---	5.0	25.8	---	30.0	2.0	---	---
Miscellan.	3.5	10.0	12.0	10.0	4.0	5.7	30.0	10.0	3.0	10.0	---
Share of the world-wide trop. timber imports [%]	2.6	33.3	4.7	20.6 (EU12)	3.8	3.4	3.5	2.7	0.7	0.1	---

Notes: ---: No information available; TT: Tropical timber; nCT: Non-coniferous timber. Tropical timber import shares: State 1990 for logs, sawnwood, veneer and plywood, converted into roundwood equivalents.

Source: FRG 1984: Own calculations according to Appendix A7. Japan: NECTOUX/KURODA (1989:52-55), USA: SPELTER/PHELPS (1984, cited in UN/ECE/FAO 1986, Vol.II:97). Europe and Great Britain: ESE (1992, Vol.IV:130-131). France, Italy, Portugal and Poland: UN/ECE/FAO (1986, Vol. II:97). The Netherlands and Switzerland: NECTOUX/DUDLEY (1987:36). Tropical timber import shares from ESE (1992, Vol.IV:6).

Tables 18 and 19 show the tropical timber end consumer structure for the Federal Republic of Germany, Japan, the USA and Europe as well as for individual

European countries. Table 18 contains data for the utilization structure of imported or home-produced sawnwood made of tropical timber. Table 19 contains the corresponding information for plywood. For plywood and in some cases also for sawnwood, only aggregate data is available on the use of non-coniferous timber of tropical and non-tropical origin.

Table 19:   Consumption Structure for Plywood Made from Tropical and Non-Tropical Timber in Selected Countries

[%]	FRG	Japan	USA	Europe	Great Britain	Italy	Por-tugal	Fin-land	Nor-way	Swe-den	Po-land
Ref. year :	1984	1980	1976	1976	1981	1979	1980	1976	1980	---	1980
Building	27.2	55.4	65.0	40.5	45.0	45.0	65.0	60.0	57.0	58.0	14.0
Furniture	31.0	30.2	12.0	30.7	15.0	13.0	20.0	13.0	10.0	15.0	25.0
Packing	3.8	3.0	4.0	9.3	21.0	25.0	---	5.0	---	20.0	29.0
Miscellan.	38.0	11.4	19.0	19.5	19.0	17.0	15.0	22.0	33.0	7.0	32.0
Share in the world-wide trop. timber imports [%]	2.6	33.3	4.7	20.6 (EU-12)	3.8	2.7	0.7	0.0	0.0	0.1	---

Notes: ---: no information available.
For the FRG 1984, plywood and veneers made only of tropical timber; miscellaneous chiefly undeclared usage is probably mostly assignable to the building sector and furniture production.

Source: FRG 1984: Own calculations according to Appendix A7. Japan: NECTOUX/KURODA (1989:52-55). USA and Europe: UN/ECE/FAO (cited in IBRD 1986:86). Great Britain: NECTOUX/DUDLEY (1987:36), Italy, Portugal, Finland, Norway, Sweden and Poland: UN/ECE/FAO (1986, Vol. II:98). See Table 18 for import shares.

Visible uses, roughly expressed as the combined consumption for „building" and „furniture", amount to the same percentages of 60% respective 90% in the European countries and in Japan. For sawnwood the Federal Republic of Germany actually lies slightly above this spectrum with a figure of 96.5%, so that uncorrected transposition of the reaction of the German tropical timber market to a certification of tropical timber for all OECD countries would tend to give an overestimate. Taking into consideration that a large volume of tropical timber consumed in the building sector or in furniture production is probably classified as „miscellaneous", the Federal Republic of Germany corresponds to the average for plywood. Consequently, extrapolation to cover all OECD countries is reasonable. However, it is necessary to bear in mind that in the USA and Italy, which together represent about 7.4% of the world-wide demand for tropical timber, a great deal of sawnwood and plywood made of tropical timber is used for packing purposes. This is an area in which a certification scheme is expected to have only slight effects (see Section 5.5).

Japan is still the world's greatest import country for tropical timber. Utilization in the building sector followed by furniture production dominates for sawnwood as well as for plywood. Japan has a long standing tradition of building timber houses which, at least for private houses has persisted until today. Apart from reinforced concrete, a timber frame construction gives good protection in earthquake regions. Plywood is used in the building sector mainly for constructional purposes, not as concrete formwork (P.T.CAPRICORN 1987:122). The quality demands of Japanese consumers are very high for furniture. In recent years the demand has shifted to tropical timber. Chiefly home-grown and imported coniferous timber is used in the paper industry. The share of wooden packing is relatively large in Japan, including tropical timber. Timber for single use chopsticks (cf. for example HOERING 1995) is usually tropical coniferous timber (POHL 1990) and thus more likely to come from plantations.

The second important determining factor for reliable transposition of Federal German demand reactions to a certification scheme for all OECD countries is the effect of the campaign against tropical timber and any change of fashion in recent years. Corresponding results of qualitative market studies for assessing the effects of a change in fashion were not available so that it was not possible to judge them on their own within the scope of this study. The effect of the campaign against tropical timber can be estimated only approximately by a comparative analysis of import development and isolated information available on market shares of tropical timber in four important end consumer fields of some European countries.

The demand for tropical timber imports has increased in recent years - as Table 20 shows - not only in the Federal Republic of Germany, but also in the USA. In contrast thereto, the import demand has fallen since 1989 on important European tropical timber markets and in Japan. However, it must be borne in mind that conclusions regarding domestic consumption drawn from considerations of tropical timber imports are somewhat dubious due to re-exports not adequately covered by the statistics. For example, tropical logs, after processing to tropical veneers in Belgium, are exported in large quantities to France. Furthermore, the import development for finished timber goods such as doors and furniture is missing in Table 20. Japan and many European countries usually import tropical timber with low finishing level, whereas for example Great Britain imports many finished joinery products made of tropical timber (for example doors) (NECTOUX/DUDLEY 1987:38).

Declining net imports without detailed qualitative and quantitative analysis of the particular market conditions does not necessarily imply the presence of effects of a campaign against tropical timber or a change in fashion. Technical changes as well as the development of the general economic situation in a country have a large effect on the demand for tropical timber. It is nevertheless striking that all European countries considered are experiencing clear declines of tropical sawnwood imports. This is partly due to export restrictions imposed, for example, by Indonesia on unprocessed sawnwood, but it is also partly due to the fact that sawnwood is used mainly for visible uses. Since the imports of plywood used mainly for non-visible uses increased at the same time, an effect of the campaign against tropical timber can well be suspected.

Table 20:   Development of Timber Imports from Tropical Countries

[%, 1992 versus 1989]	Logs	Sawnwood	Veneers	Plywood	Total
Switzerland	-39.5	-33.8	-89.4	-0.3	-37.0
Belgium/Luxemburg	-8.8	-37.5	18.2	5.1	-16.8
Germany	-24.4	-18.5	11.7	94.7	1.8
France	3.4	-23.2	-64.7	69.1	-7.2
Netherlands	-25.5	-33.7	133.3	38.5	-12.3
Great Britain	-82.1	-46.8	-38.1	3.8	-22.5
USA	---	32.8	-27.8	7.4	10.3
Japan	-38.7	-46.1	-63.3	-36.7	-39.5

Notes: ---: no information available.
Calculated on the basis of roundwood equivalents. USA, Germany and Japan: Imports.
All others: Imports minus exports.

Source: USA 1989, 1992 and Japan 1989: FAO (Yearbook of Forest Products, various years). Japan 1992: FAO (Monthly Bulletin 1992). Germany: Own calculations. All others: DE BOER (1994).

It is very difficult to make reliable statements on the effects of the campaign against tropical timber and of fashion changes for Japan and the USA, because special developments dominate their import structure. Examples of such special developments are Japan's restrictive import policy for processed tropical timber products and Indonesia's expansive export policy for plywood aimed for regional diversification. The demand for non-coniferous timber plywood in the USA is 100% covered by domestic production (DGFU/FAO 1990:290). This means that the increased plywood imports of the USA from tropical countries shown in Table 20 primarily consist of non-coniferous timber plywood. In fact, it must be pointed out again that increased total imports do not necessarily rule out the presence of declining demand on certain submarkets as a result of the campaign against tropical timber - as we have seen in the development of the German tropical timber market.

Campaigns against tropical timber have taken place particularly in central European countries. Important movements are to be found in the Federal Republic of Germany, the Netherlands and Great Britain, as well as in Belgium, Luxemburg, Austria and Switzerland. Actions against the utilization of tropical timber are also present in Portugal, Spain, Italy, Australia, Japan and the USA. In Australia the Association of Tropical Timber Importers has reacted to public pressure by publishing a regularly updated list of tropical exporting countries undertaking adequate steps for establishing sustainable forest management. Imports from all other tropical countries should be stopped (ESE 1992, Vol. II:97). Legislation is being drawn-up in the USA for establishing a labelling scheme for all tropical timber imports. This labelling is intended to provide information about the timber species and the country of origin without undertaking any environmentally relevant evaluation (ibid:107). Some states and cities in the USA have forbidden the use of tropical timber in public building projects (VARANGIS/BRAGA/TAKEUCHI 1993:17). The campaign against tropical timber received public attention in Austria in 1992 when a law requiring obligatory labelling of tropical timber and tropical timber products had to be repealed after sharp protests from Asian exporting countries (GHAZALI/SIMULA 1994:22). As seen on the whole, public pressure has been exerted against the use of tropical timber in many important consumer countries. However, since in many other countries this pressure was not as determined as in the Federal Republic of Germany, the Netherlands and Great Britain, extending the German reaction to all OECD countries would result in overestimating the effect of a certification scheme for tropical timber.

In DE BOER (1994) we find some statements concerning the market share development of tropical timber for some European countries. The development of tropical timber, non-tropical timber, PVC and other materials is investigated for the years 1992 and 1994 with respect to the production of inner doors, outer doors, windows and staircases. According to this study the shares of tropical timber remained constant in Switzerland. Belgium/Luxemburg and France suffered slight declines for outer doors and windows, France for staircases too. In Great Britain less tropical timber was used for inner doors and staircases. In the Netherlands the market shares of tropical timber for all four products showed a declining trend, but only amounted to one or two percent with respect to starting values of 46% to 83%. When interpreted cautiously, these trends suggest that the campaign against tropical timber has led to reduced consumption of tropical timber in other European countries as well as in the Federal Republic of Germany, especially in the important sectors of windows and outer doors.

The following can be said in summary: The tropical timber import volume declined between 1989 and 1992 in all important consumer countries except the USA and Germany. Consumption structures are comparable in all OECD countries meaning that visible uses dominate. Therefore, the campaign against tropical timber could find much resonance in many of these countries and produce corresponding effects. In comparison with other countries, the Federal Republic of Germany leads the field with its share of visible uses in the total domestic consumption of tropical timber. Together with the Netherlands and Great Britain, Germany also belongs to the countries with the most effective campaign against tropical timber. It can be concluded therefore that the percentage demand expansions calculated under scenario T II for the Federal Republic of Germany represent the upper bounds of the possible effect of an OECD-wide certification scheme. The T I scenario is more likely to present a realistic picture of the OECD-demand expansion to be expected when intruducing an OECD-wide certification scheme.

9 Theoretical Foundations

Sections 9.1 to 9.3 explain in detail the theoretical foundations and the procedure adopted for calculating the scenarios. Section 9.1 describes the basic procedure for determining the new equilibria of world market prices and quantities for an OECD-wide certification scheme and one restricted to the Federal Republic of Germany. Section 9.2 shows how to set up on the five submarkets and on the total market models for the costs of certification, for the additional costs caused by sustainable forest management and for willingness to pay higher prices on part of the end consumers. Section 9.3 establishes the concept of derived demand which forms the basis for determining the price elasticity of the demand for tropical timber in the five submarkets. Finally Section 9.4 explains the choice of parameters for the calculations.

9.1 Determining the Market Equilibrium on a Certified Tropical Timber Market

It is assumed that the price for tropical timber as a raw material is the same on all submarkets. The chosen submarkets cover a large part of the tropical timber imports (see Appendix A7). Therefore, a possible alternative would be the average import unit value of all imported goods made of tropical timber or - since sawnwood has an intermediate position in the processing chain and, coming before veneers, it constitutes the most important input for the chosen submarkets - the average import unit value for tropical sawnwood in the Federal Republic of Germany. The former was DM 606,70, the latter DM 599,80 per cubic metre roundwood in 1993. Therefore, the assumption of a homogeneous price can be taken as realistic, and the average import value for veneers with DM 564,60 per cubic metre roundwood lying in the same price range confirms this. Therefore, we base the following calculations on a tropical timber price of DM 600,00 per cubic metre roundwood processed into an imported product [600,00 DM/m^3(r)]. A market with a homogeneous product is assumed, i.e. that complete displacement of non-certified tropical timber from the market is assumed *in the long run*. The reasons for expecting this displacement have already been explained at the end of Chapter 2.

9.1.1   Market Equilibrium with OECD-wide Certification

When demand increases simultaneously in all OECD countries, the resulting rise of the world market price must be taken into consideration. Fig. 17 demonstrates the theoretical concept.

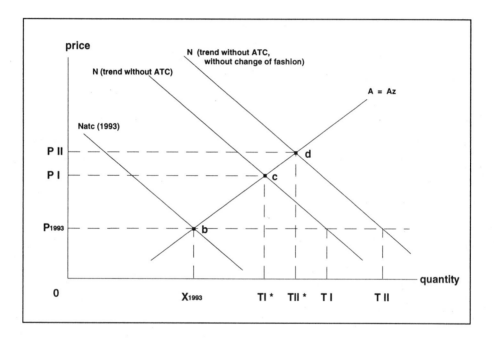

Figure 17:   Equilibrium Price Level for an OECD-Wide Certification Scheme for Tropical Timber

Note: atc: Anti-tropical timber campaign.

Let us first of all consider the aggregate German market for tropical timber. In the initial situation of 1993 the total German demand is the sum of the demand in the five investigated submarkets and all other utilization. This X_{1993} with an equilibrium price of P_{1993}. The demand expands by the aggregate additional amounts calculated in the five submarkets in the basic scenarios for T I and T II respectively after the introduction of a certification scheme.[73] The equilibrium price will become P I or P II respectively. With this increase in price levels, the quantities of the basic scenarios for T I and T II will no longer be realized completely in the market. As the result of interaction with the aggregate supply, the new equilibrium demand quantities T I* and T II* will appear.

The chosen model specification describes the market using a function of the German import demand for tropical timber and the function of the total world market supply of tropical timber. This procedure implicitly assumes that the same percentage expansion of demand as in the Federal Republic of Germany will simultaneously take place in all OECD countries. The validity of this assumption was discussed at the beginning of Part III.

In order to apply this model to the German tropical timber market, the position and reaction parameters must be determined[74] for the supply and demand functions shown in Fig. 17.

The position of the aggregate world market supply function for non-sustainably produced tropical timber (**A**) and the aggregate German tropical timber demand function in the initial situation (**Natc**) are known from the prices and quantities realized in the market in 1993. The sensitivity of the supply, that is the price elasticity of the world market supply of tropical timber, is taken from the literature (see Chapter 4 and Section 9.4). The sensitivity of the demand is taken from the literature too (see Section 9.4). Position and sensitivity of the supply of sustainably produced tropical timber (**Az**) correspond to the historic supply function of non-sustainably produced tropical timber because, as explained in Chapter 4, it is assumed within the scope of this study that the supply can be changed completely to sustainably produced tropical timber. Furthermore, it is assumed that the price elasticity observed in the past will remain the same.

When specifying the supply function it is necessary to take the changes in the export structure of the tropical timber exporting countries into consideration which are today exporting large quantities of half-finished wood products under massive export restrictions for unprocessed tropical timber. This aspect is taken into account by expressing all imports in terms of roundwood equivalents ($[m^3(r)]$).

---

[73] This is depicted graphically in Fig. 17 by parallel shifting of the demand function along the quantity axis from X_{1993} to T I or T II respectively. The demand *expansion* calculated for the establishment of a credible certification scheme for the five chief tropical timber submarkets together, for reversal of the campaign against tropical timber (T I) amounts to 269 000 $m^3(r)$ and for additional reversal of the change of fashion (T II) amounts to 435 200 $m^3(r)$ (see Table 17 at the end of Chapter 8). Since X_{1993} must be assessed with 2 005 000 $m^3(r)$, T I in Fig. 17 is consequently 2 274 000 $m^3(r)$ and T II is 2 440 000 $m^3(r)$ (see Table 33 in Section 11.1).

[74] Linear functions are used in the illustrations for simplicity. In the algebraic model the supply and demand functions are expressed as Cobb-Douglas functions featuring constant price elasticities.

The position of the function for aggregate German demand for tropical timber with a credible certification scheme - N(trend without ATC) and N(trend without ATC, without change of fashion) - is determined from the historic demand function, Natc (1993), by shifting their position parameters by the amount of the respective demand expansion in the basic scenario. The price elasticity of the original demand function is used for the new function as well.

When all position and reaction parameters of the aggregate demand and aggregate supply are known, the intersections **c** and **d** can be calculated. These intersections determine the aggregate tropical timber import quantity and the associated equilibrium price of the scenarios for an OECD-wide certification scheme.

No supply function is specified in the submarkets for the big country case of an OECD-wide certification of tropical timber. Instead, the equilibrium price determined for the aggregate market is taken over and the corresponding equilibrium quantity is looked for along the demand function in the respective submarket.

The position parameters of the demand functions in the submarkets must be determined using the same procedure described above for the total market, from the actual quantities consumed in the reference year 1993 and the estimated expansion in demand in the basic scenarios for T I and T II (see Table 17). Section 9.3 considers the determination of the sensitivity of the demand in the submarkets, that is the respective price elasticity of the demand.

With that all position and reaction parameters of the supply and demand functions in the total market and in the submarkets are known, so that the basic equilibria **c** and **d** can be specified for all markets. From this can be derived further effects, such as the costs of the certification scheme and of sustainable forest management and the possible willingness of consumers to pay a higher price for certified tropical timber. The theoretical approaches for this will be derived in Section 9.2.

9.1.2   Market Equilibrium for a Certification Scheme Confined to the Federal Republic of Germany

If certification of tropical timber is restricted to the Federal Republic of Germany, the world market price will stay at the level P_{1993}, ignoring the certification costs. The world market supply is completely elastic and depicts graphically as a horizontal line through P_{1993}. The equilibrium quantities and prices in the scenarios of the total market and submarkets are determined as the point of intersection of the respective demand function and the completely elastic supply function. Without taking into account the certification and sustainable management costs or an increased willingness to pay, the basic scenarios T I and T II are realized in the market to their full extent at a price P_{1993}.

Finally we point out again that more optimistic assumptions regarding the reaction of supply and demand to a certification scheme are conceivable, too. In some submarkets demand might rise above the level realized before the campaign against tropical timber and before the fashion change, and even above the effect resulting from the acceptance of higher prices (ecological mark-up). For example, an additional substitution effect is conceivable in which tropical timber gains an ecological advantage over the competitor aluminium which is a large consumer of energy in production. However, this possibility has not been included in the scenarios in order to preserve a cautious estimate of the effects of certification for tropical timber.

Furthermore, the position of the supply curve as shown in Fig. 17 is not necessarily the only one possible, as has already been pointed out in Chapter 4. A sustainable harvest level above the historic „reckless" level is conceivable at least on a long term basis, because sustainably forested areas can bring a greater annual growth per hectare in commercial species especially when reforestation measures are differentiated according to species. But over short and medium periods (shorter than 20 years) it is necessary to base the supply curve on the level shown.

9.2   Theoretical Description of the Supply Function with Increased Costs and the Demand Function with Increased Willingness to Pay

The theoretical approach for calculating price effects initiated by certification costs and increased willingness to pay, is shown in Fig. 18 for the **big country version** of the aggregate tropical timber market. An analogous model for the submarkets differs only in that the world market price level is taken from the respective total market scenario. So no explicit supply function is specified for the respective submarkets.

The exogenous „shocks" which appear in each submarket through the campaign against tropical timber, the fashion change and a certification scheme for tropical timber, are depicted as the movements **(1)** to **(4)** designated with arrows. The campaign against tropical timber and the fashion change first of all produce a contraction of the demand from **N(1984)** to **Natc (1993) (1)**.[75] The market equilibrium shifts with unchanged supply from **a** to **b**, the actual market state in 1993. After the introduction of a certification scheme the demand expands again to **N(basic scenario T I or T II) (2)**.[76] The movement (2) is already familiar from Fig. 17. In the interests of synoptical clarity, no distinction is here made between the basic scenarios for T I and T II.

---

[75]   The index **atc** indicates for the effect of the fashion change too.

[76]   The graphic representation of a shrinking or expanding demand is explained in Appendix A 10.

It is assumed that after introduction of a certification scheme the supply will convert completely to sustainable production (**A=Az**, see Chapter 4). The costs of the certification scheme are levied as a quantity-related charge. This results in an absolute increase of the previous market price depicted graphically such that the supply function is moved up by a constant amount (**3**). Additional costs caused by a change to sustainable forest management are modelled analogously by a constant upward movement. For a simplification, Fig. 18 refers only to the costs of the certification scheme.

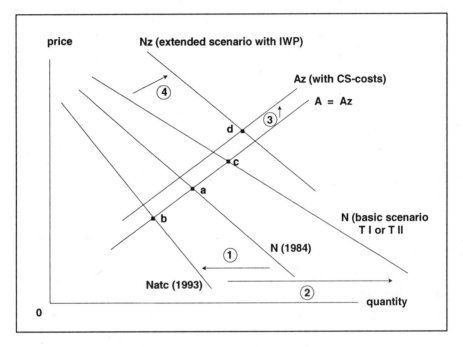

Figure 18:   Partial Model for the Certification of Tropical Timber

Notes: atc: Anti-tropical timber campaign. CS: Certification scheme. IWP: Increased willingness to pay.

The willingness of consumers to pay more for a certified tropical timber product appears graphically as an upward rotation of the demand function (**4**) for the case of a percentage surcharge.

The procedure for calculating the new equilibrium point **c** for the total market and for the individual markets has been explained in Section 9.1. The costs of the certification scheme and of a change to sustainable forest management were determined in Chapter 4. The possible willingness to pay more was estimated in

Section 5.5. With that all parameters required are known for calculating the transition from **c** to **d**.

The **small country case** of a certification scheme restricted to the Federal Republic of Germany features a fully elastic world market supply as already explained above. If the certification costs are covered by a quantity-related charge, the fully elastic (horizontal) world market supply curve for the total market shifts parallel upwards by the amount of the certification costs, and the equilibrium world market price rises by the corresponding amount. Also this applies to the additional costs caused by a change to sustainable forest management. Analogously to the procedure described above for the big country case, the world price level determined in the total market is taken over into the respective submarket scenarios, and the corresponding equilibrium demand is sought.

Willingness to pay more on the part of consumers is again shown graphically for the small country case as an upward rotation of the demand function to the right. But differing in this respect from the big country case, the willingness to pay more does not reflect as a rise in the world market price. Instead it is converted completely into higher levels of consumption.

9.3   Determining the Price Elasticity of Demand in the Submarkets

The price elasticity of the demand for tropical timber in the five end consumer categories raises the problem that these elasticities cannot be estimated directly. They have to be determined indirectly by the procedure described in this section. First of all it is necessary to specify the product and the quantity unit on which the determined price elasticity is to be based. The subject of this study is the demand reaction of end consumers to the introduction of a certification scheme in the tropical timber market. It does not make sense to use a price elasticity of demand for windows or furniture in the corresponding consumer sectors, because the materials here involved represent only a certain part, often a very small fraction, of the production costs of these products.

An econometric estimate of the price elasticity of the demand for the utilized material involves the problem that the elasticities often take very low values because, for example, luxury veneers in the production of a piece of furniture or windows in a new building represent only a very small part of the total production costs. The situation becomes even more difficult to analyse, because other factors apart from the price, such as economic or fashion trends, can act superimposed on the price effect. Both aspects imply that an econometric estimate with significant results is hardly possible.

An alternative would be to calculate the demand for tropical timber as derived demand from the demand for windows, doors, wall elements, floors, strips and furniture. However, regarding the price elasticity of the demand for windows, etc., we again end up with the same econometric problem as for tropical timber in relation to furniture. Windows constitute only a fraction of the production costs of the actual final product, a new building or a refurbished old building. Ultimately, the demand for windows, floors, etc. is derived from the demand for new building and for refurbishing of old ones.

In vertically linked markets such as the market for tropical timber and the market for building operations we can make use of the concept of derived demand introduced by Marshall and further developed by Hicks.[77] This concept is subject to the condition that the demand in the subordinate market mainly or completely consists of the input demand in the superior market. This condition is fulfilled, because the German demand for tropical timber almost completely depends on the demand for furniture and building operations (see Appendix A7).

The advantages of the concept of derived demand lie in easier empirical handling because the required input values - here among others the price elasticity of the demand for building measures and furniture and the cost share of tropical timber in the final product - are easier to observe. Price elasticities of the demand for furniture are known from the published literature. Corresponding estimates also exist for the demand for new buildings.

Fig. 19 illustrates the concept of derived demand. The final product X_2 is obtained from only two inputs, X_1 and X_4 (cf. HAYNES 1977:282).

The sale prices of the three goods are plotted on the ordinate of Fig. 19. The quantity units for the two inputs and the final product have been chosen on the abscissa such that one unit each of the two inputs together give one unit of the final product. Thus the derived demand for the input X_1, aN_1., is calculated graphically as vertical difference of the demand for the final product and the supply of X_4 . Thus aN_1 measures along the demand curve for X_2 the maximum purchase price which can be paid for the input X_1 after deducting the necessary costs for X_4. Analogously vertical subtraction of the supply curve for X_1 from N_2 gives the derived demand for X_4, aN_4.[78]

An exogenic expansion of the demand in the final product market produced in the scenarios by a certification scheme expresses itself as a shift of the direct demand function and the derived demand function to the right. Increased supply of an input (shifting of A_1 or A_4 to the right) in turn produces a shift to the right of the supply function of commodity X_2.

In the initial situation shown in Fig. 19, all three markets are in equilibrium with the prices P_1, P_2 and P_4. It must be pointed out as restriction that the consistency of the two derived demand functions aN_1 and aN_4 is ensured in this model only in the vicinity of the output equilibrium, because moving along a derived demand

[77] Cf. MARSHALL (1890: Book V, Ch. VI, pp 430-440) and HICKS (1963:241 ff. or the first edition published in 1932). A detailed discussion is also given by FRIEDMAN (1976:153 ff.).

[78] Functions are printed in bold type in the following text whereas quantities and prices are printed in normal type.

function implies that the price of the other component is determined only by moving along the supply curve whereby the demand conditions in the market for the other component do not play a significant role.

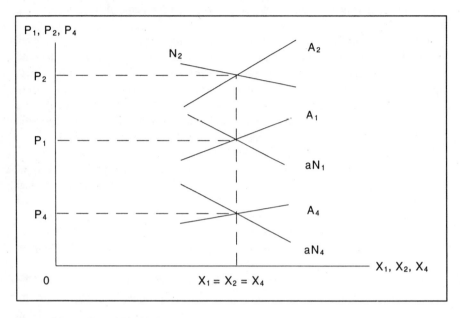

Figure 19:   Partial Model for the Derived Demand

For calculating the individual market scenarios it is necessary to set up the algebraic representation shown in Fig. 19 between the derived demand, the final product demand as well as the supply of other factors and inputs. It is helpful to picture a simple economy in which only one producer and one consumer of the commodity X_2 exist. For example, the commodity X_2 may consist of a group of new buildings and refurbishing tasks for residential and-non residential buildings, to be implemented annually in this economy. The example of tropical timber in furniture production is analogous.

It is assumed that the commodity group X_2 is homogenous and changes its structure only in steady progression. This assumption means explicitly that the trend analyses in Section 8.3 are based on a continuous quantity and structural development of the building and furniture demand as contained in the observed long-term trend of recent years. Short-term special movements which are partly due to German reunification - for example the present boom for plastic windows in the new federal states - have therefore been eliminated as far as possible. Long-term developments such as the trend towards residential buildings with more wooden windows or the trend towards refurbishing old buildings with a greater proportion of plastic windows, have been retained in the extrapolations.

Many production factors and preliminary products are at the disposal of the producer of the commodity group X_2 in the simplified economy. He can use these facilities in various combinations for the production of X_2. First of all these are the classic factors of production labour, land and capital. Preliminary products such as steel are involved for furniture and concrete in addition thereto for buildings. For example, tropical timber or coniferous timber can be used for plywood rear panels of furniture. Visible surfaces of furniture can be PVC or tropical timber. In buildings the windows can be made of plastic or tropical timber and staircases can be made of tropical timber or concrete. These examples make it clear that the inputs are partly in completely complementary relationship in the production process (for example concrete for the foundation and tropical timber for the windows) and partly in predominantly substitutive relationship (for example tropical timber or plastic for the windows).

The substitutive relationships between the various inputs are expressed by substitution elasticities in the algebraic equations. Ideally substitution elasticities should be calculated for the model taking into account all substitution pair relationships between all production factors (cf. BLACKORBY/RUSSEL 1989), but the database is not designed to handle such a procedure. Therefore, it must be assumed as a simplification that the substitution relationships of tropical timber in the various uses (windows, doors, wall elements, staircases etc.) with respect to land, labour, capital, etc. are zero, leaving only one substitution relationship between the material tropical timber and an aggregate group of various alternative materials (for example, for outer doors, tropical timber against all other possible materials such as coniferous timber, aluminium or plastic). Therefore, the following discussion always distinguishes between a „tropical timber version" and a version „all other materials".

The substitution elasticity between the „tropical timber version" and the version „all other materials" in the simplified economy considered does not describe any production-technical relation for building a house or making a piece of furniture. Of course there is no technical consideration forbidding complete replacement of all tropical timber windows of a house by coniferous timber windows, or replacing all tropical timber veneers by non-tropical non-coniferous timber veneers. Instead, the relationship describes all expected technical adjustment processes expected in all companies affected by a certain measure resulting, for example, from a fashion change in favour of tropical timber.[79]

It is furthermore assumed within the *submarket scenarios* that the supply of all inputs except the two considered material versions is infinitely elastic. This means for example that the change from a tropical timber window to coniferous timber, aluminium or plastic window is not hampered by supply-side adjustment problems with the other inputs. This assumption means that price reactions in the factor and input markets such as labour, land, concrete, etc. are ruled out. In this

---

[79] For example the capacity extensions of tropical timber veneer manufacturers and parallel shrinkage processes for manufacturers of PVC furniture surface materials.

way the model is reduced to the direct relationships between the two considered material versions within the analysed product

In the scenarios for the *aggregate German tropical timber market* in Chapter 11 it is nevertheless necessary to take adjustment processes into consideration. For this purpose an aggregate price elasticity of the total tropical timber demand in the OECD countries taken from the literature is used as basis. This aggregate price elasticity is less elastic than the price elasticity of demand in each submarket.

Hicks, who is considered to be the originator of the substitution elasticity concept, formally calculates the derived demand according to the input X_1 (here the „tropical timber version") from the optimum conditions of a profit maximizing entrepreneur producing with constant returns to scale and perfect factor and commodity markets. The price elasticity of the derived demand for tropical timber in the submarket considered is thereby determined by the following equation:[80]

$$\eta_{\alpha 1} = \frac{\sigma_{14}(\varepsilon_4 - \eta_2) + \kappa \varepsilon_4 (\eta_2 - \sigma_{14})}{\varepsilon_4 - \eta_2 + \kappa (\eta_2 - \sigma_{14})}$$

where:

$\eta_{\alpha 1}$	Price elasticity of the derived demand for commodity X_1 (tropical timber),
η_2	Price elasticity of the demand for the final product X_2 (here the group of building operations or a group of furniture productions),
ε_4	Price elasticity of the offer of the substitutive component X_4 (here the version „all other materials"),
$\kappa = \dfrac{P_1 X_1}{P_2 X_2}$	Cost share of the commodity X_1 (here for example the average share of the costs of the window material in the total costs of a building project) in the commodity group X_2 (here the building project) with $0<\kappa<1$,

---

[80]   Cf. HICKS (1932:245). Here in a presentation as customary today and deviating from Hicks, whereby the price elasticities of the demand take on negative values in the case of normal behaviour, and the substitution elasticity is negative for substitutive inputs.

$$\sigma_{14} = \frac{d\left(\dfrac{X_1}{X_4}\right)\left(\dfrac{F_1}{F_4}\right)}{d\left(\dfrac{F_1}{F_4}\right)\left(\dfrac{X_1}{X_4}\right)}$$

Elasticity of substitution between the substitutive factors X_1 and X_4 in the production of X_2 (for constant output) with $\sigma_{14} < 0$.

X_1 and X_4 are the input quantities for the two production factors. F_1 and F_4 are the derivatives of the production function for commodity X_2 according to the factors X_1 and X_4.[81]

The sign of $\eta_{\alpha1}$ is not unambiguously positive or negative. For substitutive inputs and normal reactions of the market participators with negative price elasticity of the demand and positive price elasticity of the supply, η_{α_1} is negative in every case. It is easy to see why this is so. A price increase of the input considered produces two adjustment reactions which reduce the demand for the input: The production process responds with substitution movements towards relatively cheaper inputs, and in the market for the final product the equilibrium demand decreases because the higher price is partly or completely handed down to the consumer. Therefore the final demand could react abnormally (up to a certain maximum limit) ($\eta_2 > 0$), without making the price elasticity of the derived input demand go positive, because this is over-compensated by the substitution effect.

The following relationships (see also Appendix A11) hold for the formula determining $\eta_{\alpha1}$: [82]

$\partial \eta_{\alpha1} / \partial \sigma_{14} > 0$,
This means that η_{α_1} becomes increasingly elastic, the easier the change to substitutes is.

$\partial \eta_{\alpha1} / \partial \varepsilon_4 < 0$,
This means that η_{α_1} becomes increasingly elastic, the more elastically the supply of other necessary production factors reacts.

$\partial \eta_{\alpha1} / \partial \eta_2 > 0$,
This means that η_{α_1} becomes increasingly elastic, the more elastic the demand for the final product is.

---

[81] The representation of the substitution elasticity chosen by Hicks is formally identical to the one chosen here, cf. BARTMANN (1981:129-130).

[82] It is again necessary to take the negative sign into consideration for the demand elasticities and for the substitution elasticity. cf. also HICKS (1963:245) and MARSHALL (1980: Book V, Ch. VI, p.433 ff).

$\partial \eta_{\alpha 1} / \partial \kappa < 0$, provided that $|\eta_2| > |\sigma_{14}|$, and
$\partial \eta_{\alpha 1} / \partial \kappa > 0$, provided that $|\eta_2| < |\sigma_{14}|$,

This means that if the substitution elasticity is (in absolute terms) greater than the price elasticity of the demand, $\eta_{\alpha 1}$ becomes increasingly elastic, the smaller the cost share of this factor in the value of the final product.

When the cost share of tropical timber is small, the price elasticity of the derived demand always lies close to the value of the substitution elasticity. In the analysed submarkets the magnitude (in absolute terms) of the substitution elasticity is greater than the price elasticity of the demand for the final product[83] so that we have: $\partial \eta_{\alpha 1}/\partial \kappa > 0$. The price elasticity of the derived demand therefore decreases when the cost share increases. A marginal analysis shows that it thereby approaches the price elasticity of the demand for the final product. On the face of it, this result appears to contradict intuition. However, it sounds reasonable that with increasing cost share the substitution possibilities for the producer will become exhausted and the cost increase must be passed on to the end consumer. This makes his price reaction, which has a smaller elasticity than the substitution possibilities of the producer (in absolute terms), increasingly become the determining element of the price reaction of the derived demand. HICKS (1963:246) aptly summarizes this as follows: „It is 'important to be unimportant' only when the consumer can substitute more easily than the entrepreneur".

The concept of the derived demand is based on a partially analytical approach. The calculation of the certification scenarios uses partial equilibrium models. This is justified on theoretical considerations under the following simplifying assumptions (cf. CORNWALL 1984:81-82):

- Changes in the analysed market do not induce any retroactive price effects. This means that changes in the market considered do not affect supply and demand on this market indirectly through any effects on the equilibrium prices of other factor and commodity markets.
- Changes in the analysed market do not induce any retroactive income effects. This means that only small effects on the aggregate demand of all consumers within the particular economy originate from the market considered. Furthermore, these small changes do not focus on the group of consumers chiefly consuming the considered commodity so that changes on this market do not affect it through feedback via aggregate demand.
- The foreign country supply curve is given within the period of the analysis. This means that there are no retroactive price and income effects via foreign countries and no danger of countervailing foreign trade measures. (However, as already pointed out, the costs for a certification scheme are modelled with an exogenic shifting of the world market supply.)

---

[83]   See Table 21 in the next section.

Under these aspects the partial model determines the equilibrium in the considered market independently of the other factor and commodity markets of the economy. The three assumptions seem to be justified because the German forestry
and timber industry, considering its share in the gross national income or in the
total wages and salaries, is of relatively small significance.[84] On the other hand, a
general equilibrium model would be much more difficult to handle just because of
the lacks in the database.

9.4   Selection of the Supply, Demand and Substitution Elasticities

The theoretical considerations have shown that the following information items
are required for the scenarios in the submarkets:
- Price elasticity of demand for building and civil engineering projects
- Price elasticity of demand for furnitures
- Average price elasticity of supply of all materials which can be substituted for
  tropical timber
- Average substitution elasticity between tropical timber and all substitutable
  materials
- Cost shares of tropical timber and tropical timber products in the total produc-
  tion costs of a new building or a piece of furniture

A price elasticity of -0.54 for the demand for building and civil engineering
works is used in the calculations. This value was determined by FINKE/LU/THEIL
(1984) with respect to the Federal Republic of Germany in the 1970s for the reference market of rented flats. A similar value (-0.56) of the price elasticity of the
demand for building and civil engineering works is used by other authors (cf.
HOHMEYER et al. 1995). It is extremely difficult to make a direct estimate of the
price elasticity of the demand for building and civil engineering works. The
reason for this is that the market for new buildings and refurbishing of old buildings is subject to strong government intervention (for example by promotion
schemes and by changes of taxation legislation), so that the price is not a predominant factor.

The price elasticity of the demand for furniture is also taken from FINKEL/LU/
THEIL (1984) who found a value of -0.59 for the Federal Republic of Germany in
the 1970s.

---

[84]   The share of forestry and fishing in the gross domestic product in Germany was about
0.4% in 1990 and the share of wood working and wood processing was about 0.9%
(STATISTISCHES BUNDESAMT, Statistisches Jahrbuch 1993).

Table 21:   Parameters in the Scenarios of the Submarkets

Price elasticity of demand for	
- Building projects	-0.54
- Furniture	-0.59
Price elasticity of supply of all other materials	
- Scenario A I	0.8
- Scenario A II	0.7
- Scenario A III	0.6
Substitution elasticity between tropical timber and all other materials	-0.9
Costs of certification [DM/m^3(r)]	2.4
Willingness to pay higher prices [%]	5.0

Table 22:   Cost Shares of Various Materials of the Total Manufacturing Costs for
Areas in which Tropical Timber is Important

[%] *Products:*	*Outer Windows*	*Outer doors*	*Do-It-Yourself Mouldings*	*Staircases*	*Furniture surfaces*
average cost share of timber or a substitute in the total manufacturing costs of the product **(A)**	30.0	50.0	80.0	50.0	15.0
average cost share of the product (without installation) in the total costs for a building project **(B)**	4.0	2.0	2.0	0.5	-----
average cost share of timber or a substitute in the total costs of a building project respectively of a piece of furniture **(AxB/100)**	1.2	1.0	1.6	0.25	15.0

Notes and sources: Material cost share (A) for windows and outer doors according to HOHMEYER et al. (1985). Some cost shares had to be approximated on the basis of the cost structure of the particular branch according to the STATISTISCHES BUNDESAMT. According to cost structure data (Fachserie 4, Reihe 4.3.1, 1990), the material consumption (including commercial goods and labour costs) amounts to 66.7% for the production of sawnwood and mouldings and 55.0% for the manufacture of semi-finished timber products, as a fraction of the gross production value in each case. The share of timber products in the material consumption is 88.7% for sawnwood and mouldings, 53.9% for timber half-products and 55.6% for timber building materials (Fachserie 4, Reihe 4.2.4, 1990). On the basis of this data, the cost shares for staircases and outer doors in line A were estimated with the values specified above. The cost share in the final product (B) was taken from EDITION AUM (3.3.1995), KELLER (1986:46 ff.), NEHM et al. (1994:95). The share of the surface material in the production costs for a piece of furniture was calculated from the information in the surface material market given by SEIZINGER (1995) and according to production value data in the furniture industry from the production statistics. The values for do-it-yourself mouldings are estimates by the authors made by comparison with the other components.

The average price elasticity of all substitute materials for tropical timber, such as coniferous timber and non-coniferous timber from temperate latitudes, aluminium, plastics, etc., is taken to be 0.8. Starting with the price elasticity of 0.61 estimated by JOHANSSON/LÖFGREN (1985:196) for the supply of coniferous sawnwood - one of the major substitutes - we have taken a 30% higher value of 0.8 for all materials together. The supply scenario A I (certification scheme only for tropical timber, see Chapter 4) is based on this value. The supply scenario A II in which non-tropical timber is included in the certification scheme as well is modelled by reducing the price elasticity of substitutes to 0.7. This means that the supply of non-tropical timber reacts „more sluggishly". An energy tax is taken into consideration in addition to the certification scheme (for all timber species) in the supply scenario A III. Energy taxation would primarily make aluminium and plastics more expensive. This effect is incorporated into the model by further reducing the price elasticity of supply of substitutes to 0.6.

In each case it must be assumed that the substitution elasticity between tropical timber and other materials has a comparably high value (OLLMANN 31.8.1994). In a study made by the FAO (DGFU/FAO 1990:340) for the exports of Indonesian timber products, a value of -1.3 was taken as basis for the substitution possibilities in the world markets between tropical non-coniferous sawnwood and non-tropical coniferous sawnwood. The authors considered this value to be rather high, so that a lower value should be set when the individual scenarios are concerned only with submarkets. An average value of -0.9 over all submarkets has therefore been assumed for this study.

Table 21 summarizes all values and Table 22 lists the tropical timber cost shares in the individual submarkets which are required in addition to the values in Table 21 for calculating the price elasticity of the derived demand (cf. Section 9.3).

10 Extended Scenarios for Individual Submarkets

Sections 10.1 to 10.5 develop extended certification scenarios for five important submarkets for tropical timber, including the price effects through the costs for certification, through willingness of consumers to pay higher prices and through OECD-wide introduction of a certification scheme for tropical timber (big country version). The effects on the aggregate German tropical timber market are calculated in Chapter 11.

With a certification scheme confined to the Federal Republic of Germany (small country version), there are no resulting price effects in the world market through increased or decreased German demand. The extensions of the basic scenarios for T I and T II are therefore based in the small country version on the average tropical timber price in the initial reference state ($600 \ DM/m^3(r)$). In contrast to this, the rise of the average world market price is taken into account in the big country versions of the submarkets, as calculated in Chapter 11 in the respective versions for the aggregate German tropical timber market.

For the tropical timber demand in the submarket scenarios, the calculations using the concept of the derived demand (see Section 9.3) reveal a more elastic price reaction than assumed for the aggregate tropical timber demand in the scenarios for the total market. In the big country version of the submarkets this leads to an overestimate of the reduced demand caused by the world market price increase resulting from OECD-wide certification. Therefore the demand reduction given by the sum of the reactions of the five submarkets exceeds the reduction of demand calculated in Chapter 11 for the aggregate market. In the more realistic scenario T I this overestimate is as high as 17%.

10.1 Windows

In the basic scenarios of the window market, a rise in consumption of 45.8% was calculated for the case of reversal of the effects of the campaign against tropical timber (T I), and a rise of 80.5% for the case of reversal of the effects of the fashion change and other effects[85] (T II), compared with the actual consumption in 1993 (see Table 23). The calculations for the extended scenarios for the window market show that in the small country version the certification costs lead to hardly any decline of the demand compared with the basic scenarios (-0.4%), because the price increase through the costs of certification is relatively small compared with the price for a cubic metre of tropical timber.

Table 23:   Effects of a Certification Scheme Confined to Germany on the German Market for Tropical Timber Windows

Reference situation (R): Realised price and demand in 1993				
TT price [DM/m^3(r)]		600,0		
TT demand for windows [1000m^3(r)]		323		
Basic scenario (B): CS confined to the FRG, without CS costs, without IWP			Change against R [%]	
	T I	**T II**	**T I**	**T II**
TT price [DM/m^3(r)]	600,0	600,0	0,0	0,0
TT demand for windows [1000m^3(r)]	471	583	45,8	80,5
Extended scenarios: CS confined to the FRG, with CS costs			Change against B [%]	
	T I	**T II**	**T I**	**T II**
without IWP				
equilibrium TT price [DM/m^3(r)]	602,4	602,4	0,4	0,4
TT demand [1000 m^3(r)] with a :				
- CS for tropical timber	469	581	-0,4	-0,4
- CS for all timber	469	581	-0,4	-0,4
- CS for all timber plus energy tax	469	581	-0,4	-0,4
with IWP (5%)				
equilibrium TT price [DM/m^3(r)]	602,4	602,4	0,4	0,4
TT demand [1000 m^3(r)] with a :				
- CS for tropical timber	490	607	4,1	4,1
- CS for all timber	490	607	4,1	4,1
- CS for all timber plus energy tax	490	607	4,1	4,1

Notes: TT: Tropical timber; CS: Certification scheme; IWP: Increased willingness to pay. Source: Own calculations.

However, Table 23 also shows that without the additional world market price increase, which would appear in the case of OECD-wide increased demand, willingness to pay higher prices with moderate certification costs would have a strong effect on the demand volume. The latter increases by 4.1% in T I and T II on the assumption that 5% higher prices would be accepted.

---

[85]   See Section 8.3.1 for explanations.

Table 24 illustrates the effects of an OECD-wide certification scheme on the German window market. The general OECD-wide increased demand, assumed to result initially from the certification scheme, increases the price relative to the reference situation, the average import unit value of tropical timber, by 11.7% for T I and 18.7% for T II (in each case without willingness to pay higher prices).

Table 24: Effects of an OECD-Wide Certification Scheme on the German Market for Tropical Timber Windows

Reference situation (R):				
Realised price and demand in 1993				
TT price [DM/m³(r)]		600,0		
TT demand for windows [1000m³(r)]		323		
Basic scenario (B): CS confined to the FRG,			Change	
without CS costs, without IWP			against R [%]	
	T I	**T II**	**T I**	**T II**
TT price [DM/m³(r)]	600,0	600,0	0,0	0,0
TT demand for windows [1000m³(r)]	471	583	45,8	80,5
Extended scenarios: OECD-wide CS,			Change	
with CS costs, price increase on world market			against B [%]	
	T I	**T II**	**T I**	**T II**
without IWP				
equilibrium TT price [DM/m³(r)]	670,2	712,2	11,7	18,7
TT demand [1000 m³(r)] with a :				
- CS for tropical timber	427	500	-9,4	-14,2
- CS for all timber	427	500	-9,4	-14,2
- CS for all timber plus energy tax	427	500	-9,4	-14,2
with IWP (5%)				
equilibrium TT price [DM/m³(r)]	683,3	726,1	13,9	21,0
TT demand [1000 m³(r)] with a :				
- CS for tropical timber	438	513	-7,0	-11,9
- CS for all timber	438	513	-7,0	-11,9
- CS for all timber plus energy tax	438	513	-7,0	-11,9

Notes: TT: Tropical timber; CS: Certification scheme; IWP: Increased willingness to pay.
Source: Own calculations.

This price increase resulting from the calculations of the effects of an OECD-wide certification scheme on the aggregate German tropical timber market (see Table 35 in Chapter 11), leads in turn to quantity adjustment reactions in the window market.

Compared with a certification scheme introduced only for Germany, the demand drops by 9.4% (T I) or 14.4% (T II), but it still remains significantly above the quantities consumed in 1993 for windows (reference situation **R**). The willingness on the part of consumers to accept higher prices can cover the costs of the certification scheme which amount to 0.24% with respect to the present average import value of a cubic metre of sawnwood, but it cannot compensate the world market price increase completely. The consumption under these assumptions drops by 7.0% and 11.9% according to scenario, to 438 000 and 513 000 $m^3(r)$ respectively, compared with the basic scenarios which do not consider any price effects.

Tables 23 and 24 also make it clear that the supply scenarios defined in Chapter 4 do not change the results. It is evident that the differences between a certification scheme for tropical timber only(scenario A I), a certification scheme for all timber species (scenario A II) and a price increase for all timber through certification with simultaneous price increase for alternative materials plastics and aluminium through energy taxation (scenario A III) all lie below the order of magnitude 500 $m^3(r)$. Therefore no severe distortion of competition is expected in the window market as a result of different forms of certification and taxation. This is primarily so because of the small differences in the calculated price elasticities of the derived demand for tropical timber according to certification of tropical and non-tropical timber or introduction of additional energy tax.

10.2 Outer Doors

Only scenario T II has been defined in the market for outer doors because it was not possible to separate the effects of the campaign against tropical timber and of the fashion change in producing the decline of tropical timber consumption. For a certification scheme confined to the Federal Republic of Germany (Table 25), a similar situation was found for windows. The costs of the certification scheme are hardly significant, but the marketing aspect of a certification is clearly evident. If the positive environmental protection image of convincingly certified tropical timber succeeds in making consumers willing to pay higher prices, an increase in sales amounting to 4.6% can be expected (226 against 216).

This result is strongly compromised in the case of an OECD-wide certification scheme (see Table 26). The demand expansion which can be initiated with a certification scheme is relatively small. The substitution process towards other materials induced by the price effect of an OECD-wide certification scheme leads to a new equilibrium which lies below the level realized in 1993.

The price increasing effect of an OECD-wide certification scheme cannot be compensated by consumer willingness to pay higher prices. The new equilibrium quantitatively lies 1.5% below the initial state of 1993 (191 versus 194). The reason for this is that the market has been affected only to a relatively small extent by the campaign against tropical timber and the fashion change. Consequently a certification scheme reversing these two effects can induce only a comparatively small demand expansion which is over-compensated by the demand attenuating effect of the world market price increase.

As already discussed for windows and discussed below as well for the other submarkets, no differences are found in both versions (big country/small country) by including non-tropical timber or by introducing an additional energy tax.

Table 25:   Effects of a Certification Scheme Confined to Germany on the German Market for Tropical Timber Outer Doors

Reference situation (R): Realised price and demand in 1993		
TT price [DM/m^3(r)]	600,0	
TT demand for outer doors [1000m^3(r)]	194	
Basic scenario (B): CS confined to the FRG, without CS costs, without IWP		Change against R [%]
	T II	**T II**
TT price [DM/m^3(r)]	600,0	0,0
TT demand for outer doors [1000m^3(r)]	217	11,9
Extended scenarios: CS confined to the FRG, with CS costs		Change against B [%]
	T II	**T II**
without IWP		
equilibrium TT price [DM/m^3(r)]	602,4	0,4
TT demand [1000 m^3(r)] with a :		
- CS for tropical timber	216	-0,4
- CS for all timber	216	-0,4
- CS for all timber plus energy tax	216	-0,4
with IWP (5%)		
equilibrium TT price [DM/m^3(r)]	602,4	0,4
TT demand [1000 m^3(r)] with a :		
- CS for tropical timber	226	4,1
- CS for all timber	226	4,1
- CS for all timber plus energy tax	226	4,1

Notes: TT: Tropical timber; CS: Certification scheme; IWP: Increased willingness to pay. Source: Own calculations.

Table 26:   Effects of an OECD-Wide Certification Scheme on the German Market for
Tropical Timber Outer Doors

Reference situation (R): Realised price and demand in 1993		
TT price [DM/m³(r)]	600,0	
TT demand for outer doors [1000m³(r)]	194	
Basic scenario (B): CS confined to the FRG, **without CS costs, without IWP**		Change against R [%]
	T II	**T II**
TT price [DM/m3(r)]	600,0	0,0
TT demand for outer doors [1000m³(r)]	217	11,9
Extended scenarios: OECD-wide CS, **with CS costs, price increase on world market**		Change against B [%]
	T II	**T II**
without IWP equilibrium TT price [DM/m³(r)]	712,2	18,7
TT demand [1000 m³(r)] with a :		
- CS for tropical timber	186	-14,2
- CS for all timber	186	-14,2
- CS for all timber plus energy tax	186	-14,2
with IWP (5%) equilibrium TT price [DM/m³(r)]	726,1	21,0
TT demand [1000 m³(r)] with a :		
- CS for tropical timber	191	-11,9
- CS for all timber	191	-11,9
- CS for all timber plus energy tax	191	-11,9

Notes: TT: Tropical timber; CS: Certification scheme; IWP: Increased willingness to pay.
Source: Own calculations.

10.3 Staircases

For staircases the development of tropical timber utilization up to 1994 showed an
absolute decline as well as a relative decline with respect to the total timber consumption. Only one basic scenario, for T II, was defined representing both effects,
because it was not possible to separate the effects of the campaign against tropical
timber and those of the fashion change. The demand in this scenario, which does
not yet consider any price effects, lies 7.6% above the reference situation of the
demand realized in 1993.

Table 27:   Effects of a Certification Scheme Confined to Germany on the German
Market for Tropical Timber Staircases

Reference situation (R): Realised price and demand in 1993		
TT price [DM/m³(r)]	600,0	
TT demand for staircases [1000m³(r)]	82	
Basic scenario (B): CS confined to the FRG, without CS costs, without IWP		**Change against R [%]**
	T II	T II
TT price [DM/m³(r)]	600,0	0,0
TT demand for staircases [1000m³(r)]	88	7,6
Extended scenarios: CS confined to the FRG, with CS costs		**Change against B [%]**
	T II	T II
without IWP		
equilibrium TT price [DM/m³(r)]	602,4	0,4
TT demand [1000 m³(r)] with a :		
- CS for tropical timber	87	-0,4
- CS for all timber	87	-0,4
- CS for all timber plus energy tax	87	-0,4
with IWP (5%)		
equilibrium TT price [DM/m³(r)]	602,4	0,4
TT demand [1000 m³(r)] with a :		
- CS for tropical timber	91	4,1
- CS for all timber	91	4,1
- CS for all timber plus energy tax	91	4,1

Notes: TT: Tropical timber; CS: Certification scheme; IWP: Increased willingness to pay.
Source: Own calculations.

The staircase market reacts similarly to the outer door market. The certification
costs are hardly significant in any of the versions. In the small country version
(see Table 27) the acceptability of higher prices leads to increased sales by 4.6%
(91 versus 87). Again - due to the relatively small consumption increase in the
basic scenario compared with the reference situation - the world market price
increase in the case of an OECD-wide introduction of the certification scheme
results in decreased demand even when higher prices are acceptable. The decline
in this case is 6.1% below the level of the reference situation (77 versus 82, see
Table 28). Compared with the basic scenarios, the decline of -12.0% and -14.3%
respectively is even more distinct.

Table 28:   Effects of an OECD-Wide Certification Scheme on the German Market for Tropical Timber Staircases

Reference situation (R): Realised price and demand in 1993		
TT price [DM/m^3(r)]	600,0	
TT demand for staircases [1000m^3(r)]	82	
Basic scenario (B): CS confined to the FRG, without CS costs, without IWP		Change against R [%]
	T II	T II
TT price [DM/m^3(r)]	600,0	0,0
TT demand for staircases [1000m^3(r)]	88	7,6
Extended scenarios: OECD-wide CS, with CS costs, price increase on world market		Change against B [%]
	T II	T II
without IWP equilibrium TT price [DM/m^3(r)]	712,2	18,7
TT demand [1000 m^3(r)] with a :		
- CS for tropical timber	75	-14,3
- CS for all timber	75	-14,3
- CS for all timber plus energy tax	75	-14,3
with IWP (5%) equilibrium TT price [DM/m^3(r)]	726,1	21,0
TT demand [1000 m^3(r)] with a :		
- CS for tropical timber	77	-12,0
- CS for all timber	77	-12,0
- CS for all timber plus energy tax	77	-12,0

Notes: TT: Tropical timber; CS: Certification scheme; IWP: Increased willingness to pay. Source: Own calculations.

10.4 Do-It-Yourself Mouldings

In the market for do-it-yourself mouldings, only the basic scenario of a reversal of the campaign against tropical timber by a certification scheme has been defined, because this market was strongly affected by that campaign, but fashion change effects are not apparent. The expected rise of demand through a certification scheme is very large in absolute (96 000 m^3(r)) and relative (320%) terms. One reason for this is the low initial basis. Apart from this, a large demand reaction must be expected because, as has already been pointed out, environmental labels meet with considerable acceptance on the part of hobby and building market customers.

The large increase of consumption in the basic scenario made the new equilibrium quantities lie above the reference level, for the tropical timber certification scheme confined to the Federal Republic of Germany (see Table 29) as well in the case of a world market price increase due to OECD-wide introduction of the certification scheme. The worst case of OECD-wide certification taking into consideration the certification costs without willingness on the part of consumers to accept higher prices, the market growth is still 280% compared with the present level (114 versus 30, see Table 30).

Table 29:   Effects of a Certification Scheme Confined to Germany on the German Market for Tropical Timber Do-It-Yourself Mouldings

Reference situation (R): Realised price and demand in 1993		
TT price [DM/m³(r)]	600,0	
TT demand for DIY mouldings [1000m³(r)]	30	
Basic scenario (B): CS confined to the FRG, without CS costs, without IWP		Change against R [%]
	T I	T I
TT price [DM/m³(r)]	600,0	0,0
TT demand for DIY mouldings [1000m³(r)]	126	320,0
Extended scenarios: CS confined to the FRG, with CS costs		Change against B [%]
	T I	T I
without IWP		
equilibrium TT price [DM/m³(r)]	602,4	0,4
TT demand [1000 m³(r)] with a :		
- CS for tropical timber	126	-0,4
- CS for all timber	126	-0,4
- CS for all timber plus energy tax	126	-0,4
with IWP (5%)		
equilibrium TT price [DM/m³(r)]	602,4	0,4
TT demand [1000 m³(r)] with a :		
- CS for tropical timber	131	4,1
- CS for all timber	131	4,1
- CS for all timber plus energy tax	131	4,1

Notes: TT: Tropical timber; CS: Certification scheme; IWP: Increased willingness to pay; DIY: Do-It-Yourself.
Source: Own calculations.

Table 30: Effects of an OECD-Wide Certification Scheme on the German Market for Tropical Timber Do-It-Yourself Mouldings

Reference situation (R): Realised price and demand in 1993		
TT price [DM/m³(r)]	600,0	
TT demand for DIY mouldings [1000m³(r)]	30	

Basic scenario (B): CS confined to the FRG, without CS costs, without IWP		Change against R [%]
	T I	T I
TT price [DM/m³(r)]	600,0	0,0
TT demand for DIY mouldings [1000m³(r)]	126	320,0

Extended scenarios: OECD-wide CS, with CS costs, price increase on world market		Change against B [%]
	T I	T I
without IWP		
equilibrium TT price [DM/m³(r)]	670,2	11,7
TT demand [1000 m³(r)] with a :		
- CS for tropical timber	114	-9,4
- CS for all timber	114	-9,4
- CS for all timber plus energy tax	114	-9,4
with IWP (5%)		
equilibrium TT price [DM/m³(r)]	683,3	13,9
TT demand [1000 m³(r)] with a :		
- CS for tropical timber	117	-7,0
- CS for all timber	117	-7,0
- CS for all timber plus energy tax	117	-7,0

Notes: TT: Tropical timber; CS: Certification scheme; IWP: Increased willingness to pay; DIY: Do-It-Yourself.
Source: Own calculations.

10.5 Furniture Surfaces

In the market for tropical timber furniture surface materials, again two scenarios have been calculated. Reversal of the effects of the campaign against tropical timber and of the fashion change through a certification scheme contribute equally to the demand expansion of altogether 178.6%. Here too it can be assumed that consumers react quickly and flexibly to the incentive to buy furniture with tropical timber surfaces, because this material has many visual and technical advantages.

The results of the scenarios are similar to those already found for the other submarkets, for example the almost non-existent difference between various certification schemes and energy taxation. In total, the market for tropical timber furniture surfaces - like the market for windows and do-it-yourself mouldings, but

differing from the market for outer doors or staircases - already features a sufficiently large (percentage) expansion as a result of a certification scheme, so that
the demand reducing effect of the certification costs and the world market price
increase (in the big country case) can be over-compensated. Therefore all scenarios show increased demand compared with the reference situation of the demand
realized in 1993. In the least case compared with the reference situation, the expected growth is 71% (48 versus 28, T I under the big country assumption, see
Table 32). In the best case the growth is 189% (81 versus 28, T II under the small
country assumption, see Table 31).

Table 31:   Effects of a Certification Scheme Confined to Germany on the German
Market for Tropical Timber Furniture Surfaces

Reference situation (R): Realised price and demand in 1993				
TT price [DM/m3(r)]	600,0			
TT demand for furniture surfaces [1000m³(r)]	28			
Basic scenario (B): CS confined to the FRG, without CS costs, without IWP			Change against R [%]	
	T I	**T II**	**T I**	**T II**
TT price [DM/m³(r)]	600,0	600,0	0,0	0,0
TT demand for furniture surfaces [1000m³(r)]	53	78	89,3	178,6
Extended scenarios: CS confined to the FRG, with CS costs			Change against B [%]	
	T I	**T II**	**T I**	**T II**
without IWP				
equilibrium TT price [DM/m³(r)]	602,4	602,4	0,4	0,4
TT demand [1000 m³(r)] with a :				
- CS for tropical timber	53	78	-0,3	-0,3
- CS for all timber	53	78	-0,3	-0,3
- CS for all timber plus energy tax	53	78	-0,3	-0,3
with IWP (5%)				
equilibrium TT price [DM/m³(r)]	602,4	602,4	0,4	0,4
TT demand [1000 m³(r)] with a :				
- CS for tropical timber	55	81	3,9	3,9
- CS for all timber	55	81	3,9	3,9
- CS for all timber plus energy tax	55	81	3,9	3,9

Notes: TT: Tropical timber; CS: Certification scheme; IWP: Increased willingness to pay.
Source: Own calculations.

Table 32:   Effects of an OECD-Wide Certification Scheme on the German Market for Tropical Timber Furniture Surfaces

Reference situation (R):				
Realised price and demand in 1993				
TT price [DM/m^3(r)]	600,0			
TT demand for furniture surfaces [1000m^3(r)]	28			
Basic scenario (B): CS confined to the FRG,			Change	
without CS costs, without IWP			against R [%]	
	T I	**T II**	**T I**	**T II**
TT price [DM/m^3(r)]	600,0	600,0	0,0	0,0
TT demand for furniture surfaces [1000m3(r)]	53	78	89,3	178,6
Extended scenarios: OECD-wide CS,			Change	
with CS costs, price increase on world market			against B [%]	
	T I	**T II**	**T I**	**T II**
without IWP				
equilibrium TT price [DM/m^3(r)]	670,2	712,2	11,7	18,7
TT demand [1000 m^3(r)] with a :				
- CS for tropical timber	48	67	-8,9	-13,5
- CS for all timber	48	67	-8,9	-13,5
- CS for all timber plus energy tax	48	67	-8,9	-13,5
with IWP (5%)				
equilibrium TT price [DM/m^3(r)]	683,3	726,1	13,9	21,0
TT demand [1000 m^3(r)] with a :				
- CS for tropical timber	49	69	-6,6	-11,3
- CS for all timber	49	69	-6,6	-11,3
- CS for all timber plus energy tax	49	69	-6,6	-11,3

Notes: TT: Tropical timber; CS: Certification scheme; IWP: Increased willingness to pay.
Source: Own calculations.

11 Extended Scenarios of the Aggregate Timber Market

In this chapter scenarios are calculated for tropical timber certification in the aggregate German timber market. The German tropical timber market (Section 11.1) stands in the foreground. As already found for the scenarios of the submarkets, the distinction between an OECD-wide certification scheme and one confined to the Federal Republic of Germany, is of special importance for the aggregate market consideration too. Different conditions affecting tropical timber demand resulting from certification of all timber species or from energy taxation are not considered for the total market scenarios because - as can be seen in the submarket scenarios - only small differences arise from these causes. Instead, a brief analysis of the effects on the German market for non-tropical timber follows in Section 11.2.

11.1 Extended Scenarios of the Aggregate Tropical Timber Market

This Chapter is concerned with the aggregate German tropical timber market. The scenarios are based on a highly aggregated world market supply of tropical timber and an agregated German tropical timber import demand. Basically, import demand consists of the actual demand in the reference year 1993 increased by the accumulated expansions of demand calculated in the five submarkets for the basic scenarios T I and T II (see the Chapter before).

In the small country version (certification scheme confined to the Federal Republic of Germany) the behaviour of the world market supply is characterized by the feature that any extent of expansion of the German demand for tropical timber can be satisfied without price increase, due to the small German share (2.6%) in the world market of tropical timber. But, in case of a certification surcharge and additional costs caused by sustainable forest management, the world market price will rise exactly by that amount.

In the big country version (OECD-wide certification), the demand expansion in the German tropical timber market and simultaneously in the markets of the other OECD countries leads to an increase of the world market price. Therefore the calculation of the new market equilibrium must take into consideration the price elasticity of the world market supply of tropical timber.

In both cases scenarios are calculated with and without certification costs, with and without additional costs caused by sustainable forest management as well as with and without willingness to pay higher prices. Table 33 lists the underlying parameters. The procedure for determining the equilibrium quantities and prices for the various scenarios has already been described in Sections 9.1 to 9.3. The equilibrium prices determined in this Chapter for the aggregate market with an OECD-wide certification scheme are used in the respective scenarios for the individual submarkets in Chapter 10.

It must always be borne in mind that in the basic scenarios an increase of the aggregate demand for tropical timber is assumed to result solely from the five submarkets. These actually cover most of the visible uses and thus a large part of the area in which a certification scheme produces effects, but the demand for tropical timber may increase on other sectors too.

Table 33:   Data for the Initial Situation and the Basic Scenarios for the Aggregate German Tropical Timber Market

	Reference situation: actual situation 1993	Reversal of effects of the ATC	Reversal of effects of the ATC and of the fashion change
	R	*T I*	*T II*
Import quantity [1000 m³(r)]	2 005	2 274	2 440
Import rise [% versus **R**]		13.4	21.7
average price for Tropical timber [DM/m³(r)]	600		
average price elasticity of the world-wide supply of all tropical timber products		0.7	0.7
average price elasticity of the OECD demand for all tropical timber products		-0.46	-0.46

Notes: ATC: Anti-tropical timber campaign.
Source: Own calculations and sources stated in the text.

For the price elasticity of the world market supply of tropical timber a value of 0.7 was chosen, oriented according to the price elasticity of the supply of tropical sawnwood from the Asian region (according to econometric estimates by

SIDABUTAR 1988). For the price elasticity of the OECD demand and the aggregate German tropical timber demand we did not take an averaged or aggregate value of the derived demands from the submarkets, but instead a value assessed by the UNO for the European demand for tropical sawnwood (UN/ECE/FAO 1986:165). This procedure is based on the one hand on the assumption that a price increase for tropical timber will induce parallel substitution processes in all individual end consumer areas, which in the aggregate effect will lead to production capacity shortages for plastics and aluminium. This makes substitution processes more difficult and consequently the aggregate derived demand for tropical timber becomes less price-elastic. On the other hand this procedure also takes into consideration the consumed quantities outside the five investigated end consumer areas. An elasticity is chosen for sawnwood because it has an intermediate position between roundwood on the one hand and plywood, mouldings and finished wood products on the other hand.

The calculations for an OECD-wide certification of tropical timber are based on the assumption that the other OECD countries manifest an analogous and simultaneous percentage increase of tropical timber consumption in response to a certification scheme (see Section 9.1.1). With the calculated relative changes of the equilibrium import quantities and prices in the German tropical timber market, related to the absolute import quantities in the other OECD countries, it was thus possible to estimate the absolute changes of the demand for tropical timber on all OECD markets which could be achieved by a certification scheme. It is thereby necessary to take into consideration the differences in the tropical timber market structure and the effectiveness of the campaign against tropical timber in OECD countries, as presented in the introduction to Part III. The described differences between the OECD countries strongly suggest that scenario T I depicts the world market price changes induced by an OECD-wide certification scheme more realistically than scenario T II. The latter represents the reactions to be expected in the extreme case.

Table 34 summarizes the results of a certification scheme confined to the Federal Republic of Germany. Since it is assumed in this version that a world market price increase is only due to the certification costs or the costs of a change to sustainable forest management, the increased demand induced by the introduction of a certification scheme and by an increased willingness to pay higher prices can take full effect. By introducing the scheme new equilibrium German demand for tropical timber lies between 12.8% and 24.2% above the reference situation which is the actual demand in 1993.

The assumed willingness of consumers to accept 5% higher prices induces an additional increase in equilibrium demand, depending on the particular scenario, of 2.5 to 2.8 percentage points (15.3% versus 12.8% in T I, 23.8% versus 21.0% in T II).

The possible reductions in equilibrium demand resulting from the increased production costs after a change to sustainable timber production are relatively small. They amount to 0.4 to 0.5 percentage points only (e.g. 15.3% vs 15.8% in

T I respectively 23.8% vs 24.2% in T II). The effect of the increased production costs on the development of world market prices is considerably higher amounting 0.8 percentage points (1.2% vs 0.4%).

Table 34:   Effects of a Certification Scheme Confined to Germany on the Aggregate German Market for Tropical Timber

| | Import quantity | | Import price | | Import quantity | | Import price | |
| | 1000 $m^3(r)$ | | DM/$m^3(r)$ | | % versus **R** | | | |
Version:	T I	T II	T I	T II	T I	T II	T I	T II
Reference situation (**R**): Actual situation for 1993, no CS	2005	2005	600.0	600.0				
Basic scenario, CS confined to the FRG	2274	2440	600.0	600.0	13.4	21.7	0.0	0.0
Extended scenarios, CS confined to the FRG								
- with CS costs, no IWP	2270	2436	602.4	602.4	13.2	21.5	0.4	0.4
- with CS costs, with IWP	2321	2491	602.4	602.4	15.8	24.2	0.4	0.4
- with CS and SFM costs, no IWP	2261	2426	607.4	607.4	12.8	21.0	1.2	1.2
- with CS and SFM costs, with IWP	2313	2482	607.4	607.4	15.3	23.8	1.2	1.2

Notes: CS:Certification scheme; IWP: Increased willingness to pay higher prices; SFM: Sustainable forest management. Assumptions: In the basic scenarios the certification costs are zero and higher prices are not accepted. In the extended scenarios the costs for the certification scheme amount to 2.4 DM/$m^3(r)$, the additional costs for sustainable forest management to 5 DM/$m^3(r)$, and end consumers will accept 5% higher prices for sustainably produced tropical timber products.
Source: Own calculations.

Table 35 summarizes the results for the big country case. In view of the restrictions explained above, scenario T I is placed in the foreground for the following discussion. The increased demand through the OECD-wide certification alone produces a world market price increase of approx. 11.5% compared with the certification scheme restricted to the Federal Republic of Germany. This price increase induces adaptation reactions in consumption so that the final consumption drops by 4.9% compared with the small country case (2163 in row 3 vs 2274 in row 2). Nevertheless, it still remains clearly 7.9% above the initial situation in 1993 in which no certification scheme was in effect.

In the extreme case when all OECD countries react to the certification scheme in a way similar to the German demand for tropical timber in its best scenario (additional reversal of the fashion change, T II), equilibrium demand would decrease by an greater *percentage* compared with restriction of the certification scheme to the Federal Republic of Germany (8.1%, 2257 in row 3 vs 2440 in row 2). Nevertheless, here too the equilibrium consumption still is greater than in the initial situation (12.6%).

Table 35:   Effects of an OECD-Wide Timber Certification Scheme on the Aggregate German Market for Tropical Timber

	Import quantity 1000 m^3(r)		Import price DM/m^3(r)		Import quantity % versus **R**		Import price % versus **R**	
Version:	T I	T II	T I	T II	T I	T II	T I	T II
Reference situation (**R**): Actual situation for 1993, no CS	2005	2005	600.0	600.0				
Basic scenario („small country"), CS confined to the FRG	2274	2440	600.0	600.0	13.4	21.7	0.0	0.0
Extended scenarios („big country"), OECD-wide CS								
- no CS costs, no IWP	2163	2257	668.8	710.7	7.9	12.6	11.5	18.5
- with CS costs, no IWP	2161	2255	670.2	712.2	7.8	12.5	11.7	18.7
- with CS costs, with IWP	2191	2286	683.3	726.1	9.3	14.0	13.9	21.0
- with CS and SFM costs, no IWP	2157	2251	673.3	715.2	7.6	12.3	12.2	19.2
- with CS and SFM costs, with IWP	2186	2282	686.3	729.1	9.0	13.8	14.4	21.5

Notes: CS:Certification scheme; IWP: Increased willingness to pay higher prices; SFM: Sustainable forest management. Assumptions: In the basic scenarios the certification costs are zero and higher prices are not accepted. In the extended scenarios the costs of a certification scheme amount to 2.4 DM/m^3(r), the additional costs for sustainable forest management to 5 DM/m^3(r), and end consumers will accept 5% higher prices for sustainably produced tropical timber products.
Source: Own calculations.

The results change only insignificantly when the costs of the certification scheme are taken into consideration. Willingness on the part of end consumers to accept higher prices - as an ecological mark-up here cautiously estimated as 5% - fully compensates the price increase and induces an additional increase in demand of 1.4% (2191 in row 5 versus 2161 in row 4).

In contrast to a certification scheme confined to Germany, within an OECD-wide certification scheme the increase in costs for sustainably produced timber of 5 DM/m^3(r) cannot be fully passed on to the end consumers. The new equilibrium price is only 3 DM/m^3(r) above the price in the corresponding scenario not reflecting increases in production costs (729.1 in row 7 vs 726.1 in row 5). This reduces the new equilibrium German imports by 0.2 to 0.3 percentage points (9.0% vs 9.3% respectively 13.8% vs 14.0%). In either case increased willingness to pay is able to compensate most of the cost increases from both the certification scheme and the change to sustainable forest management.

On the whole an OECD-wide certification scheme taking into account an increased willingness to pay as well as the costs of the certification scheme and the costs of sustainable timber production indicates an increase in German imports of tropical timber of 9.0% in the more realistic scenario T I. Yet, this increase in import volume goes, due to a considerable increase in the OECD-wide demand, hand in hand with a massive increase in prices of 14.4%.

11.2 Tropical Timber Certification and the Demand for Non-Tropical Timber

The basic scenarios of the individual submarkets assume that a certification scheme can restore the share of tropical timber in the total timber consumption of the respective submarkets to the long-term trend which existed before the campaign against tropical timber and before the change of fashion (see Section 8.1). These substitution movements are exogenous changes of demand *within* the group of all timber species.[86] This means that in the basic scenarios the demand for non-tropical timber is expected to decrease by the same amount as the demand for tropical timber increases as a result of the certification scheme (*substitution effect*).

The extended scenarios model additional aspects which can affect tropical and non-tropical timber to the same extent. Certification costs as well as costs of a change to sustainable forest management which unilaterally increase the price of tropical timber or the price of non-tropical timber do not play any significant role, as the calculations made above have shown. In addition to the effects of reversing the campaign against tropical timber and the fashion change, the willingness to pay higher prices assumed in some extended scenarios greatly increases the demand for tropical timber. The model leaves open the question, to what extent this demand increase reduces the demand for non-tropical timber or for non-timber materials.

Assuming in the scenarios of an OECD-wide certification scheme that not only the substitution effect, but also the additional demand resulting from increased

---

[86] No assumption is made in the basic scenarios, how the group of all timber species could gain ground over other materials through a certification scheme. This distribution is taken as given according to the observed long-term trend.

willingness to accept higher prices, results *exclusively* in reducing the demand for non-tropical timber, the calculations made in this study give a maximum increased demand volume for tropical timber respectively a maximum decreased demand volume for non-tropical timber amounting to about 0,186 Mio $m^3(r)$ (see Table 35, T I: 2005 versus 2191).

In the case of certification of all timber species these losses could be compensated by a possible expansion of the demand for non-tropical timber as a result of the image gain of timber compared with non-timber materials such as plastics, glass, aluminium, etc. (*timber image effect*).

Assuming for example that a certification scheme will also make consumers more willing to accept higher prices for non-tropical timber and that non-timber materials become relatively less attractive, the demand for non-tropical timber could increase too. Willingness to accept 5% higher prices could then increase consumption by about 1.5%[87], taking into consideration the supply-conditioned price increase. This additional volume would be realized mainly at the expense of plastics, aluminium and glass.

The following rough estimate determines the quantity corresponding to this 1.5% increase. In order to achieve a comparison with the typical utilization regions for tropical timber, the calculation concentrates on the production of logs, sawnwood, plywood and products made from non-tropical timber.

The home market consumption of imported and home-grown coniferous and non-coniferous saw- and veneer logs in German sawmills and veneer factories as well as in the German production of railway sleepers and masts amounted to approx. 22 million m^3 roundwood in 1992 (HUCKERT 1993). To this must be added the net imports of sawnwood, panels, other half-finished and finished timber products including furniture, altogether amounting to 17 million $m^3(r)$ (*all timber species*) (OLLMANN 1993b). After deducting the net imports of tropical timber in the form of logs, sawnwood and plywood and products made of them amounting to 2.1 million $m^3(r)$, this leaves a home market consumption of non-tropical logs, sawnwood and plywood and related products amounting to about 36.9 million $m^3(r)$. In comparison, the volume of non-tropical timber which could be displaced by the tropical timber expansion amounts to only 0.5%.

Assuming now that visible uses and other uses which react sensitively to a certification scheme, make up 30% of the 36.9 million $m^3(r)$,[88] a 1.5 percent increase in consumption in these uses could generate a volume increase of 0.166 million $m^3(r)$. This corresponds roughly to the increase in consumption of tropical timber in the realistic scenario T I of an OECD-wide certification scheme amounting to approx. 0.186 million $m^3(r)$, which is going at the expense of non-tropical timber as explained above. So the substitution effect and the timber image effect will more or less cancel mutually.

---

[87] Calculated on the following assumptions: OECD-wide certification scheme, certification costs not taken into consideration, price elasticity of supply 0.7, price elasticity of demand -0.46.

[88] Own estimate, based on MÜLLER (1987).

However, it is necessary to take into consideration that this rough calculation is limited to the possible effects in the utilization areas for non-tropical timber in raw form, because these are the areas in which tropical timber is used too. If it is additionally assumed that certification of all timber species will also have a positive effect on the demand for cellulose, paper and paperboard, a still greater increase in demand for certified non-tropical timber could be the result. However, in this area it will hardly be possible to induce a general increase in demand for non-tropical timber. Instead, it is to be expected that substitution will merely take place between certified and non-certified timber. It is nevertheless conceivable that an increased volume can be achieved by displacing old paper and/or old clothes as raw material for paper and paperboard production. Whether this is realistic and sensible can be determined only by a more detailed study beyond the scope of the present one.

All assumptions about the reactions of non-tropical timber consumers to a certification scheme, which exceed the above estimate of the consumers' willingness to accept 5% higher prices for certified non-tropical timber, appear to be highly speculative without previous investigations of the respective submarkets.

12 Conclusions

This study investigates the effects of a certification system for tropical timber and tropical timber products from sustainable forest management. The purpose of this study is to concentrate on the German tropical timber market. Attention is thereby focused on the demand side. Therefore an adequate supply of sustainably produced tropical timber and an established and credible certification scheme are assumed at the outset.

The chosen method of approach is based on the individual analysis of various important submarkets for tropical timber in the Federal Republic of Germany. The possible effects on demand of a certification scheme are derived from the observed trends in the individual markets. Particular mention is made of the negative effects of the campaign against tropical timber and of a change of fashion favouring lighter coloured timber species.

The submarkets for which it is possible to calculate scenarios altogether cover about 50% of the entire German demand for tropical timber. A fundamental principle of the method of approach in this study consists of the assumption that a credible certification scheme can reverse the negative effects of the campaign against tropical timber and of the fashion change observed in the submarkets, in favour of tropical timber. Since visible uses of tropical timber dominate in the chosen submarkets, it is reasonable to assume that they cover much more than 50% of all uses, for which in recent years negative effects of the campaign against tropical timber and of the change of fashion towards lighter coloured timber might have appeared.

The calculations of the scenarios are based on the common reference year (1993). Growth effects in the German tropical timber market until the actual introduction of a certification scheme are not taken into account, so that the analysis concentrates on the effects of certification.

Evaluation of experience gathered especially in the Federal Republic of Germany with environmental labels indicates that credibly certified products are usually preferred by consumers when these products are priced at the same level as non certified products. In some circumstances an environmental label can even entice a consumer's willingness to pay slightly more. Therefore this study also considers scenarios in which it is assumed that end consumers of tropical timber will accept 5% higher prices.

The analysis of the utilization trends shows that some German submarkets for tropical timber were strongly affected by the campaign against tropical timber and the change of fashion (for example the window market and the market for do-it-yourself mouldings). These are therefore also the submarkets which will expand significantly as a result of timber certification.

One important result of the scenarios of certification is that the costs of the certification scheme and the additional costs brought about by a change to sustainable forest management are of minor significance. Tropical timber's ability to compete as a raw material is neither impaired nor improved substantially by including non-tropical timber in the certification scheme or by energy taxation, which mainly affects the non-timber substitute materials plastics and aluminium by making them more expensive.

It was furthermore found that a moderate willingness of end consumers to accept on the average 5% higher prices is able to compensate the additional costs of a certification scheme and of a change to sustainable forest management in all scenarios and can in several scenarios even further stimulate the tropical timber market.

The main parameter in modeling the scenarios is the distinction between a certification scheme confined to the Federal Republic of Germany and an OECD-wide scheme (see Table 36). Since the German tropical timber demand amounts to only 2.6% of the world-wide demand and is therefore relatively insignificant, demand changes induced by a certification scheme confined to Germany would not have any effect on the development of the price in the world market. The demand stimulating effects of the certification scheme and the willingness to accept higher prices lead in this case to an increase of between 15.3% and 23.8% in the German demand for tropical timber.

In the calculations for a certification scheme confined to Germany, the scenarios T I and T II cover a realistic bandwidth of the possible reactions of the total market and the submarkets. T I assumes that a certification scheme will at least reverse the effects of the campaign against tropical timber. In T II it is more optimistically assumed that a certification scheme will influence a change of fashion already becoming evident in the German tropical timber market, so that consumers will again favour coloured and darker timber species, and thus i.a. tropical timber. Consequently T II simulates that a certification scheme will raise the tropical timber consumption in the analysed submarkets from the present low level back to the long-term trend observed before the campaign against tropical timber *and* the fashion change.

For an OECD-wide certification scheme, T II must be considered as an extreme case on account of some special aspects of the German tropical timber market which restrict the applicability of German reactions to a certification scheme to all OECD countries. Scenario T I produces a more realistic development. A distinct rise of the price of tropical timber by 14.4% is found. This price increase considerably weakens the expansive demand effects which a certification scheme restricted to the Federal Republic of Germany induces. The entire import demand increases by 6.3 percentage points less (9.0% instead of 15.3%).

Table 36:   Survey of the Effects of a Timber Certification Scheme on the German Tropical Timber Market

scenario: scope of certification:	initial situation 1993	T I		T II		T I		T II	
		FRG	OECD	FRG	OECD	FRG	OECD	FRG	OECD
consumption in the market for:		volume [1000 m³(r)]				change vs initial situation [%]			
- windows	323	490	438	607	513	51.7	35.6	87.9	58.8
- outer doors	194	n.d.	n.d.	226	191	n.d.	n.d.	16.5	-1.5
- staircases	82	n.d.	n.d.	91	77	n.d.	n.d.	11.7	-5.5
- do-it-yourself mouldings	30	131	117	n.d.	n.d.	336.7	290	n.d.	n.d.
- furniture surfaces	28	55	49	81	69	96.4	75.0	189.3	146.4
total submarkets	657								
total market						change vs initial situation [%]			
import quantity [1000 m³(r)]	2005	2313	2186	2482	2282	15.3	9.0	23.8	13.8
average import price [DM/m³(r)]	600	607.4	686.3	607.4	729.1	1.2	14.4	1.2	21.5

Source: Own calculations.
Notes: n.d.: Scenario not defined. Assumptions for all executed scenarios: Costs of a certification scheme 2,4 DM/m³(r). End consumers are willing to accept 5% higher prices for a sustainably produced tropical timber product. Additional assumption for the total market scenarios: Additional costs due to a change to sustainable forest management 5 DM/m³(r). For technical reasons, the reductions in the scenarios of the submarkets are systematically overestimated. In the more realistic big country scenario T I this overestimate is as high as 17% (see introduction to Chapter 10).

If in the case of an OECD-wide certification scheme a still greater price increase occurs in the extreme case (T II), the price-conditioned decline of demand will on some individual German submarkets even lead to a new equilibrium level below the actual consumption in the reference year 1993 (outer doors -1.5% and staircases -5.5%). Under normal conditions, however, the consumption will rise in the analysed submarkets in response to an OECD-wide certification of tropical timber. This is particularly the case for the window market and in the market for do-it-yourself mouldings, which were both strongly affected by the campaign against tropical timber.

In the politically more realistic case of OECD-wide certification, an increased consumption in the total market by about 9% and a price increase of about 14% is to be expected as reaction to a certification scheme. This holds for certification costs amounting to 2.4 DM/m^3(r), additional sustainable management costs amounting to 5 DM/m^3(r), and if consumers are willing to accept 5% higher prices.

The reduced consumption of non-tropical timber in Germany, which is to be expected as a result of the expansion of tropical timber consumption induced by an OECD-wide certification scheme, is only slight compared with the entire home-market consumption of non-tropical timber (about 0.5%). This reduced consumption can be compensated if in the case of extension of the certification scheme to non-tropical timber, willingness on the part of the end consumers to pay 5% higher prices is assumed for non-tropical timber too.

The scenarios show that a certification scheme for tropical timber confined to the Federal Republic of Germany can have a strongly expansive effect on the demand because it avoids inducing price effects in the world market. This is true in particular for the case in which it can be made clear to end consumers what personal advantage they might enjoy with the certification scheme, thus making them willing to accept higher prices. The extent to which a credible certification scheme which is an effective instrument for preserving the tropical rain forests can motivate consumers should not be underestimated.

However, such a scheme also entails costs which would amount to about DM 5 million annually for a German tropical timber import volume of at present roughly 2 million m^3 roundwood equivalent. If on the average 5% higher prices are accepted, these costs can be passed down completely to the consumers without inducing a decline in demand.

Appendix

A1   Procedure for Evaluating the Foreign Trade Statistics

The procedure described below was used to determine the price and quantity data for the imports and exports of the relevant products for 1984 and 1989 to 1993. This procedure is based on that of OLLMANN (1993a).

- For goods categories labelled „made of tropical timber", the total quantities and total values for import and export are taken from the foreign trade statistics. Exports of products „made of tropical timber" are added to the final consumption abroad.
- Additional quantities of tropical timber products can be approximated for the imports. For this purpose, the imports originating from the tropical countries listed below are taken over for categories of goods described as „made of non-coniferous timber" or „made of other timber" or stating no kind of timber. In these countries timber products for export are usually made mainly of tropical non-coniferous timber. Categories which explicitly specify coniferous timber products are not included, not even for countries in the list shown below (this also applies to plywood with at least one outer layer of coniferous timber). This approach is based on the assumption explained in Chapter 6 that exported coniferous timber usually comes from plantations and not from natural forests.
    - **List of countries considered for determining the German imports of tropical timber:** *From Latin America and the Caribbean:* Antigua and Barbuda, Bahamas, Bolivia, Brazil, Costa Rica, Dominica, Dominican Republic, Ecuador, El Salvador, French Guayana, Grenada, Guatemala, Guyana, Haiti, Hoduras, Jamaica, Columbia, Cuba, Martinique, Mexico, Nicaragua, Panama, Paraguay, Peru, Puerto Rico, St. Kitts-Nevis, St. Lucia, St. Vincent, Surinam, Trinidad and Tobago, Venezuela (not included: Argentine, Chile, Uruguay). *From Africa:* Angola, Equatorial Guinea, Ethiopia, Benin, Botsuana, Burkina Faso, Burundi, Djibuti, Ivory Coast, Gaboon, Gambia, Ghana, Guinea, Guinea-Buissau, Cameroon, Cape Verde, Congo, Liberia, Madagascar, Mali, Mauretania, Mauritius, Mocambique, Namibia, Niger, Nigeria, Ruanda, Zambia, Senegal, Sierra Leone, Zimbabwe, Somalia, Sudan, Tansania, Togo, Chad, Uganda, Zaire, Central African Republic (not included: South African Republic, Swaziland, North African States). *From Asia and the Pacific area:* Bangladesh, Bhutan, Brunei, Hongkong, India, Indonesia, Cambodia, Laos, Malaya, Myanmar, Nepal, Pakistan, Papua New Guinea, Philippines, Singapore, Sri Lanka, South Korea, Taiwan,

Thailand, Vietnam (not included: Australia, China, Japan, New Zealand, Middle East).
- Not included but treated separately on the basis of specific information: Non-tropical non-coniferous veneers from Brazil which usually consist of American Oak (OLLMANN 16.12.1994), charcoal, cellulose, fibre-boards and particle boards (see Section 7.2).
- Where quantities are not specified in [m^3] in the statistics, but instead for example in [m^2], [pieces], etc., they are converted to timber content [m^3] and to roundwood equivalents [m^3(r)] using the conversions factors listed in Appendix A5.

The described procedure has to contend with the following sources of error:

- The exports of tropical timber goods, particularly half-finished and finished goods, are underestimated. Usually no separate category „made of tropical timber" is listed for these goods, for example windows and window parts. No information is available on the export share of the relevant tropical timber product. Thus the fraction consumed in the producing country is systematically overestimated.
- Other types of timber are included with goods which are not explicitly declared in the foreign trade statistics as „made of tropical timber" or „made of coniferous timber", but instead as „non-coniferous timber" and „other timber" and for which tropical non-coniferous timber is assumed according to country of origin. The other types might be imported and further processed non-tropical non-coniferous timber or home-grown coniferous timber. The latter may originate from natural forests or from plantations, and detailed information is rarely available for this distinction. Therefore, a systematic overestimation of imported tropical timber is possible.
- A systematic underestimation of the tropical timber imports results through imports from non-tropical countries which import tropical timber and then export it, either unchanged or after further processing to Germany. These quantities can only be covered when the product is listed in the statistics in a category as „made of tropical timber". Especially goods from Japan and France as well as the considerable furniture exports from Italy are involved here. Specific information is not available on German imports of half-finished and finished tropical timber products from non-tropical countries (OLLMANN 31.8.1994).

A2   Production Quantities and Values of Lacquer of German Production

Erzeugnis	Mengen in Tonnen							Wert in 1000 DM							Wert pro kg						
	1987	1988	1989	1990	1991	1992	1993	1987	1988	1989	1990	1991	1992	1993	1987	1988	1989	1990	1991	1992	1993
Lösungsmittelarme bzw. -freie Lacke																					
Dispersionslackfarben	16439	19872	24686	28982	28991	30885	32769	77320	93974	129473	162482	194601	216394	261239	4,70	4,73	5,24	5,61	6,71	7,01	7,97
High-Solids	4439	4940	6534	6853	12872	8640	13224	29636	34787	43239	45927	k.A.	k.A.	69220	6,68	7,04	6,62	6,70		8,20	5,23
Pulverlacke	24615	28341	33425	38462	43096	44242	46866	199009	225787	267784	311362	k.A.	362580	380354	8,08	7,97	8,01	8,10			8,12
Elektrolyselacke	49170	49642	52921	56172	67098	71503	59209	291989	300020	323888	363257	k.A.	k.A.	394893	5,94	6,04	6,12	6,47			6,67
Lösemittelhaltige Lacke *																					
Alkydharzlacke	171539	168617	177245	171289	186409	172078	148109	1096444	1106254	1167865	1166369	1252637	1155971	1006201	6,39	6,56	6,59	6,81	6,72	6,72	6,79
Oelfarben u. -lacke	8917	7791	6552	7509	k.A.	k.A.	4218	46828	44007	39528	45978	k.A.	k.A.	25539	5,25	5,65	6,03	6,12	k.A.	k.A.	6,05
Zelluloselacke nicht-pigmentiert	46056	47416	48057	44346	55426	55436	47862	217534	231245	243193	233567	274857	281642	263654	4,72	4,88	5,06	5,27	4,96	5,08	5,51
Zelluloselacke pigmentiert	14735	14760	14899	14386	16885	13247	13303	101509	101542	105468	105273	125989	91926	92030	6,89	6,88	7,08	7,32	7,46	6,94	6,92
Bitumen u. teerhalt. Lacke	6779	6780	5910	4905	4602	k.A.	3679	23036	22669	19025	18311	16375	k.A.	12723	3,40	3,34	3,22	3,73	3,56	k.A.	3,46
Metall. pigmentierte Anstrichstoffe	8823	9124	8647	9573	k.A.	k.A.	10688	59763	64701	67315	75947	k.A.	k.A.	87415	6,77	7,09	7,78	7,93	k.A.	k.A.	8,18
Leuchtfarben	47	38	24	93	k.A.	k.A.	14	1355	929	664	2860	k.A.	k.A.	399	28,83	24,45	27,67	30,75	k.A.	k.A.	28,50
Lacke u.a. spachtel	19087	19087	19262	23493	k.A.	k.A.	22291	75333	78998	79304	96364	k.A.	k.A.	99671	3,95	4,14	4,12	4,10	k.A.	k.A.	4,47
sonst. Lacke	1366	1576	1894	4885	k.A.	8855	7473	9956	11755	13760	44196	98349	58628	57749	7,29	7,46	7,27	9,05	k.A.	6,62	7,73
Phenol-, Harnstoff- u. Melaminharzlacke	10003	11573	14740	15153	18449	k.A.	12914	64111	70370	82087	84483	k.A.	k.A.	83696	6,41	6,08	5,57	5,58	5,33	k.A.	6,48
Polyesterharzlacke	70323	77589	77687	80963	k.A.	k.A.	69634	590699	655109	664924	721848	k.A.	k.A.	676714	8,40	8,44	8,56	8,92	k.A.	k.A.	9,72
Epoxidharzlacke	30599	31281	29896	42977	k.A.	k.A.	30234	221262	226396	223915	323391	k.A.	k.A.	231642	7,23	7,24	7,49	7,50	k.A.	k.A.	7,66
Polyurethanharzlacke	40155	45667	50173	58228	61402	57191	55196	315281	346609	391588	442052	482226	460711	450337	7,85	7,59	7,80	7,59	7,85	8,06	8,16
Polystrol- u. Polyvinylharzlacke	8315	8106	8284	16433	k.A.	k.A.	24946	58193	54182	56404	139470	k.A.	k.A.	258919	7,00	6,68	6,81	8,49	k.A.	k.A.	10,38
sonst. Lacke auf synth. Basis	78633	84589	88171	77843	77276	71656	63984	619964	665714	703850	622830	596469	560389	497624	7,88	7,87	7,98	8,00	7,72	7,82	7,78
Summen bzw. durchschnittlicher Wertkg																					
Lösungsmittelarme bzw. -freie Lacke	94663	102795	117566	130469	152057	155270	152068	597864	654568	764384	883028	k.A.	k.A.	1105706	6,4	6,4	6,5	6,7	k.A.	k.A.	7,0
# Dispersionslacke	16439	19872	24686	28982	28991	30885	32769	77320	93974	129473	162482	194601	216394	261239	4,7	4,7	5,2	5,6	6,7	7,0	8,0
Lösungsmittelhaltige Lacke	515277	533994	551441	572076	k.A.	k.A.	514545	3501268	3680480	3658890	4121939	k.A.	k.A.	3844313	7,9	7,6	7,9	8,5	k.A.	k.A.	8,5
# Alkydharze	171539	168617	177245	171289	186409	172078	148109	1096444	1106254	1167865	1166369	1252637	1155971	1006201	6,4	6,8	6,6	6,6	6,7	6,7	6,8
Gesamtmarkt	610040	636789	669007	702545	726000	710677	666613	4099132	4335048	4623274	5004967	k.A.	k.A.	4950019	6,7	6,8	6,9	7,1	k.A.	k.A.	7,4

Quelle: Stat.Bundesamt Fachs.4, Reihe 3.1; Verband der Lackindustrie e.V., Jahresbericht 1993; eigene Berechnungen

Anmerkungen: In den lösemittelfreien bzw. -armen Lacken sind die praktisch lösemittelfreien Dispersionsfarben und kunstharzgebundenen Putze nicht berücksichtigt; k.A.= keine Angaben

A3   List of Goods Categories in the Foreign Trade Statistics as Information Source for Tropical Timber

Tables A3.1 to A3.3 list the typical uses of the tropical timber species distinguished in the foreign trade statistics as to saw- and veneer logs, sawnwood and veneers. It is evident that the species are not grouped according to similar characteristics, but instead according to the geographic region of their origin. Thus valuable information is lost. Since the regional association can easily be reconstructed via the exporting countries, it would be desirable to develop a categorization of the foreign trade statistics according to utilization.

The tables do not show separate categories of goods for windows, parquet, furniture, furniture parts, other building carpentry products and other goods *made of tropical timber*. Yet, such a differentiation is extremely useful. Subdividing the last two categories seems to be desirable as each of them has nowadays reached a considerable volume in international trade (see Appendix A4).

Table A3.1:   Tropical Non-Coniferous Logs Imported into
the Federal Republic of Germany and its Typical Uses

Timber Species	Origin	Typical Use (Source)
Dark Red Meranti	Asia	Interior and exterior of buildings; lamellated square sawn timber (VDH, Blatt 5)
Light Red Meranti	Asia	Veneer sheets; sawnwood for interior furnishing (VDH, Blatt 5)
Meranti Bakau	Asia	Similar to Dark Red Meranti and Light Red Meranti (VDH, Blatt 5)
White Lauan	Asia	Solid timber (framework, furniture, shelves, packings); peeled veneers (shells, panelling, rear panels) (VDH, Blatt 102)
White Meranti	Asia	Peeled and sliced veneers for shell boards and inside surfaces of furniture (VDH, Blatt 31)
White Seraya	Asia	Solid timber (framework, furniture, shelves, packings): peeled veneers (shells, panelling, rear panels) (VDH, Blatt 102)
Yellow Meranti	Asia	Solid timber (light constructions, window shutters, wall and ceiling coverings, furniture parts); veneers (furniture and interior furnishings, shell boards) (VDH, Blatt 32)
Alan	Asia	Interior and exterior of buildings; lamellated square sawn timber (VDH, Blatt 5)

Continuation of Table A 3.1		
Keruing	Asia	Carriage floors, ramps, railway sleepers, technical plywood (VDH, Blatt 48)
Ramin	Asia	Solid timber (strips, frames, profile boards, shelves, furniture parts, round rods, tool handles); veneers (covering veneers) (VDH, Blatt 27)
Kapur	Asia	Carriage floors, ramps, railway sleepers, steps of staircases: technical plywood (VDH, Blatt 49)
Teak	Asia	Solid timber (windows, gates, doors, staircases, parquet, furniture, shipbuilding, works of art); decorative veneers (furniture, panels) (VDH, Blatt 42)
Jongkong Merbau	Asia	Outside of buildings (windows, doors, gates); inside of buildings (floors, steps of staircases, strong furniture) (VDH, Blatt 33)
Jelutong Kempas		
Okoumé	Africa	Veneers (veneer plywood and other boards, door wings); solid timber (door jambs) (VDH, Blatt 79)
Obéché (Abachi)	Africa	Only interior of buildings: Solid timber (strips, profile timber, sauna construction); veneers for veneer plywood (VDH, Blatt 58)
Sipo	Africa	Windows, doors, gates, wall elements, staircases (VDH, Blatt 1)
Makoré	Africa	Visible veneers (furniture, panelling, separating walls); veneer plywood for boat construction; plywood for concrete casting moulds; solid timber for exterior of buildings (windows, doors, gates) and interior of buildings (staircases, furniture parts, parquet) (VDH, Blatt 16)
Sapelli	Africa	Covering veneers for furniture, doors, panelling; staircases, parquet (VDH, Blatt 2)
Acajou d'Afrique (Khaya, African Mahogany	Africa	Solid timber (furniture, boats, frames); veneers (furniture, panelling) (VDH, Blatt 39)
Iroko	Africa	Outdoor construction (gates, posts, doors, park benches; staircases, parquet, special containers for chemicals (VDH, Blatt 3)
Limba (Fraké)	Africa	Only for interior furnishing: Solid timber (strips, frames, door jambs, furniture parts); veneers (veneer plywood, doors, concrete casting shell boards) (VDH, Blatt 19)

		Continuation of Table A3.1
Tiama	Africa	Solid timber (furniture parts, staircase sidepieces, frame constructions, boat construction); decorative veneer (VDH, Blatt 40)
Mansonia	Africa	Decorative veneer (furniture, wall and ceiling coverings, door wings); solid timber (seating furniture, furniture parts, brush handles) (VDH, Blatt 34)
Ilomba	Africa	Only for interior furnishing: Solid timber (strips); veneers (veneer plywood and blockboard for rear panels and internal floors) (VDH, Blatt 24)
Dibétou	Africa	Decorative veneers (furniture, interior furnishing); solid timber (furniture, furniture parts, strips) (VDH, Blatt 41)
Azobé (Bongossi)	Africa	Outdoor constructional timber; hydraulic and dyke engineering; coachbuilding; heavily stressed floors; railway sleepers (VDH, Blatt 7)
Baboen (American Mahogany)	Latin America	(Particularly outdoors) windows, doors, gates, profile boards, seating furniture, tables; boat construction; veneers (high quality furniture) (VDH, Blatt 18)
Imbuia	Latin America	
Balsa Rio-Palisander	Latin America	Decorative veneers (high quality furniture, panelling); handles, woodwind musical instruments (VDH, Blatt 53)
Rosewood	chiefly Latin America	Decorative veneers (high quality furniture, panelling; handles, woodwind musical instruments (VDH, Blatt 53)

Note: The timber species within each box constitute a single category in the foreign trade statistics.

Source: STATISTISCHES BUNDESAMT (1993).

Table A3.2:   Tropical Non-Coniferous Sawnwood Imported into
the Federal Republic of Germany

Dark Red Meranti, Light Red Meranti
White Lauan, White Meranti
Meranti Bakau, White Seraya, Yellow Meranti, Alan, Keruing, Ramin, Kapur, Teak, Jongkong, Merbau, Jelutong, Kempas
Okoumé, Obéché (Abachi), Sapelli, Sipo, Acajou d'Afrique (Khaya, African Mahogany), Makoré, Iroko, Tiama, Mansonia, Ilomba, Dibétou, Limba (Fraké), Azobé (Bongossi)
Baboen, (American) Mahogany, Imbuia, Balsa
Rio-Palisander, Rosewood
Note: The timber species in each box constitute a single category in the foreign trade statistics. See Table A 3.1 for the possible uses of the timber species.

Source: See Table A 3.1

Table A3.3:   Tropical Non-Coniferous Veneers Imported
into the Federal Republic of Germany

Dark Red Meranti, Light Red Meranti, White Lauan, Sipo, Limba (Fraké), Okoumé, Obéché (Abachi), Acajou d'Afrique (Khaya, African Mahogany), Sapelli, Baboen, (American) Mahogany, Rio-Palisander, Rosewood
Makoré, Iroko, Tiama, Mansonia, Ilomba, Dibétou, Azobé (Bongossi), Meranti Bakau, White Meranti, White Seraya, Yellow Meranti, Alan, Keruing, Ramin, Kapur, Teak, Jongkong, Merbau, Jelutong, Kempas, Imbuia, Balsa
Note: The timber species in each box constitute a single category in the foreign trade statistics. See Table A 3.1 for the possible uses of the timber species.

Source: See Table A 3.1

A4   Net Imports of Tropical Timber into the Federal Republic of Germany

[1000 m3(r)]	1984	1989	1990	1991	1992	1993
Roundwood	447.641	345.118	321.731	292.947	268.313	199.779
Sleepers, etc.	18.601	5.493	6.248	2.482	933	1.335
Sawnwood	713.981	640.608	568.473	478.712	467.799	328.361
Mouldings	22.280	53.690	52.507	72.517	96.621	74.367
Peeled veneers	70.699	89.143	106.040	105.151	120.172	84.631
Plywood	176.162	249.362	339.856	456.866	497.403	470.564
Doors	9.052	12.364	1.700	-1.009	20.268	13.218
Windows	0	569	966	5.158	730	1.056
Other joinery items	5.815	1.093	8.124	55.509	194.731	282.134
Parquet	1.358	8.534	17.361	28.037	39.193	53.451
Interior furnishing, other timber goods	13.326	3.881	7.452	21.777	26.543	17.826
Household utensils	17.643	29.675	30.292	50.553	44.183	35.500
Decorative objects	0	11.808	17.947	25.548	20.246	22.096
Packing material	171	2.169	595	3.092	6.974	3.541
Wooden handles, shoe expanders, etc.	22.131	29.563	43.047	43.791	40.330	43.019
Seating furniture	6.111	15.029	20.541	30.171	32.861	41.560
Office furniture	65	188	280	2.390	5.176	7.457
Domestic furniture	2.784	8.927	8.762	24.336	43.319	63.561
Other furniture	4.078	7.711	10.667	29.734	33.158	41.286
Furniture parts	7.230	14.085	12.305	23.568	23.077	20.419
Other timber goods	45.634	137.603	164.802	156.444	144.409	81.483
Rest	9.450	2.092	7.352	16.251	15.729	14.816
Total	1.594.211	1.668.704	1.747.046	1.924.025	2.142.167	1.901.459

Source: STATISTISCHES BUNDESAMT, Fachserie 7, Reihe 2, various years. Own calculations.

A5   Conversion Factors for Evaluating the Foreign Trade Statistics

Goods Category (original unit of measurement) Conversion to:	m^3	$m^3(r)$
Fuelwood (m^3)	0.6	0.6
Waste wood (100kg)	0.16	0.16
Charcoal (100kg)	0.6	0.6
Sawnwood, roughly squared, non-coniferous (100kg)	0.14	0.24
Wooden railway sleepers (m^3)	1.0	1.7
Dark Red Meranti sawn lengthwise (m^3)	1.0	1.5
Okoume/Baboen/miscellaneous, sawn lengthwise (m^3)	1.0	1.5
Wooden planks <6mm (100kg)	0.2	0.46
Red Meranti, Okoume: Planed parquet lath (100kg)	0.185	0.37
Red Meranti , sawn lengthwise, finger-jointed (100kg)	0.185	0.37
Red Meranti, sawn lengthwise, planed (100kg)	0.135	0.27
Red Meranti, sawn lengthwise, ground (100kg)	0.2	0.4
Other tropical timber, sawn lengthwise, finger-jointed, >6mm (100kg)	0.185	0.37
Other tropical timber, sawn lengthwise, planed >6mm (100kg)	0.135	0.27
Other tropical timber, sawn lengthwise, ground >6mm (100kg)	0.2	0.4
Other tropical timber, sawn lengthwise, finger-jointed <6mm (100kg)	0.17	0.4
Other tropical timber, sawn lengthwise, planed <6mm (100kg)	0.135	0.27
Other tropical timber, sawn lengthwise, ground <6mm (100kg)	0.20	0.45
Tropical timber veneer sheet <1mm (m^3)	1.0	1.8
Tropical timber veneer sheet >1mm (m^3)	1.0	1.8
Non-coniferous timber veneer sheet <1mm (m^3)	1.0	1.8
Non-coniferous timber veneer sheet >1mm (m^3)	1.0	1.8
Framing strips (m)	0.0005	0.001
Other timber strips and other profile timber (100kg)	0.21	0.49
Wooden parquet strips (m^2)	0.015	0.035
Plywood <6mm outer layer tropical timber (m^3)	1.0	2.3
Plywood <6mm outer layer non-coniferous timber (m^3)	1.0	2.3
Plywood, middle layer non-coniferous timber (m^3)	1.0	2.0
Plywood, outer layer non-coniferous timber (m^3)	1.0	2.0
Wooden blocks, slabs, etc. (100kg)	0.067	0.2
Wooden frames (100kg)	0.325	0.65
Crates, etc. (100kg)	0.19	0.38
Flat pallets (100kg)	0.19	0.38
Box pallets (100kg)	0.19	0.38
Wooden handles, etc. (100kg)	0.28	0.56
Shoe expanders, etc. (100kg)	0.28	0.56

Continuation of Table A 5		
Wooden windows and doors (100kg)	0.19	0.38
Tropical timber doors (100kg)	0.19	0.38
Other wooden doors and frames (100kg)	0.19	0.38
Mosaic parquet panels (m^2)	0.014	0.028
Other parquet panels (m^2)	0.015	0.029
Blatts for concrete formwork (100kg)	0.19	0.38
joinery components (100kg)	0.19	0.38
Objects for use in households (100kg)	0.28	0.56
Ornamental objects (100kg)	0.28	0.56
Intarsia (m^3)	1.0	2.0
Indoor furnishings (100kg)	0.28	0.56
Clothes hangers (100 pieces)	0.035	0.07
Round rods (100kg)	0.28	0.56
Timber goods (100kg)	0.28	0.56
Upholstered seating furniture (100kg)	0.1	0.2
Other seating furniture (100kg)	0.28	0.56
Office writing tables <80cm (100kg)	0.125	0.25
Other office furniture <80cm (100kg)	0.125	0.25
Office wardrobes >80cm (100kg)	0.125	0.25
Other office furniture >80cm (100kg)	0.125	0.25
Kitchen furniture (100kg)	0.125	0.25
Bedroom furniture (100kg)	0.125	0.25
Dining room and living room tables (100kg)	0.125	0.25
Shop furniture (100kg)	0.125	0.25
Other furniture (100kg)	0.28	0.56
Furniture parts (100kg)	0.28	0.56
Prefabricated buildings (100kg)	0.19	0.38

Source: According to OLLMANN (1993a) with extensions by the authors.

A6   Recovery Rates

from:	into:	Reference	Value [%]	Source
Tropical non-coniferous log	Trop. non-conif. sawnwood	Switzerland 1992	75.0	de Boer (1994:21)
		FRG 1992	60.0	de Boer (1994:33)
Tropical log	Tropical timber veneer	Switzerland 1992	53.0	de Boer (1994:21)
		FRG 1992	50.0	de Boer (1994:33)
		FRG 1984	48.0	Müller (1987:26)
Roundwood	Charcoal	FRG 1984	28.4	Müller (1987:73)
Roundwood	Telegraph poles, line masts	FRG 1984	90.0	Ollmann (cited in Müller 1987:49)
Roundwood	Stakes	FRG 1982	80.0	CMA (1983, cited in Müller 1987:51)
Roundwood	Sawnwood	FRG 1984	65.0	Ollmann (cited in Müller 1987:34)
		FRG 1986-88	66.7	Kroth/Kollert/Filippi (1991:34)
Roundwood	Veneer plywood	FRG 1978	40-48	Albin (1978, cited in Müller 1987:163)
Roundwood	blockboard	FRG 1978	46-50	Albin (1978, cited in Müller 1987:163)
Roundwood	Form parts	FRG 1978	34-38	Albin (1978, cited in Müller 1987:163)
Veneer	Veneer plywood	FRG 1978	80.0	Müller (1987:163 according to Albin 1978)
Veneer	Blockboard	FRG 1978	80.0	Müller (1987:163 according to Albin 1978)
Veneer	Form parts	FRG 1978	65.0	Müller (1987:163 according to Albin 1978)
Roundwood	Particle board	FRG 1986-88	77.0	Kroth/Kollert/Filippi (1991:34)
Roundwood	Other timber boards	FRG 1986-88	50.0	Kroth/Kollert/Filippi (1991:34)
Roundwood	Parquet	FRG 1986-88	45.5	Kroth/Kollert/Filippi (1991:34)
Roundwood	Window profiles	FRG 1986-88	34.5	Kroth/Kollert/Filippi (1991:34)
Sawnwood	Mouldings	FRG 1984	87.0	Ressel (1985, cited In Müller 1987:42)
Roundwood	Glued timber construction	FRG 1984	44.0	Ressel (1986:39)
Sawnwood	Glued timber construction	FRG 1984	73.0	Ressel (1986:39)
Half-finished timber goods	Furniture	FRG 1984	55.7	Müller (1987:113)

A7   Domestic Final Consumption of Tropical Timber in the Federal Republic of Germany in 1984

Table A7.1:   Absolute Domestic Final Consumption of Tropical Timber in the Federal Republic of Germany in 1984

[1000 m3(r)]	Sleepers	Mouldings	Sawnwood	high-grade Veneer	Plywood	total
Do-It-Yourself		55.8	44.8			100.6
Garden furniture			4.6			4.6
Other furniture			68.7	52.9	65.7	187.3
Sleepers	12.2					12.2
Packings					14.5	14.5
Construction			51.8			51.8
Parquet			6.9			6.9
Panelling, Cassettes		144.2		19.4	35.7	199.3
Staircases			89.2		2.3	91.5
Outer doors, gates			73.8			73.8
Inner doors			153.6	27.8		181.4
Windows			308.0			308.0
Sauna			9.2			9.2
Concrete formwork etc.					18.6	18.6
undefined		6.2	8.6		145.2	160.0
total	12.2	206.2	819.2	100.1	282.0	1 419.7

Notes: The entire domestic final consumption of tropical timber in the Federal Republic of Germany in 1984 amounted to estimated 1 419 700 $m^3(r)$. This amount must be distinguished with respect to other specifications of the gross imports of tropical timber (e.g. OLLMANN 1993a: Table 1 with 1 701 000 $m^3(r)$). The final consumption reported includes exports of tropical timber and tropical timber product specified in the foreign trade statistics as well as estimated exports in important categories such as doors and windows for which the foreign trade statistics do not itemize according to timber species.

Source: Own calculations according to Figure 6.

Table A7.2: Structure of the Domestic Final Consumption of Tropical Timber in the Federal Republic of Germany in 1984

[%]	Sleepers	Mouldings	Sawnwood	high-grade Veneer	Plywood	total
Do-It-Yourself		3.9	3.2			7.1
Garden furniture			0.3			0.3
Other furniture			4.8	3.7	4.6	13.2
Sleepers	0.9					0.9
Packings					1.0	1.0
Construction			3.6			3.6
Parquet			0.5			0.5
Panelling, cassettes		10.2		1.4	2.5	14.0
Staircases			6.3		0.2	6.4
Outer doors, gates			5.2			5.2
Inner doors			10.8	2.0		12.8
Windows			21.7			21.7
Sauna			0.5			0.5
Concrete formwork etc.					1.3	1.3
undefined		0.4	0.6		10.2	11.3
total	0.9	14.5	57.7	7.1	19.9	100.0

Source: Own calculations according to Figure 6.

A8   Half-Finished Tropical Timber Products: Chief Uses and Substitutes

Wood Product	Main Uses	Wood Substitutes	Non-wood Substitutes
Sawnwood	*Construction* structural building elements, boards, for flooring, walls, joinery, panelling, scantling, lining. *Engineering* bridges, wharves, piers, piling, railway sleepers, mining timbers. *Packing* boxes, crates, pallets, dunnage. *Manufacturing* furniture, boats, toy handles.	veneer, plywood (mainly in panelling, joinery, furniture, flooring). paper, paper-board and fibre-board (mainly in packing). particle board.	concrete, bricks, steel, aluminium (construction, egineering) Plastic (furniture, packing).
Veneer and Plywood	*Construction* walls, doors, decorative. panelling *Packing* crates, boxes, tea chests. *Manufacturing* furniture, boats, caravans.	sawnwood (as above) paper overlay (panelling and packing).	polyster overlay, fibreglass, concrete (construction) plastic (manufacturing and packing) steel, aluminium (construction)
Particle Board and Blockboard	*Construction* building elements, walls, panelling, weather boarding. *Manufacturing* furniture boards. *Packing* boxes, crates.	sawnwood, veneer and plywood (packing, construction and manufacturing).	steel, aluminium and concrete (construction). plastic (furniture and packing).
Poles	*Construction* telephone and power lines, sheds, store houses, bridges, wharves, beam posts.		steel, concrete, aluminium.
Mouldings	*Construction* door jambs, groove, panelling, level sidings, architraves. *Manufacturing* drawer sides.		

Source: KUMAR (1986:34-36) on Malaysian tropical timber according to various sources.

A9   Finished Timber Products on the German Market Containing No or Negligible Tropical Timber from Natural Forests

Product	from imports	from domestic production	Source and material specification when available
Wood fibre	x		Amelung/Diehl (1992:22)
Cellulose	x		Steinlin (1987:51)
Fuel wood	x		Amelung/Diehl (1992:22)
Charcoal	x		Amelung/Diehl (1992:22)
Wood wool		x	Müller (1987:60): Spruce
Light wood wool boards		x	Müller (1987:60)
Coffins		x	Blosen (28.7.1994): Pine, Oak
Wooden packings and storage containers (including pallets)		x	Müller (1987:128), Blosen (28.7.1994): Low quality timber from forest clearance, sidelines, weak timber
Mining pit timber, pylon timber, sawnwood in mining		x	CMA 1983 (cited in Müller, 1987:111): Spruce, Pine, Oak
Pianos		x	Wittgen (2.8.1994): Home-grown hardwood species
Wooden facades in domestic and non-domestic building		x	Kroth/Kollert/Filippi (1991:152-153)
Roof interior lining in domestic buildings		x	Kroth/Kollert/Filippi (1991:41)
Tool handles	x		Vormann (2.8.1994)
Power line masts, telegraph poles	x	x	Müller (1987:74): Spruce, Pine
Stakes, palisades, fences		x	CMA (1983, according to Müller 1987:75): Pine, Spruce
Glued timber constructions		x	Schwaner (2.8. 1994): Spruce, Larch
Brushes and paintbrushes		x	Mieth (2.8.1994)
Ladders and clothes hangers		x	Müller (1987:121)
Floor boards		x	Müller (1987:42)

A10 Graphic Depiction of a Contracting or Expanding Demand

Customers lost due to the campaign against tropical timber and/or a change in fashion, and customers gained through a reversal of these effects, are modelled by a corresponding percentage decrease or increase in the original demand quantities. Algebraically the percentage decrease of the demanded quantities (for all prices P) is given as $N_1(P) = (1-a)N_0(P)$ where a is the fractional decrease, N_0 is the original demand function depending on the price, and N_1 is the demand function after onset of the campaign against tropical timber and/or the fashion change. This compresses the demand function horizontally in a quantity/price diagram.[1] Fig. A 10.1 demonstrates this. N_0, the aggregate demand, is determined as the (horizontal) sum of all $n = 1,2,...m$ individual demands. If half of the customers are lost ($a = 0.5$), N_0 is compressed to N_1.

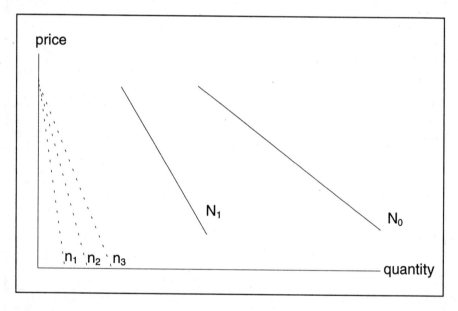

Figure A10.1: Aggregate Demand and the Campaign Against Tropical Timber

---

[1]   For the theoretical background and construction of the aggregate demand function, see Varian (1992:152ff).

A11   Determining the Reaction Directions
of the Derived Demand

The following relationship derived by HICKS (1963:241ff.) in the partial model holds for the price elasticity of the derived demand after an input X_1 (see Section 9.3 for the explanation of the variables):

$$\eta_{\alpha 1} = \frac{\sigma_{14}(\varepsilon_4 - \eta_2) + \kappa \varepsilon_4(\eta_2 - \sigma_{14})}{\varepsilon_4 - \eta_2 + \kappa(\eta_2 - \sigma_{14})} \quad .$$

The differentiation according to the price elasticity of final demand is positive:

$$\frac{\partial \eta_{\alpha 1}}{\partial \eta_2} = \frac{\left[(-\sigma_{14} + \kappa \varepsilon_4)(\varepsilon_4 - \eta_2 + \kappa(\eta_2 - \sigma_{14}))\right] - \left[(\kappa - 1)(\sigma_{14}(\varepsilon_4 - \eta_2) + \kappa \varepsilon_4(\eta_2 - \sigma_{14}))\right]}{(\varepsilon_4 - \eta_2 + \kappa(\eta_2 - \sigma_{14}))^2}$$

$$= \kappa \frac{\sigma_{14}^2 + \varepsilon_4^2}{(\varepsilon_4 - \eta_2 + \kappa(\eta_2 - \sigma_{14}))^2} \qquad\qquad > 0 \ .$$

The differentiation according to the substitution elasticity is positive too:

$$\frac{\partial \eta_{\alpha 1}}{\partial \sigma_{14}} = \frac{\left[(\varepsilon_4 - \eta_2 - \kappa \varepsilon_4)(\varepsilon_4 - \eta_2 + \kappa(\eta_2 - \sigma_{14}))\right] + \left[\kappa(\sigma_{14}(\varepsilon_4 - \eta_2) + \kappa \varepsilon_4(\eta_2 - \sigma_{14}))\right]}{(\varepsilon_4 - \eta_2 + \kappa(\eta_2 - \sigma_{14}))^2}$$

$$= (1 - \kappa) \frac{(\varepsilon_4 - \eta_2)^2}{(\varepsilon_4 - \eta_2 + \kappa(\eta_2 - \sigma_{14}))^2} \qquad\qquad > 0 \ .$$

The differentiation according to the price elasticity of supply of substitutive input is negative:

$$\frac{\partial \eta_{\alpha 1}}{\partial \varepsilon_4} = \frac{\left[(\sigma_{14} + \kappa(\eta_2 - \sigma_{14}))(\varepsilon_4 - \eta_2 + \kappa(\eta_2 - \sigma_{14}))\right] - \left[(\sigma_{14}(\varepsilon_4 - \eta_2) + \kappa \varepsilon_4(\eta_2 - \sigma_{14}))\right]}{(\varepsilon_4 - \eta_2 + \kappa(\eta_2 - \sigma_{14}))^2}$$

$$= \kappa(\kappa - 1) \frac{(\sigma_{14} - \eta_2)^2}{(\varepsilon_4 - \eta_2 + \kappa(\eta_2 - \sigma_{14}))^2} \qquad\qquad < 0 \ .$$

The sign of the differentiation of the cost share of the input in the final product is ambiguous:

$$\frac{\partial \eta_{\alpha l}}{\partial \kappa} = \frac{\left[\left(\varepsilon_4(\eta_2 - \sigma_{14})\right)\left(\varepsilon_4 - \eta_2 + \kappa(\eta_2 - \sigma_{14})\right)\right] + \left[\left(\sigma_{14} - \eta_2\right)\left(\sigma_{14}(\varepsilon_4 - \eta_2) + \kappa\varepsilon_4(\eta_2 - \sigma_{14})\right)\right]}{\left(\varepsilon_4 - \eta_2 + \kappa(\eta_2 - \sigma_{14})\right)^2}$$

$$= \frac{\left(\sigma_{14} - \eta_2\right)\left(\eta_2 - \varepsilon_4\right)\left(\varepsilon_4 - \sigma_{14}\right)}{\left(\varepsilon_4 - \eta_2 + \kappa(\eta_2 - \sigma_{14})\right)^2} \ .$$

The sign of this differentiation is negative only when supply and demand react normally and also the price elasticity of the final demand is more elastic than the substitution elasticity ($|\eta_2| > |\sigma_{14}|$). Under these conditions the demand becomes more price elastic, the greater the cost share of the input X_1.

Summary

Background and Objectives of the Research

A boycott of tropical timber, promoted by many ecological groups in the Federal Republic of Germany (FRG) and other industrialized countries and presently followed by private consumers, trade and local authorities, has been increasingly criticized. One important argument is that a boycott reduces the value of the rain forest and increases the attractivity of other land uses, e.g. farming and agriculture. The possible consequences could be that a boycott promotes even further destruction of the tropical rain forest. Thus the aim of a certification scheme for tropical timber produced by sustainable forestry is to increase the demand for tropical timber as long as it is produced according to certain standards of sustainability. This scheme raises the economic value of land cultivated by sustainable forest management and provides an incentive to manage forests sustainably, rather then overexploiting the forests or burning them down for subsequent agricultural uses.

The benefit a sustained forest management and a certification scheme bring to producers of tropical timber depends considerably on how the consumer reacts to such a scheme. Therefore, the Federal Ministry of Economy asked the Centre for European Economic Research (ZEW) to investigate the impact of a certification of tropical timber and tropical timber products from sustainable forest management on demand. Specifically this involved investigating the effects of a certification scheme on the German tropical timber market on a long term basis with attention focused on the demand side.

Methodology

Because this study focuses on the demand side, an established and credible certification scheme as well as a sufficient supply of tropical timber produced under
sustainable and ecological forest management are assumed. Preliminary investigations of costs and yields of sustainable management of natural forests in the
tropics indicate that in the long term a sufficient supply of tropical timber from
sustained forestry can be provided at competitive production costs.

The estimated costs of the certification scheme, i.e the costs of controlling the
maintenance of defined production standards and the costs of controlling the
flows from the forestry to the end consumer, are estimated to be relatively low,
approximately around DM 2.4 per cubic metre of roundwood equivalent. Compared to the average German import price of tropical timber of all processing stages
this equals only 0.4%. Thereby the costs of certification might have a considerably less impact in the market than for example the fluctuation of the exchange
rate of the US$.

The same holds true for additional logging costs which might arise from a
change to sustainable forest management. Based on an evaluation of logging costs
in Indonesia, one of the most important tropical timber producing countries, and
the assumption that a change will induce a long-term increase in production costs
by 10%, additional costs amounting to 5 DM/m^3 roundwood are estimated. In
relation to the average German import unit value for tropical timber this equals an
increase of 0.8%.

Experience with eco-labels in Germany indicate that private as well as commercial consumers are generally in favour of reliably labelled products, provided
they are being sold at the same price. However, if being sold at a higher price,
commerce and industry in particular will tend to buy the competitive non-labelled
product.

In general, it is only possible to realize higher prices for the end consumers
when they have developed an awareness for environmental damages caused by a
product or its production and are willing to pay more to support an intact environment. This is especially the case, when the consumer is directly affected by the
environmental damages of the product. An example is provided by ecologically
friendly emulsion paints labelled with a „Blue Angel" (a German symbol attached
to a product guaranteeing environmental friendliness). These products sell more
easily at higher prices than certified tropical timber. The end consumer himself
can directly feel the effects of pollution caused by solvents, whereas the effects of
the destruction of the rain forest are only perceived indirectly at a later stage. On
the other hand, the discussion about the anthropogenic green house effect and the
destruction of the rain forest is still strong. Rightly so, because the latest figures of
the FAO show that the average annual deforestation rate of tropical forests in the
eighties has been around 0.8%. Based on the experience made with ecological
labels in Germany and in the United Kingdom, it seems quite reasonable to con-

clude that, on the average, the consumer accepts an increased price of 5% for a certified tropical timber product.

In recent years, there has been a considerable slump in the German use of tropical timber in some end-use sectors (e.g. for do-it-yourself building materials and for windows) caused by a fashion trend favouring bright woods and by the anti-tropical-timber campaign. At the same time, the total German imports of tropical timber products increased until 1992. Obviously, in some sectors there must have been an increased use, assumably areas where the use of tropical timber is not visible. Changing fashions and the anti-tropical-timber campaign showed their effects especially on the visible use of tropical timber. Most of the markets affected are investigated in this study (windows, panels, inner doors, outer doors, furniture, and staircases as well as the sales of mouldings through do-it-yourself (DIY) supermarkets). They cover approximately 80% of all German imports of tropical timber products of all processing stages.

The chosen method for calculating the effects induced by a certification scheme is based on the assumption that a reliable certification scheme can reverse the negative impacts of the anti-tropical-timber campaign and of the change in fashion towards bright woods, or can influence the change in fashion in favour of tropical timber respectively.

To analyse the effects a certification scheme may have on the German tropical timber market, the latest development and trends associated with the use of tropical timber are investigated and the effects of the changing trend in fashion as well as the effects of the anti-tropical-timber campaign are identified (trend analysis). This is done thoroughly for the total German market for tropical timber as well as for the following submarkets: windows, outer doors, staircases, surfaces of furniture and do-it-yourself mouldings. Those five markets represent roughly 50% of the German import demand for tropical timber. Because these are mainly visible uses of tropical timber, they might cover a significantly higher percentage of the volume affected by the anti-tropical-timber campaign and the changing trends in fashion.

Based on the market analysis two different basic scenarios of a certification of tropical timber are defined for the total market and for the five submarkets. Scenario T I assumes that a reliable certification scheme is well capable of reversing the observed decline in the demand caused by the anti-tropical-timber campaign. Scenario T II assumes that, in addition, the effect of the changing trend in fashion can be reversed as well.

Consequently, the two basic scenarios describe possible increases in the demanded quantities as a reaction to a certification scheme. Based on the two basic scenarios several extended scenarios for the total German tropical timber market as well as for the five submarkets are defined. Extensions are made to cover the costs of the certification scheme, so that there is a scenario with and without certification costs. In addition, the scenarios of the total market include computations of the possible effects of increased logging costs due to a change to sustainable forest management. Secondly, scenarios are quantified with and without an increase in the willingness to pay more for environmentally friendly goods (5%). Thirdly, the effects of a certification scheme extended to all timber species as well as the effects of an energy tax are estimated, which increases the price for the non-wood substitutes aluminium and plastics. Fourth, the scope of the certification scheme is modified by establishing a certification scheme limited only to the German market on the one hand, and an OECD-wide introduction of a certification scheme on the other hand. The latter has the significant consequence that an OECD-wide additional demand leads to an increase in the world market price of tropical timber.

The calculations are based on the same reference year (1993). This has the effect that economic growth, which will take place independently of a certification scheme, is neutralized. In doing so, a concentration of the analysis on the effects of a certification scheme has been achieved.

The theoretical analysis is characterized as follows: Based on a partial-analytical framework several features are modelled for the aggregate German timber market as well as for the five submarkets. The supply function shifts as a consequence of the certification costs and the additional costs of sustainable forest management. The demand function shifts as a consequence of the change in fashion, the anti-tropical-timber campaign, the introduction of a credible certification scheme, the increased willingness to pay, and the increased costs for substitutes (certification costs for non-tropical timbers, energy tax). The points of intersection of the corresponding demand and supply functions are used to calculate the new equilibrium quantities and prices of the different scenarios.

Results

The results indicate that the costs of a certification scheme as well as the costs brought about by a change to sustainable forest management are of minor importance as they are relatively low compared to current prices of tropical timber. If the end user tolerates paying on average a moderate increase of 5% for an environmentally friendly product, the additional costs can be compensated leaving additional demand to even increase the volume of the tropical timber market in svereral scenarios.

Furthermore, the scenarios show that the market position of the raw material tropical timber will neither improve nor get worse substantially by including non-tropical timber in the certification scheme or by introducing an energy tax which raises the price for the non-wood substitutes plastics and aluminium. This is due to the fact that the costs for the materials used for building windows, staircases, doors etc. are relatively low in comparison to the total costs of a construction project.

In the case of a certification scheme limited to the Federal Republic of Germany, the demand expansion due to the introduced certification scheme and to the increased willingness to pay will not cause a rise in world market prices, as the total German demand for tropical timber represents only 2.6% of world demand only. Thus, a certification scheme limited to the FRG can induce an increase in imports of tropical timber by about 15% as an effect of reversing the anti-tropical-timber campaign (T I: FRG, see figure S1, respectively table S1). In addition, if a fashionable trend towards tropical timber can be initiated by means of a certification scheme, a growth of approximately 24% can be expected (T II: FRG).

With the introduction of a certification scheme limited to the FRG the scenarios T I and T II give a realistic spectrum of the possible outcome. Analysing an OECD-wide certification, the scenario T II represents an extreme case, as the structure of German demand for tropical timber is not fully symmetric to the demand in other OECD countries. However, T I seems to be a realistic scenario, and the following interpretation of the results of an OECD-wide certification will be concentrated on T I.

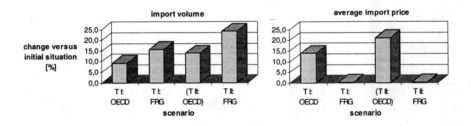

Figure S1:   Impacts of a Certification Scheme for Tropical Timber on the Aggregate German Market for Tropical Timber

Source: See Table S1.

When certified timber is introduced on an OECD-wide basis, a significant increase of the tropical timber price of about 14% will be induced (T I, see figure S1). This price rise will lead to a smaller increase in demand compared to a certification limited to Germany (9.0% instead of 15.3%). An extreme expansion of OECD tropical timber demand according to T II would cause the world market price for tropical timber to increase by 21.5%. This would lower German timber demand in some submarkets below the initial 1993 level without any certification scheme (see figure S2).

In the end, an OECD-wide certification of tropical timber has the effect that in most of the submarkets demand will exceed the initial level. This can be seen quite clearly in the market for windows and in the do-it-yourself sector, which is strongly influenced by the anti-tropical timber campaign.

An OECD-wide certification scheme seems to be more realistic than a scheme limited to the FRG as far as political considerations are concerned. Assuming a willingness to pay an extra 5% by consumers, certification costs of 2.4 DM/m³(r) and additional costs by a change to sustainable forest management of 5 DM/m³(r), the introduction of an OECD-wide certification scheme will lead to an additional consumption in the German timber market of approx. 9% with prices climbing approx. 14%.

The expansion of tropical timber consumption in the German market induced by an (OECD-wide) certification will result in a lower consumption of temperate timber. Nevertheless, compared to the total volume of temperate timber consumed in Germany this reduction is of minor importance (approx. 0.5%). If a willingness to pay an extra 5% is stimulated - at least in visible uses - by an extension of the certification scheme to temperate timber the losses will be completely compensated.

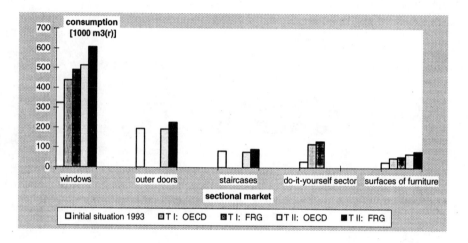

Figure S2:   Impacts of a Certification Scheme for Tropical Timber on Five Important German Submarkets

Source: See Table S1.
Note: Several scenarios have not been defined, so the corresponding columns are not shown in the figure.

The scenarios indicate that a certification scheme for tropical timber limited to Germany can have a strong expansive effect on demand as substantial price effects on the world market are avoided. This is especially true when consumers can be convinced of a personal advantage they could expect from a certification scheme, thereby inducing them to tolerate higher prices. Thus, the impact of the credibility of a certification scheme on its effectiveness as a means for the preservation of the tropical rain forest should not be underestimated.

A German certification scheme will induce additional costs of DM 5 million per year given a German import volume of tropical timber of presently 2 million m^3 roundwood equivalent. If, by means of a credible certification scheme, the consumer's willingness to pay is increased by 5%, the certification costs can be passed on to the consumers without a decrease in the volume of demand.

Table S1:   Survey of the Effects of a Timber Certification Scheme on the German Tropical Timber Market

scenario:	initial situation 1993	T I		T II		T I		T II	
scope of certification:		FRG	OECD	FRG	OECD	FRG	OECD	FRG	OECD
consumption in the market for:		volume [1000 m^3(r)]				change vs initial situation [%]			
- windows	323	490	438	607	513	51.7	35.6	87.9	58.8
- outer doors	194	n.d.	n.d.	226	191	n.d.	n.d.	16.5	-1.5
- staircases	82	n.d.	n.d.	91	77	n.d.	n.d.	11.7	-5.5
- do-it-yourself mouldings	30	131	117	n.d.	n.d.	336.7	290	n.d.	n.d.
- furniture surfaces	28	55	49	81	69	96.4	75.0	189.3	146.4
total submarkets	657								
total market						change vs initial situation [%]			
import quantity [1000 m^3(r)]	2005	2313	2186	2482	2282	15.3	9.0	23.8	13.8
average import price [DM/m^3(r)]	600	607.4	686.3	607.4	729.1	1.2	14.4	1.2	21.5

Source: Own calculations.
*Notes:*n.d.: Scenario not defined. Assumptions for all executed scenarios: Costs of a certification scheme 2,4 DM/m^3(r). End consumers are willing to accept 5% higher prices for a sustainably produced tropical timber product. Additional assumption for the total market scenarios: Additional costs due to a change to sustainable forest management 5 DM/m^3(r). For technical reasons, the reductions in the scenarios of the submarkets are systematically overestimated. In the more realistic big country scenario T I this overestimate is as high as 17%.

Bibliography

AMELUNG, T./DIEHL, M. (1992), Deforestation of Tropical Rain Forests: Economic Causes and Impact on Development. Kieler Studien Nr. 241. Tübingen

ANONYMOUS (1989), Zur Frage der Substitution von tropischen Hölzern und Holzprodukten durch europäische Laub- und Nadelhölzer. In: Internationaler Holzmarkt, Vol. 80, Nr. 22, S. 1-3

ANONYMOUS (1991), Im Fensterbau stehen die Nadelhölzer jetzt an erster Stelle. In: Holz-Zentralblatt vom 29.5.1991, Jhg. 117, Nr. 64/65, S. 1033-1034

ANONYMOUS (1994a), Umweltzeichen für ökologisch unbedenkliche Produkte. In: Holz-Zentralblatt vom 29.7.1994, Jhg. 120, Nr. 90, S. 1413,1426

ANONYMOUS (1994b), Parkett und Ausbauprodukte stark gefragt. In: Holz-Zentralblatt vom 26.10.1994, Jhg. 120, Nr. 128, S. 2123

ANONYMOUS (1994c), Es gibt keinen überzeugenden Grund für einen Verzicht auf Tropenholz. In: Holz-Zentralblatt vom 14.12.1994, Jhg. 120, Nr. 149, S. 2510

ANONYMOUS (1994d), Malaysia vertritt seine Forstpolitik offensiv. In: Holz-Zentralblatt vom 5.8.1994, Jhg. 120, Nr. 93, S. 1446

ANONYMOUS (1994e), Neue Hölzer und mehr Farbe bei Büromöbeln. In: Holz-Zentralblatt vom 19.10.1994, Jhg. 120, Nr. 125, S. 2045

ANONYMOUS (1994f), Holz ist mehr als nur „heimelig". In: Holz-Zentralblatt vom 16.9.1994, Jhg. 120, Nr. 111, S. 1753

ANONYMOUS (1994g), Neues Weltabkommen für tropische Hölzer. In: Nachrichten für den Außenhandel vom 2.2.1994

ANONYMOUS (1994h), Holz und Holzprodukte sollen mit dem Ursprungsland und Handelsnamen gekennzeichnet werden. In: Holz-Zentralblatt vom 3.8.1994, Jhg. 120, Nr. 91/92, S. 1435

ATLANTA/INPROMA (1987), Wood Processing Industry Sector Study Indonesia. Main Report and Volume I-IX. Report prepared for the Directorate General of Multifarious Manufacturing Industries/Ministry of Industry. Hamburg, Jakarta

BACH, S. et al. (1994), Wirtschaftliche Auswirkungen einer ökologischen Steuerreform. Deutsches Institut für Wirtschaftsforschung. Gutachten im Auftrag von Greenpeace e.V. Berlin

BARTMANN, H. (1981), Verteilungstheorie. München

BECKER, K. (1994), Furnier im Wettbewerb der Materialien. In: Holz-Zentralblatt vom 19.8.1994, Jhg. 120, Nr. 99, S. 1513-1515

BHAGWATI, J.N. (1971), The Generalized Theory of Distortions and Welfare. In: Bhagwati et al. (eds.), Trade, Balance of Payments and Growth. Amsterdam. S. 69-90

BLACKORBY, C./RUSSELL, R.R. (1989), Will the Real Elasticity of Substitution Please Stand up?. In: American Economic Review, Vol. 79, Nr. 4, S. 882-888

BLOSEN 28.7.1994. Personal communication with M. Blosen, Bundesverband der Holzpackmittel, Paletten, Exportverpackung e.V.

BML (Bundesministerium für Ernährung, Landwirtschaft und Forsten) (1993), Statistisches Jahrbuch über Ernährung, Landwirtschaft und Forsten der Bundesrepublik Deutschland. Münster-Hiltrup

BOJÖ, J./MÄLER, K.-G./UNEMO, L. (1990), Environment and Development: An Economic Approach. Dordrecht

BRUENIG, E.F. (1990 a), Möglichkeiten nachhaltiger Forstwirtschaft in Regenwaldgebieten. In: Nord-Süd aktuell, Vol. 4, Nr. 1, S. 93-97

BRUENIG, E.F. (1990 b), Tropical Forest Resources. In: Furtado, J.I. et al. (eds.), Tropical Resources, Ecology and Development. Philadelphia. S. 67-95

BRUENIG, E.F. (1994), Costs and Benefits of Reduced Impact Timber Harvesting (RIL) in Mixed Dipterocarp Forest in Accord with Criteria and Standards of Sustainability and Cost of Timber Certification. Mimeo

CORNWALL, R.R. (1984), Introduction to the Use of General Equilibrium Analysis. Amsterdam

DAHMS, K.-G. (1980), Sorge um Exotenhölzer ist nicht berechtigt. In: Holz- und Kunststoffverarbeitung, Vol. 15, Nr. 6, S. 520-525

DE BOER 19.9.1994, 13.12.1994. Ir. R.C. de Boer, Stichting Bos en Hout, Wageningen/Niederlande. Personal communication 19.9.1994 and letter dated 13.12.1994

DE BOER, R.C. (1994), Tropical Timber Market. In: 7 European Countries in 1992. Stichting Bos en Hout/Wageningen/Niederlande. International Tropical Timber Organization PD 9/93 Rev. 1 (M): "Market Intelligence; Tropical Timber Market Information System", Part I. Wageningen

DEPPE 18.1.1995. Personal communication with Prof. Hans-Joachim Deppe, Bundesanstalt für Materialforschung und -prüfung, Berlin

DEPPE, H.-J. (1988), Entwicklungstendenzen bei Herstellung und Verbrauch von Holzwerkstoffen für den Innenraumbereich. In: Forstarchiv, Jhg. 59, Nr. 1, S. 28-31

DEUTSCHER FORSTVEREIN (1986), Ausschuß für internationale forst- und holzwirt-schaftliche Zusammenarbeit, Erhaltung und nachhaltige Nutzung tropischer Regenwälder, Forschungsberichte des Bundesministeriums für wirtschaftliche Zusammenarbeit, Bd. 74. München

DEUTSCHER STÄDTE- UND GEMEINDEBUND, Pressemitteilung Nr. 1/89 vom 19.1.1989

DGFU/FAO (Directorate General of Forest Utilization/Food and Agriculture Organization) (1990), Situation and Outlook of the Forestry Sector in Indonesia. Indonesia UTF/INS/065/INS: Forestry Studies Technical Report No. 1 (Volume 3 of 4). Jakarta

DIEHL, M. (1991), Holzwirtschaft in den tropischen Ländern: Ursache für die Zerstörung der Regenwälder oder Entwicklungsgrundlage? In: Die Weltwirtschaft, 1991, Heft 1, S. 211-222

DMD (1995 a), EuroDoor (interior) Deutschland 1995. Detail-Marketing-Dienste, Essen

DMD (1995 b), EuroDoor Deutschland 1995. Detail-Marketing-Dienste, Essen

DMD (1995 c), EuroStair Deutschland 1995. Detail-Marketing-Dienste, Essen

DMD (1995 d), EuroWindow Deutschland 1995. Detail-Marketing-Dienste, Essen

EDITION AUM (3.3.1995). Schriftliche Mitteilung der Edition AUM, München, über aktuelle Preise von Fenstern und Außentüren verschiedener Materialien (Auszug aus einer detaillierten Baupreisliste)

EHRENTREICH 11.1.1995. Personal communication with W. Ehrentreich, Holz-Zentralblatt, Stuttgart

ENQUETE-KOMMISSION (1990), „Vorsorge zum Schutz der Erdatmosphäre" des Deutschen Bundestages (Hrsg.), Schutz der tropischen Wälder. 2. Bericht. Bonn

ENQUETE-KOMMISSION (1991), „Vorsorge zum Schutz der Erdatmosphäre" des Deutschen Bundestages (Hrsg.), Schutz der Erde. 3. Bericht, Teilband I. Bonn

ENVIRONMENT WATCH: Western Europe, vom 16.12.1994

ENVIRONMENT WATCH: Western Europe, vom 2.6.1995

ESE (Environmental Strategies Europe) (1992), Identification and Analysis of Measures and Instruments Concerning Trade in Tropical Wood. Report Submitted to the European Communities; Vol. I, Executive Report; Vol. II, Overview of Existing and Potential Instruments; Vol. IV, Statistical Overview. Brüssel

FAO (1993), Forest Resources Assessment 1990, Tropical Countries, FAO Forestry Paper 112. Rom

FAO, Monthly Bulletin, Tropical Forest Products in World Timber Trade, Trade in Tropical Timber: 1992 Annual Totals. FAO:MISC/93/3

FAO, Yearbook of Forest Products, diverse Jahrgänge. Rom

FAO-Aktuell Nr. 11/91 vom 15.3.1991

FINKE, R./LU, W.-L./THEIL, H. (1984), A Cross-Country Tabulation of Own-Price Elasticities of Demand. In: Economics Letters, Vol. 14, No. 1, S. 137-142

FRIEDMAN, M. (1976), Price Theory. 2nd edition. Chicago.(1962 1st. ed.)

GHAZALI, B./SIMULA, M. (1994), Certification Schemes for all Timber Products. Report prepared for the ITTO. Yokohama

GRAMMEL, R./KARMANN, M. (1994), Ecolabel auch für mitteleuropäisches Holz? In: Holz-Zentralblatt vom 30.9.1994. Jhg. 120, Nr. 117, S. 1893-1898

GRAY, J.A./HADI, S. (1990), Fiscal Policies and Pricing in Indonesian Forestry. Indonesia UTF/INS/065/INS/: Forestry Studies Field Document No. VI-3 (DGFU/FAO), Jakarta.

GREFERMANN, K. (1988), Holzbearbeitung. Berlin

HÄBER, J. (1988), Der Markt für Holzwerkstoffe in der Bundesrepublik; Teil 1. In: Holz-Zentralblatt vom 13.7.1988, Jhg. 114, Nr. 83/84, S. 1241-1242; Teil 2 in: Holz-Zentralblatt vom 22.7.1988, Jhg. 114, Nr. 88, S. 1281-1283

HÄBER, J. (1990), Holzwerkstoffe für Bau und Ausbau. In: Holz-Zentralblatt vom 28.12.1990, Jhg. 116, Nr. 155/156/157, suppl. S. 13-14

HAYNES, R. (1977), A Derived Demand Approach to Estimating the Linkage Between Stumpage and Lumber Markets. In: Forest Science, Vol. 23, S. 281-288

HERKER, A. (1993), Die Erklärung des umweltbewußten Konsumverhaltens. Eine internationale Studie. Frankfurt a.M.

HERKNER, W. (1981), Einführung in die Sozialpsychologie. Bern

HERRMANN 1.2.1995. Personal communication with W. Herrmann, Fa. Danzer, Reutlingen

HESS 19.9.1994. Personal communication with G. Hess, Vereinigung Deutscher Furnierwerke e.V.

HICKS, J.R. (1932), The Theory of Wages. 1st edition (2nd edition 1963). London.

HOERING, U. (1995), Urwaldriesen zu Eßstäbchen. In: Frankfurter Rundschau vom 13.2.1995

HOHMEYER, O. et al. (1985), Employment Effects of Energy Conservation Investments in EC Countries. ISI, Karlsruhe

HOHMEYER, O. et al. (1995), Umweltauswirkungen einer ökologischen Steuerreform, Mannheim (unveröffentlicht)

HOLZ-LEXIKON. 3. Auflage 1988. Stuttgart

HUCKERT, H. (1993), Aufkommen und Verwendung von Nadel- und Laubrohholz 1992 in der Bundesrepublik Deutschland. In: Holz-Zentralblatt vom 10.12.1993, Jhg. 119, Nr. 148, S. 2425

HÜSER, A. (1993), Institutionelle Regelungen und Marketinginstrumente zur Überwindung von Kaufbarrieren auf ökologischen Märkten. In: Zeitschrift für Betriebswirtschaft, Jhg. 63, Heft 3, S. 267-287

IBRD (International Bank for Reconstruction and Development) (1986), Price Prospects for Major Primary Commodities, Volume III: Agricultural Raw Materials. Washington

IBRD (International Bank for Reconstruction and Development) (1990), Indonesia. Sustainable Development of Forests, Land and Water. Washington

IPOS (Institut für praxisorientierte Sozialforschung) (1993), Einstellungen zu Fragen des Umweltschutzes 1993. Nr. 876/875. o.O.

ITTO (International Tropical Timber Organization) (1990), ITTO Guidelines for the Sustainable Management of Natural Tropical Forests. ITTO Technical Series No. 5. Yokohama

ITW (Initiative Tropenwald) (1994), Timber Certification, Proposals and Positions. Position Paper of Initiative Tropenwald, presented to the Working Party on Certification of all Timber and Timber Products, 12.-14.5.1994. Cartagena de Indias/Kolumbien

JOHANSSON, P.-O./LÖFGREN, K.-G. (1985), The Economics of Forestry and Natural Resources. Oxford

JOHNSON, N./CABARLE, B. (1993), Surviving the Cut: Natural Forest Management in the Humid Tropics. World Resources Institute

KAMM, G. (1991), Absatzwege und Verwendungsbereiche für Furniere, eine Bestands-aufnahme. In: Holz-Zentralblatt vom 9.9.1991, Jhg. 117, Nr. 108, S. 1677-1678

KARGER, H.-J. (1978), Development Prospects and Investment Opportunities in the Wood Working and Wood Processing Industries in Indonesia. HWWA-Bericht an die GTZ. Hamburg

KELLER, S. (1986), Baukostenplanung für Architekten. Wiesbaden

KNAUER, N. (1988), Holz als nachwachsender Rohstoff

KRAFT, H. (1975), Analytische Untersuchung der Distribution des Holzes in der Bundes-republik Deutschland - Grundlagen und Problematik - dargestellt an den Ergebnissen des Jahres 1970. Freiburg i.Br.

KREIS, C./FILIPPI, M. (1991), Holzverwendung im Brückenbau. In: Holz-Zentralblatt vom 20.9.1991, Jhg. 117, Nr. 113, S. 1745-1747

KROTH, W./BARTELHEIMER, P. (1993), Holzmarktlehre. Hamburg/Berlin

KROTH, W./KOLLERT, W./FILIPPI, M. (1991), Analyse und Quantifizierung der Holzverwendung im Bauwesen. Untersuchung im Auftrag des BMELF. München

KUMAR, R. (1982), World Tropical Wood Trade. In: Resources Policy, Vol. 8, Nr. 3, S. 177-192

KUMAR, R. (1986), The Forest Resources of Malaysia. Oxford

LEUKENS, U. (1993), Holzwerkstoffe - ökologisch bewusste Baustoff-Auswahl mit der SIA-Deklaration. In: Schweizer Holzbau, Jhg. 1993, Nr. 8, S. 32-35

LORENZ 2.8.1994. Personal communication with H.-J. Lorenz, Verband deutscher Papierfabriken e.V., Bonn

MANTEL, K./SCHNEIDER, A. (1967), Holzverwendung in der Bauwirtschaft. München

MARSHALL, A. (1890), Principles of Economics. London

MATTOO, A./SINGH, H.V. (1994), Eco-Labelling: Policy Considerations. In: Kyklos, Vol. 47, Nr. 1, S. 53-65

MEFFERT, H./ KIRCHGEORG, M. (1993), Marktorientiertes Umweltmanagement. Stuttgart

MIETH 2.8.1994. Personal communication with S. Mieth, Bundesverband der Deutschen Bürsten- und Pinselindustrie e.V.

MORSCHHÄUSER, B. (1988), Strukturwandel ohne Staatshilfe: Das Beispiel der Holz-verarbeitenden Industrie in der Bundesrepublik Deutschland (1976-1985). München

MÜLLER, H. (1987), Distribution des Holzes in der Bundesrepublik Deutschland 1984. Freiburg

NAUMANN 2.8.1994. Personal communication with S. Naumann, Verband der Deutschen Möbelindustrie e.V.

NECTOUX, F./DUDLEY, N. (1987), A Hard Wood Story, an Investigation into the European Influence on Tropical Forest Loss. Study by Earth Resources Research Ltd. undertaken for Friends of the Earth, ohne Ort

NECTOUX, F./KURODA, Y. (1989), Timber from the South Seas. An Analysis of Japan's Tropical Timber Trade and its Environmental Impact. Gland

NEHM et al. (1994), Baukostenberatung Architektenkammer Baden-Württemberg. Gebäudekosten 1995, Teil 1, planungsorientiert nach Kostengruppen. Stuttgart

NEISSER, S./BOTZEM, C. (1992), Die Situation der Tropenhölzer in Deutschland. In: Holz-Zentralblatt vom 21.8.1992, Jhg. 118, Nr. 101, S. 1518-1519

NEUGEBAUER (undatiert), Wald und Marktwirtschaft, Zertifizierung, ein Weg zur nach-haltigen Nutzung? Veröffentlichung in Vorbereitung. ohne Ort

OBERLE 28.7.1994. Personal communication with N. Oberle, Bundesfachverband Saunabau e.V.

OBERNDÖRFER, D. (1989), Schutz der tropischen Regenwälder (Feuchtwälder) durch ökonomische Kompensation. In: Freiburger Universitätsblätter, Vol. 28, Heft 105, S. 91-117

OECD (1991), Environmental Labelling in OECD Countries. Paris

OLLMANN 31.8.1994 AND 16.12.1994. Personal communication with Prof. Dr. Heiner Ollmann of the Federal Research Centre for Forestry and Forest Products in Hamburg

OLLMANN, H. (1993a), Die Tropenholzeinfuhr der Bundesrepublik Deutschland 1960 - 1992. Hamburg

OLLMANN, H. (1993b), Holzbilanzen 1991 und 1992 für die Bundesrepublik Deutschland. In: Holz-Zentralblatt vom 22.12.1993, Jhg. 119, Nr. 153/154, S. 2488

OLLMANN, H. (1994), Entwicklung und Perspektiven der Holzverwendung. Hamburg, mimeo

OLSEN 2.8.1994. Personal communication with R. Olsen, Verband der Fenster- und Fassadenhersteller e.V., Frankfurt a.M.

P.T. CAPRICORN Indonesia Consult Inc. (1987), A Study on the Market for Plywood in Indonesia 1987. Jakarta

PANAYOTOU, T./ASHTON, P.S. (1992), Not By Timber Alone, Economics and Ecology for Sustaining Tropical Forests. Washington D.C.

PEARCE, D.W./TURNER, R.K. (1990), Economics of Natural Resources and the Environment. New York

PETERS, G.-A./PETERS-TIEDEMANN, W. (1989), Imageverlust durch Tropenholzdiskussion? In: Holz-Zentralblatt vom 23.8.1989, Jhg. 115, Nr. 100/101, S. 1491

PINZLER, P. (1994), Kleinholz für die Reichen. In: Die Zeit vom 23.9.1994

PLOTKIN, M./FAMOLARE, L. (Hrsg.) (1992), Sustainable Harvest and Marketing of Rain Forest Products. Washington

POHL, M. (1990), Japanische Tropenholzimporte, Stand und Probleme. In: Nord-Süd aktuell, Jg. IV, Nr. 1, S. 98-101

PRABHU, B.R./WEIDELT, H.-J./LEINERT, S. (1993), Erfahrungen und Möglichkeiten einer nachhaltigen Bewirtschaftung von artenreichen tropischen Regenwäldern, eine Untersuchung anhand von vier Fallbeispielen. München

RAL (Deutsches Institut für Gütesicherung und Kennzeichnungen e.V.) (1993), Umweltzeichen. Produktanforderungen, Zeichenanwender und Produkte. St. Augustin

REPETTO, R.(1990), Die Entwaldung der Tropen: Ein ökonomischer Fehlschlag. In: Spektrum der Wissenschaft, Juni 1990, S. 122-129

RESSEL, J. (1986), Energieanalyse der Holzindustrie der Bundesrepublik Deutschland. Bundesministerium für Forschung und Technologie Forschungsbericht T 86-184. Hamburg

RISTAU 1.3.1995. Personal communication with W. Ristau, Geschäftsführer des Bundesverbandes deutscher Heimwerker- und Baumärkte e.V.

SARTORIUS, P./ HENLE, H. (1968), Forestry and Economic Development. New York/ Washington/London

SCHARDT, S. (1994), Holzzertifizierung - Chance und Herausforderung für die Holzwirtschaft. In: Holz-Zentralblatt vom 18.11.1994, Jhg. 120, Nr. 137/138, S. 2283, 2286

SCHIPPMANN, U. (1994), Tropenhölzer und internationaler Artenschutz. Teil 1 in: Holz-Zentralblatt vom 8.7.1994, 120. Jhg., Nr. 81, S. 1317-1326. Teil 2 in: Holz-Zentralblatt vom 8.7.1994, 120. Jhg., Nr. 82, S. 1333-1338

SCHOLZ, H./KYNAST, R. (1994), Die Holz-Zertifizierung wird kommen. In: Holz-Zentralblatt vom 28.11.1994, Jhg. 120, Nr. 142, S. 2382

SCHWANER 2.8.1994. Personal communication with K. Schwaner, Studiengemeinschaft Holzleimbau e.V.

SEIZINGER, H.-J. (1995), Strukturanalyse des Möbeloberflächenmarktes. In: Holz-Zentralblatt vom 13.1.1995. Jhg. 121, Nr. 6, S. 80-81

SHAMS, R. (1995), Eco-Labelling and Environmental Policy Efforts in Developing Countries. In: Intereconomics, Vol. 30, Nr. 3, S. 143-149

SIDABUTAR, H.P. (1988), An Investigation of the Impacts of Domestic Log Processing and Log Export Restrictions on Indonesia's Export Earnings from Logs, Lumber, and Plywood. University of Washington

SOETOPO, M. (1978), Sawmilling in Indonesia. Proceedings of the Eighth World Forestry Congress, Jakarta, 16.-28.10.1978

SPEIDEL, G. (1984), Forstliche Betriebswirtschaftslehre. Hamburg/Berlin

STATISTISCHES BUNDESAMT (1993), Gütersystematik, Warenverzeichnis für die Außenhandelsstatistik, Ausgabe 1994. Stuttgart

STATISTISCHES BUNDESAMT, Fachserie 4, Reihe 3.1: Produktion im Produzierenden Gewerbe des In- und Auslandes. Stuttgart

STATISTISCHES BUNDESAMT, Fachserie 4, Reihe 4.2.4: Material- und Wareneingang im Bergbau und im Verarbeitenden Gewerbe. Stuttgart

STATISTISCHES BUNDESAMT, Fachserie 4, Reihe 4.3.1: Kostenstruktur der Unternehmen im Bergbau, Grundstoff- und Produktionsgütergewerbe. Stuttgart

STATISTISCHES BUNDESAMT, Fachserie 4, Reihe 8.3: Rohholz und Holzhalbwaren. Stuttgart

STATISTISCHES BUNDESAMT, Fachserie 7, Reihe 2: Außenhandel nach Waren und Ländern (Spezialhandel). Stuttgart

STATISTISCHES BUNDESAMT, Statistisches Jahrbuch für die Bundesrepublik Deutschland, 1993. Wiesbaden

STAUPE, J. (1990): Die Entwicklung der Kriterien zur Vergabe des Umweltzeichens. In: Bundesministerium für Umwelt, Naturschutz und Reaktorsicherheit (Hrsg.), Dokumentation zur Internationalen Konferenz zum Umweltzeichen. S. 37-44. Bonn

STEINLIN, H. (1987), Kommerzielle Nutzung und Export von Hölzern aus tropischen Feuchtwäldern. In: Allgemeine Forst- und Jagdzeitung, Vol. 158, Nr. 2/3, S. 50-55

STEINLIN, H. (1989), Tropenwälder. In: Freiburger Universitätsblätter, Vol. 28, Heft 105, S. 23-62

STENDER-MONHEMIUS, C. (1995), Divergenzen zwischen Umweltbewußtsein und Kaufverhalten. In: UmweltWirtschaftsForum, 3. Jhg., Heft 1, S. 35-43

TAKEUCHI, K. (1983), Mechanical Processing of Tropical Hardwood in Developing Countries: Issues and Prospects for the Plywood Industry's Development in the Asia-Pacific Region. In: IBRD (ed.), Case Studies on Industrial Processing of Primary Products, Volume I: Bauxite, Rubber, Tropical Hardwood. Washington. S. 215-364

THOMAS 2.8.1994. Personal communication with Dr. K. Thomas, Verband Deutscher Papierfabriken e.V., Vorsitzender des Fachausschusses Faserholz

TÖPFER, K. (1990), Das Umweltzeichen im Kontext einer vorsorgeorientierten Umweltpolitik. In: Bundesministerium für Umwelt, Naturschutz und Reaktorsicherheit (Hrsg.): Dokumentation zur Internationalen Konferenz zum Umweltzeichen, S. 11-16

TÖTSCH, W./DUBE, R. (1990), Werkstoffe für den Möbel- und Innenausbau. Fachbericht D zu „Erfassung und Bewertung von Schadstoffen in der Raumluft" (BMFT-Förderkennzeichen 0768002), Karlsuhe/Berlin

TRÜBSWETTER, T. (1989), Tropenholz in der handwerklichen Praxis. In: Holz-Zentralblatt vom 15.9.1989, Jhg. 115, Nr. 70, S. 1669-1670

UBA (Umweltbundesamt, Hrsg.) (1993), UBA-Jahresbericht 1993. Berlin

UBA (Umweltbundesamt, Hrsg.) (1994), Das Umweltverhalten der Verbraucher - Daten und Tendenzen. Texte 75/94. Berlin

UN/ECE/ FAO (1986), European Timber Trends and Prospects to the Year 2000 and Beyond, Vol. II. New York

UN/ECE/ FAO (1992), The Forest Resources of the Temperate Zones, Main Findings of the UN-ECE/FAO Forest Resource Assessment. ECE/TIM 60. New York

UNIDO (1983), First World-Wide Study of the Wood and Wood Processing Industries. Sectoral Studies Series No. 2, UNIDO/IS.398. Wien

VARANGIS, P.N./BRAGA, C.A.P./TAKEUCHI, K. (1993), Tropical Timber Trade Policies, What Impact Will Eco-Labeling Have? World Bank, Policy Research Working Papers No. 1156, Washington D.C.

VARIAN, H.R. (1992), Microeconomic Analysis. 3rd edition, New York, London

VDH (Verein Deutscher Holzeinfuhrhäuser e.V.) (Hrsg.), Informationsdienst Holz, Merkblattreihe Holzarten, diverse Blätter, diverse Jahre

VERBAND DER FENSTER- UND FASSADENHERSTELLER e.V. (1994), Die Entwicklung des Westdeutschen Fenstermarktes von 1971 bis 1995. Mimeo

VERBAND DER LACKINDUSTRIE e.V. (1993), Jahresbericht 1993

VICTOR, P.A./HANNA, E./KUBURSI, A. (1994), How Strong is Weak Sustainability? In: Pearce, D./Faucheux, S. (eds.), Proceedings of an International Symposium on „Models of Sustainable Development". 16.-18.3.1994. Paris. S. 93-114

VORMANN 2.8.1994. Personal communication with L. Vormann, Bundesverband Holzwaren-Industrie e.V.

WEGELT 28.7.1994. Personal communication with H. Wegelt, Verband der Deutschen Parkett-Industrie e.V.

WEGENER, G. (1989), Die Holzverwendung an der Schwelle zum 21. Jahrhundert. In: Allg. Forstzeitschrift, Vol. 44, Nr. 50, S. 1347-1351

WENKE, M. (1993): Konsumstruktur, Umweltbewußtsein und Umweltpolitik: Eine makro-ökonomische Analyse des Zusammenhanges in ausgewählten Konsumbereichen. Berlin

WITTGEN 2.8.1994. Personal communication with H.-H. Wittgen, Fachverband Deutsche Klavierindustrie e.V.

By virtue of its high density, tropical timber has a long life and exhibits good resistance to negative ambient influences. Apart from these frequently found **material characteristics**, there are also many outstanding features of individual tropical non-coniferous timer kinds by virtue of the large diversity of species. Some kinds decay quite quickly, others remain unchanged almost for ever. The ease of sawing, peeling or slicing differs greatly. The range of stability, colour and grain is also very large (TAKEUCHI 1983:318).

The technical constructional properties of building timber - regardless whether of tropical or non-tropical origin - were mostly assessed positively, according to the results of a survey carried out by KROTH/KOLLERT/FILIPPI (1991) among German architects and manufacturers of prefabricated houses for the year 1989. Particular emphasis was placed on the good processing possibilities, the high thermal insulation performance and the good ratio of weight to load supporting capability. Timber is a timeless building material with numerous characteristics and no known undesired side effects. However, some disadvantages of timber were mentioned too. One disadvantage is the often large effort for chemical protection of timber entailing the need to use chemicals in building construction. The effort required for protecting timber in exterior uses also deters many house builders from using timber. Both aspects apply to non-tropical more than to tropical timber. On the economic side, according to the architects questioned, building with timber is usually more expensive than using non-timber materials. The price to performance ratio is correct only for wood-based panels. Furthermore, the numerous legal statutes and regulations often make architects refrain from using timber (ibid: 114,124).

As far as demand is concerned, timber still has a large **image** lead on other materials, in spite of the setbacks suffered through the campaign against tropical timber and the formaldehyde debate.[59] In a Swiss survey of the subjective assessment of various building materials, timber scored well ahead of stone and brickwork, metal, plastics and concrete (ANONYMOUS 1994f.).

Basically, the survey made by KROTH/KOLLERT/FILIPPI (1991:109-111) showed that the utilization of timber in building construction is influenced by very divergent and often highly subjective factors. Emotional attitudes play a great role. For example, it was said that timber confers a warm and cosy domestic atmosphere. A random sample interrogation of end consumers on seven Bavarian building and home worker markets also showed clearly that the primary associations with timber are „nature", „forest", „warmth" and „cosy dwelling". Three out of four questioned persons asserted that their attitude towards timber had not changed as a result of the tropical forest discussion (PETERS/PETERS-TIEDEMANN 1989). However, in connection with these opinions it must be borne in mind that the persons concerned, as visitors of a building material and home worker market, are a selected group in the sense that they are experienced in handicraft and therefore

---

[59] With regard to the subject complex of wood and environmental protection in the Federal Republic of Germany (wood dust, formaldehyde, energy consumption), see GREFERMANN (1988:72ff.) and the comprehensive article by WEGNER (1989).

inclined to have a positive attitude towards the relatively easy to handle material timber. Furthermore, the campaign against tropical timber was still in its first stages in 1989.

In recent times there has been a **trend** for the Federal Republic of Germany, away from the long-standing preference for lighter timbers and back to medium and dark colours (cf. KAMM 1991, ANONYMOUS 1994e, OLSEN 2.8.1994). At present mainly non-coniferous timber from temperate climatic regions are profiting from this trend, chiefly beech (ANONYMOUS 1994b). Walnut and beech are often stained darker (HERRMANN 1.2.1995). Many darker tropical timbers could profit again too from this recent change of fashion, under a credible certification scheme.

Since several years tropical timber products compete increasingly in the Federal Republic of Germany with products made from temperate non-coniferous timber, coniferous timber products and non-timber products. On some market segments **strong substitution movements towards non-timber products** are evident. Examples are the substitution of plastics for furniture construction or aluminium and plastics for windows (see also Appendix A8).

In other fields in which special timber species with specific technical characteristics are employed, such as shipbuilding and hydraulic engineering, tropical timber can be replaced primarily with non-timber materials such as concrete and steel (ANONYMOUS 1989:2). For boat construction tropical timber has been replaced in recent years by polyester or epoxy resin reinforced with glass or carbon fibre (OLLMANN 16.12.1994). Some tropical timbers will keep for an unlimited time without protection when in contact with the soil (three examples are bongossi, bangkirai and basralokus). Such timbers are often used for fences, noise shielding walls and bridges. Increasing substitution with steel, concrete and plastics is found in this sector. Impregnated domestic timber which has already had a traditional market share in this sector, is gaining ground in this area too. It has thereby been found that the keeping qualities of non-tropical timber in outdoor uses can be increased by improved timber building methods (ESE 1992, Vol.II:58).

There are only a few areas in which substitution for tropical timber hardly seems possible. One of these areas is the construction of musical instruments for which a wide range of different kinds of tropical timbers has always been used (TRÜBSWETTER 1989). In certain uses in shipbuilding, for staircases and for tool handles, etc., substitution for tropical timber with other timber species or non-timber materials impairs the technical quality of the products (ESE 1992, Vol.II:58-59).

The substitution pressure on timber as a whole exerted by the advance of plastics is being combated by the timber industry with marketing campaigns. Danzer, a leading German producer of veneers, recently launched an advertising campaign together with a large furniture manufacturer, to boost the image of timber veneers. The state group Badenia in the Federal Association of the German Timber Trade last year introduced the initiative project „pro timber window" in order to strengt-